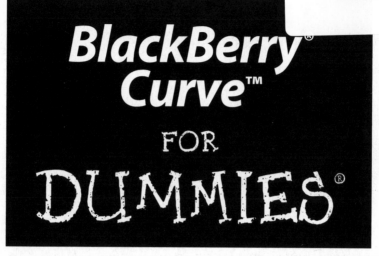

BlackBerry® Curve™ FOR DUMMIES®

by Robert Kao & Dante Sarigumba

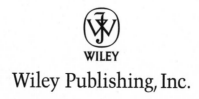

WILEY

Wiley Publishing, Inc.

BlackBerry® Curve™ For Dummies®
Published by
Wiley Publishing, Inc.
111 River Street
Hoboken, NJ 07030-5774
www.wiley.com

Copyright © 2010 by Wiley Publishing, Inc., Indianapolis, Indiana

Published by Wiley Publishing, Inc., Indianapolis, Indiana

Published simultaneously in Canada

For general information on our other products and services, please contact our Customer Care Department within the U.S. at 877-762-2974, outside the U.S. at 317-572-3993, or fax 317-572-4002.

For technical support, please visit www.wiley.com/techsupport.

Wiley also publishes its books in a variety of electronic formats. Some content that appears in print may not be available in electronic books.

Library of Congress Control Number: 2009939786

ISBN: 978-0-470-58744-7

Manufactured in the United States of America

10 9 8 7 6 5 4 3 2 1

WILEY

About the Authors

Robert Kao is one well-rounded professional. His ability to translate his technical knowledge and communicate with users of all types led him to cowrite *BlackBerry For Dummies* and *BlackBerry Pearl For Dummies*. He started out as a BlackBerry developer for various financial firms in New York City, that truly global city. Kao is currently the founder of a mobile software start-up. A graduate of Columbia University, with a Computer Engineering degree, he currently lives in South Brunswick, New Jersey.

Dante Sarigumba is a long-time user of BlackBerry and a gizmo enthusiast. He is a cohost of the Mobile Computing Authority biweekly podcast. He works for a major investment bank in New York as a software developer and lives in South Brunswick, New Jersey, with his wife, Rosemarie, and two sons, Dean and Drew.

Dedication

I would like to thank my father (MHK), my mother (SYT), and the rest of the Kao family for everything they've done for me. I wouldn't be here without their kindness and understanding. I would also like to thank my lovely wife, Marie-Claude, and little Jade for all their support. In addition, thanks to Manon Lalancette and the rest of Gamelin family for all your cheers!

— Robert Kao

To Yosma, Dean, and Drew: My greatest treasures. Thank you for your thoughts, understanding, and support.

— Dante Sarigumba

Author's Acknowledgments

Collectively, we want to give a big thanks to our new acquisition editor Katie Mohr and wish her the best of luck in bringing a new life into the world! In addition, we'd like to thank the following people:

- Tiffany Ma, for stepping in when Katie was on maternity leave.
- Mary Bednarek, for making sure we were headed in the right direction while Katie was away.
- Susan Pink, our editor, for making us look good.
- Kevin Michaluk, a.k.a. CrackBerry Kevin, for making us better.
- Carol McClendon, our agent, for presenting our proposal to the right people.
- Victoria Berry, PR of Research In Motion, for getting us access to the proper channels at the right time.

In addition, we thank the rest of the Wiley staff. Without you all, this book would not have been possible.

— Rob and Dante

Publisher's Acknowledgments

We're proud of this book; please send us your comments at http://dummies.custhelp.com. For other comments, please contact our Customer Care Department within the U.S. at 877-762-2974, outside the U.S. at 317-572-3993, or fax 317-572-4002.

Some of the people who helped bring this book to market include the following:

Acquisitions and Editorial

Project Editor: Susan Pink

Acquisitions Editors: Katie Mohr, Tiffany Ma

Copy Editor: Susan Pink

Technical Editor: Richard Evers

Editorial Manager: Jodi Jensen

Editorial Assistant: Amanda Graham

Sr. Editorial Assistant: Cherie Case

Cartoons: Rich Tennant (www.the5thwave.com)

Composition Services

Project Coordinator: Katherine Crocker

Layout and Graphics: Ana Carrillo, Carrie A. Cesavice, Ashley Chamberlain, Joyce Haughey, Melissa K. Jester

Proofreader: Kathy Simpson

Indexer: Christine Karpeles

Special Help: Amanda Graham, Annie Sullivan

Publishing and Editorial for Technology Dummies

   Richard Swadley, Vice President and Executive Group Publisher

   Andy Cummings, Vice President and Publisher

   Mary Bednarek, Executive Acquisitions Director

   Mary C. Corder, Editorial Director

Publishing for Consumer Dummies

   Diane Graves Steele, Vice President and Publisher

Composition Services

   Debbie Stailey, Director of Composition Services

Table of Contents

Introduction

*H*i there, and welcome to *BlackBerry Curve For Dummies*. If you already have a BlackBerry Curve, this is a great book to have around when you want to discover new features or need something to slap open and use as a quick reference. If you don't have a Curve yet and have some basic questions (such as "What is a BlackBerry Curve?" or "How can a BlackBerry Curve help me be more productive?"), you can benefit by reading this book cover to cover. No matter what your current BlackBerry user status (BUS, for short), this book helps you get the most out of your BlackBerry Curve.

Right off the bat, BlackBerry Curve isn't a fruit you find at the supermarket but rather an always-connected smartphone that has e-mail capabilities and a built-in Internet browser. With your BlackBerry Curve, you're in the privileged position of always being able to receive e-mail and browse the Web.

On top of that, a BlackBerry Curve has all the features you expect from a personal organizer, including a calendar, to-do lists, and memos. Oh, and did we mention that a BlackBerry Curve also has a built-in mobile phone? Talk about multitasking! Imagine being stuck on a commuter train: With your Curve by your side, you can compose e-mail while conducting a conference call, all from the comfort of your seat.

That's not all. BlackBerry Curve goes a step further to make it more fun for you to own this device. You can snap a picture with its camera, record a funny video, listen to your music collection, and enjoy watching that video on YouTube.

In this book, you find all the basics, but we also go the extra mile and highlight some of the lesser-known (but still handy) features of the BlackBerry Curve. Your Curve can work hard for you when you need it to and can play hard when you want it to.

About This Book

BlackBerry Curve For Dummies is a comprehensive user guide as well as a quick user reference. The book is designed so that you can read it cover to cover if you want, but you don't need to read one chapter after the other. Feel free to jump around while you explore the different functionalities of your BlackBerry Curve.

We cover basic and advanced topics, but we'll stick to those that we think are the most practical and frequently used. If you use or want to use a certain function of your BlackBerry Curve, it's likely covered here.

Who Are You?

We tried to be considerate of your needs, but because we've never met you, our picture of you is as follows. If you find that some of these images are true about you, this might just be the book for you:

- You have a BlackBerry Curve and want to find out how to get the most from it.

- You don't have a BlackBerry Curve yet and are wondering what one could do for you.

- You're looking for a book that doesn't assume that you know all the jargon and tech terms used in the PDA industry. (*PDA* stands for *personal digital assistant,* by the way. Take that, you jargon, you!)

- You want a reference that shows you, step by step, how to do useful and cool things with a BlackBerry Curve without bogging you down with unnecessary background or theory.

- You are tired of hauling your 10-pound laptop with you on trips and are wondering how to turn your BlackBerry Curve into a miniature traveling office.

- You no longer want to be tied to your desktop system for the critical activities in your life, such as sending and receiving e-mail, checking your calendar for appointments, getting directions, and surfing the Web.

- You like to have some fun, play games, and be entertained from a device but don't want to carry an extra game gadget in your bag.

What's in This Book

BlackBerry Curve For Dummies consists of six parts, and each part consists of different chapters related to that part's theme.

Part I: Getting Started with BlackBerry Curve

Part I starts with the basics of your Curve. You know: what it is, what you can do with it, and what elements make it up. We describe how you navigate using the QWERTY keyboard. We also show you how to personalize and express yourself through your BlackBerry Curve. This part wraps up with must-knows about security and where to go for help when you get into trouble with your BlackBerry Curve.

Part II: Organizing with Curve

Part II deals with the fact that your BlackBerry Curve is also a full-fledged PDA. We show you how to get your Curve to keep your contacts in Contacts as well as how to manage your appointments and meetings in Calendar. You also find out how to use the Clock application to set an alarm, set a timer, and set your device to Bedside mode. You explore the Password Keeper application to centralize your passwords. And finally, you see that most BlackBerry applications interconnect, working hard for you.

Part III: Getting Online with Your Curve

Part III shows you what made BlackBerry what it is today: always-connected e-mail. We also get into the other strengths of the BlackBerry — Web surfing functionality — but we don't stop there. We point out how you can use other forms of messages, such as text messaging and instant messaging. You also find out about unique forms of messages on the BlackBerry, PIN-to-PIN messages and BlackBerry Messenger. And if you have a BlackBerry Curve 8900, rest assured that your BlackBerry will be a good companion when you're traveling because we show you how to use its GPS. (The BlackBerry Curve 8500 doesn't have an internal GPS.)

Part IV: Music, Pictures, and Movies on Your Curve

You find the fun stuff in Part IV. Rock your world and use your Curve to play music, watch videos, and take pictures. You also get the scoop on how to record videos and sample ring tones. Plus you get timesaving shortcuts on the Media applications.

Part V: Working with BlackBerry Desktop Manager

In Part V, you find details of BlackBerry Desktop Manager and some of the hoops you can put it through with your BlackBerry Curve, including making backups and installing BlackBerry applications from your desktop to your Curve. You also find out how to port data from older devices — BlackBerry or not — to your new Curve. And we didn't forget to cover important stuff, such as data-syncing your appointments and contacts with desktop applications, such as Outlook.

Part VI: The Part of Tens

All *For Dummies* books include The Part of Tens, and this book is no different. In Part V, we show you places to get cool BlackBerry Curve accessories, where to get great applications, and useful mobile Web sites to visit.

Icons Used in This Book

This icon indicates that the paragraph applies to the BlackBerry Curve 8500 series. The 8500 series has a trackpad.

If a paragraph sports this icon, it means the paragraph is applicable only to the BlackBerry Curve 8900 series. The 8900 Curve has a camera and sports a trackball instead of a trackpad.

The text following this icon applies only to the older version of the operating system of your BlackBerry Curve, specifically OS 4.6. Ignore the discussion if you have OS 5.0.

This icon likewise signifies that the discussion applies to version 5.0 of the operating system. You may ignore the text if your Curve has OS 4.6.

If a paragraph sports this icon, it means we're talking about BlackBerry devices that are provided by your employer.

This icon highlights an important point that you don't want to forget because it just might come up again. We'd never be so cruel as to spring a pop quiz on you, but paying attention to these details can definitely help you.

 This book rarely delves into the geeky, technical details, but when it does, this icon warns you. Read on if you want to get under the hood a little, or just skip ahead if you aren't interested in the gory details.

 Here's where you can find not-so-obvious tricks that can make you a BlackBerry Curve power user in no time. Pay special attention to the paragraphs with this icon to get the most out of your Curve.

 Look out! This icon tells you how to avoid trouble before it starts. Be sure to read and follow the accompanying directions.

Where to Go from Here

If you want to find out more about the book or have a question or comment for us, please visit us at either of the following:

- ✔ www.BlackBerryForDummies.com
- ✔ www.BlackBerryGoodies.com — where we answer your submitted questions

Now you can dive in! Give Chapter 1 a quick look to get an idea of where this book takes you and then feel free to head straight to your chapter of choice.

Part I

Getting Started with BlackBerry Curve

The 5th Wave   By Rich Tennant

KENNETH BUYS HIS FIRST SMART PHONE

Exercise more.

In this part . . .

The road to a happy and collaborative relationship with your BlackBerry Curve starts here. Chapter 1 covers all the nuts and bolts: how the BlackBerry Curve works, its look and feel, and its connectivity. Chapter 2 describes how to navigate the Curve using the QWERTY keyboard. Chapter 3 discusses customizing your Curve and offers timesaving shortcuts.

Chapter 1

Can't Go Wrong with the Best-Selling Smartphone

***

In This Chapter

▶ Checking out your BlackBerry Curve behind the scenes

▶ Seeing what your BlackBerry Curve can do

▶ Handling the hardware

***

As of May 2009, the BlackBerry Curve family was deemed the best-selling smartphones in the United States. We're curious — what convinced you to buy this particular handheld mobile device? Was it the stats? The BlackBerry Curve 8500's cool optical trackpad? The compact size? The always-connected e-mail? The multimedia player to replace your iPod or iPhone? Or did you get a really good deal? The list goes on and on — and we might never hit on the exact reason you got yours. For whatever reason you bought your BlackBerry Curve, congratulations; you made an intelligent choice.

The same smarts that made you buy your BlackBerry Curve are clearly at it again. This time, your intelligence led you to pick up this book, perhaps because your intuition told you there's more to your BlackBerry Curve than meets the eye.

Your hunch is right. Your BlackBerry Curve *can* help you do more than you thought. For example, your BlackBerry Curve is a whiz at making phone calls, but it's also a computer that can check your e-mail and surf the Web. We're talking *World Wide* Web here, so the sky's the limit. Help is always at your fingertips instead of sitting on some desk at home or at the office:

✔ Need to check out the reviews of that restaurant on the corner?

✔ Need to know — right now — what's showing in your local movie theaters, or what the weather will be like tonight, or what's the best place to shop the sales?

✔ Need to know your current location and get directions to that cozy bed-and-breakfast, or retrieve news headlines, or check stock quotes?

> ✔ Want to do some online chatting or view some pictures online?
>
> ✔ Hanker to network with your old classmates?

You can do all these things (and more) with your BlackBerry Curve.

BlackBerry Curve is also a full-fledged *personal digital assistant (PDA)*. Out of the box, it provides you with the organizational tools you need to set up to-do lists, manage your appointments, take care of your address books, and more.

Being armed with a device that's a phone, an Internet connection, a PDA, a GPS device (Curve 8900), and a full-on media player makes you a powerful person. With your BlackBerry Curve (along with this resourceful book), you really can increase your productivity and become better organized. Watch out, world! BlackBerry Curve–wielding powerhouse coming through!

If you stick with us, you find out all you need to get the most out of your device or maybe even save a troubled relationship. (Well, the last one is a bit of an exaggeration, but we got your attention, right?)

How It All Works: The Schematic Approach

If you always ask, "How do they do that?" you don't have to go far. This section is just for you.

The role of the network service provider

Along with wondering how your BlackBerry Curve actually works, you might be wondering why you received your BlackBerry Curve from a network service provider such as T-Mobile or AT&T rather than from RIM (Research In Motion). After all, RIM makes the BlackBerry Curve. Why did you need to go through a middle person?

That's an excellent question, and here's the quick-and-dirty answer: RIM needs a delivery system — a communication medium, as it were — for its technology to work. Not in a position to come up with such a delivery system all by its lonesome, RIM partnered (and built alliances across the globe) with what developed into its network service providers — the big cellphone companies. These middlemen support the wireless network for your BlackBerry Curve so that you can connect to the BlackBerry Internet service and get all those wonderful e-mails (and spend so much valuable time surfing the Internet). See Figure 1-1 for an overview of this process.

Figure 1-1:
Your e-mail travels to your BlackBerry Curve through service providers.

Web servers

BlackBerry Internet Service

Wireless network

E-mail servers (personal and Enterprise)

Network service providers don't build alliances for nothing, right? In return, RIM gave them the right to customize the BlackBerry Curve firmware and add their carrier version of Application Center.

Connecting to your computer

Nowadays, a personal computer is a household necessity. You probably spend a lot of time using one, and it holds information you need. No surprise that BlackBerry works hand in hand with your PC and Mac. The USB cable that comes with your BlackBerry Curve does more than just charge your device.

Part V helps you use your PC connection with the help of BlackBerry Desktop Manager and all the utilities that come with it. For instance, in Chapter 16, you find how to sync your device with the personal information manager (PIM) data that you keep in your PC. You can also read Chapter 17 for directions about switching from another device (even a non–BlackBerry device) to a new BlackBerry Curve. For example, you find out how to import your contacts list into your new BlackBerry Curve. Chapter 18 tells you how to protect your data. Last, Chapter 19 talks about installing new applications on your BlackBerry Curve with the help of your PC.

If you have a Mac, you'll be happy to hear that RIM has rolled out BlackBerry Desktop Manager on the Mac. Read more in Chapter 17.

Rule the world with BlackBerry Curve in your hands

If you got your BlackBerry Curve from AT&T, chances are that your BlackBerry Curve will continue to work when you travel to, say, London or Beijing. All you need to worry about is remembering to turn on your BlackBerry Curve (and maybe the extra roaming charges).

Because your BlackBerry Curve is quad band, it works in more than 90 countries. What is *quad band?* Basically, different cellphone networks in different countries operate on different frequencies. For example, the United States and Canada operate on 850 and 1900 MHz, and Europe and Asia Pacific operate on 900 and 1800 MHz.

Your quad-band BlackBerry Curve is designed to work on 850 MHz, 900 MHz, 1800 MHz, and 1900 MHz, so you're covered almost wherever you go. Just to be sure, however, check with your network service provider to see whether your BlackBerry Curve will work at your destination before you hop on a plane.

Nothing stands still in this world, and this saying is proved by the fact that Global System for Mobile Communication (GSM) has spawned *High Speed Downlink Packet Access (HSDPA),* which is a technology that has been growing because it works on the same GSM phone infrastructure. HSDPA is available in the United States through most major network service providers and competes in the marketplace against EvDo (Evolution Data Optimized) from Code Division Multiple Access (CDMA).

What's all this alphabet soup mean to you? CDMA and GSM aren't compatible. Your phone works on only one technology. When you travel outside North America, you face the burning question: CDMA or GSM? (Read: Will my BlackBerry Curve work on this country's network?)

Your BlackBerry Curve runs on GSM, so you should be okay to travel outside the United States. Most non–North American countries are on GSM networks. If you're a CDMA kind of person, you might have some "issues," as they say. When in doubt, talk to your network service provider.

Know your BlackBerry history

Your BlackBerry Curve is truly a wondrous thing, boasting many features beyond your ordinary mobile phone. And its "sudden" popularity didn't happen overnight. Like any other good product, BlackBerry has come a long way from its (relatively humble) beginnings.

In the days when the PalmPilot ruled the PDA world, RIM was busy in its lab, ignoring the then-popular graffiti input method and designing a device with a QWERTY keyboard (the kind of keyboard people were already used to from working on their computers). RIM didn't stop there, however. It added an always-connected e-mail capability, making this device a must-have among government officials as well as finance and health professionals.

To meet the needs of government officials and industry professionals, RIM made reliability, security, and durability the priorities when manufacturing its devices. Today, the BlackBerry Curve comes from the same line of RIM family products, inheriting all the good genes while boosting usability and adding more functions to its core BlackBerry applications. As a result, BlackBerry is popular among both *prosumers* (professional customers) and consumers. Starting with BlackBerry Pearl, RIM has been targeting the mainstream consumer market. Clearly, with BlackBerry Curve, RIM is winning the hearts of consumers while maintaining its hold on the enterprise market.

Oh, the Things You Can Do!

Always-connected e-mail used to be one of the primary factors that made BlackBerry very attractive and was likely first in the long list of reasons you got yours. And if you need to go global, you can use your BlackBerry in more than 100 countries. Just hop off your flight, turn on your BlackBerry Curve, and voilà: You can receive and send e-mails whether you're in Hong Kong, London, or Paris. Your significant other can get in touch with you wherever you are — just to say hi or to remind you that you promised Aunt Edna a bottle of Chanel No. 5.

Make sure that your network service provider has the technology to go global. See the preceding section for more info. Generally, you can receive and send e-mails just like you do when you're at home. Whether you have T-Mobile in the United States or Rogers in Canada, your BlackBerry Curve will work if you have a full data and voice plan. Check with your carrier before you start your trip.

Although e-mail and communication are your BlackBerry Curve's strengths, they aren't the only things it can do. The following sections go beyond e-mail to point out some of the device's other major benefits.

All-in-one multimedia center

Previously, many people hesitated to buy a BlackBerry because of the lack of multimedia functions. They wanted a camera and audio and full video playback. BlackBerry has changed all that and has more features than you may expect. Not only does your BlackBerry Curve have a high-resolution megapixel camera (see Chapter 13) — but it also has a memory slot for a microSD chip (see Chapter 2).

Your BlackBerry Curve can function as the following:

- A music player
- A video player and recorder
- A digital camera
- A portable flash drive
- Your personal photo collection

Internet and social networking at your fingertips

Yup, with the new BlackBerry Curve on a 3G network, you can surf the Internet nearly as smoothly as you do on a desktop computer. You'll get an alert when your stock is tanking. True, that isn't fun, but you want this information as quickly as possible. With your BlackBerry Curve, you can continue chatting with your friends through all types of instant messaging applications, just as if you never left your desktop PC, and your friends will thank you for persuading them not to buy that losing stock.

Intrigued? Read how BlackBerry Curve can take full advantage of the Web in Chapter 11.

On-the-go GPS

Your BlackBerry Curve (only the 8900 and some 8500 models) comes with an onboard GPS that allows you to pinpoint your location with the BlackBerry Map application and other third-party applications such as Google Maps and TeleNav.

Me and my great personal assistant

You might be saying, "But I'm really a busy person, and I don't have time to browse the Web. What I *do* need is an assistant to help me better organize my day-to-day tasks." If you can afford one, by all means go ahead and hire a personal assistant. The next best thing is a personal *digital* assistant (PDA). Just as people come in many types, so do many PDAs.

Whip out that BlackBerry Curve of yours and take a closer look. That's right; your BlackBerry Curve is also a full-fledged PDA, helping you increase productivity:

- ✔ Remember all your acquaintances (Chapter 4)
- ✔ Manage your appointments (Chapter 5)
- ✔ Securely keep a list of passwords (Chapter 6)

A computer in the palm of your hand

Remarkable communication device? Check.

Full-fledged PDA? Check.

Full-featured media player? Check.

These capabilities are just the tip of the iceberg. Don't underestimate the device because of its size: Your BlackBerry Curve is also a powerful computer.

Need convincing? Here goes. Out of the box, with no fiddling, it comes with a great set of organizational and productivity tools. Software developers besides RIM are taking advantage of this growing market, which means that hundreds of applications are out there for you. For example, you can download graphics-intensive games or a mortgage calculator.

Download? Absolutely! BlackBerry Curve supports the downloading of applications through BlackBerry Browser. And, of course, downloading the application can be accomplished both wired and wirelessly (or over the air [OTA]). In April 2009, RIM rolled out BlackBerry App World (the company's response to the popular Apple's App Store),which allows BlackBerry owners to easily browse for BlackBerry applications on their device and download them directly. Other third-party BlackBerry application stores are tremendously popular in the BlackBerry community, such as the CrackBerry.com App Store powered by MobiHand. (For more information on downloading third-party applications, see Chapter 19.)

What's the difference between BlackBerry App World and BlackBerry Application Center?

- ✔ Application Center most likely came with your BlackBerry Curve.
- ✔ Application Center contains only applications that your network service provider wants you to see.
- ✔ App World needs to be manually downloaded by you from RIM's Web site.
- ✔ App World has an unfiltered list of BlackBerry applications for you.

Look, Dad! No hands!

Your BlackBerry Curve can be equipped with a stereo headset that doubles as a mic for hands-free talking. This accessory is your doctor's prescription for preventing the stiff neck that comes from wedging your BlackBerry Curve against your ear with your shoulder. It helps free your hands so that you can eat Chinese takeout. Some places require you by law to use an earphone while driving and talking on a cellphone.

Avoid using your cellphone while driving, hands-free or not.

But RIM didn't stop with just your standard wired earphones. BlackBerry Curve also supports cool wireless earphones based on Bluetooth technology. How could a bizarrely colored tooth help you here? *Bluetooth* is the name for a (very) short-distance wireless technology that connects devices. See Chapter 7 for how to connect your BlackBerry Curve to a Bluetooth headset.

Putting a sentry on duty

The virtual world isn't exempt from general human nastiness; in fact, every day a battle is fought between those trying to attack a system and those trying to protect it. A computer connected to the Internet faces an extra risk of being cracked by a hacker or infected by a virus. (Viruses try to replicate themselves and generally bug you.)

Fortunately, security is a BlackBerry strong point. Viruses often come as e-mail attachments. However, BlackBerry supports very few file types out of the box (mostly images and documents). You won't face threats from e-mails with these attachments. And in an enterprise environment, the data that you send to or get from the PDA is *encrypted* (coded) to prevent snooping.

Saving power

Anyone with previous BlackBerry experience knows that BlackBerry is typically a highly efficient power consumer. With the older BlackBerry, you can go for five days on a single charge. The addition of a color, high-resolution screen, GPS (only Curve 8900 and some 8500 models) and Bluetooth support have weakened the power efficiency. Power requirements have increased so much that you need to recharge roughly every two days. But hey, now you have a GPS on deck!

RIM also has a Signature process for application developers that forces developers to identify themselves and their programs if they're developing any applications for the BlackBerry that need to integrate with either BlackBerry core applications or the OS.

Remember the *I love you* and *Anna Kournikova* viruses? These are virtual evils transmitted through e-mail, scripts, or sets of instructions in the e-mail body or attachment that can be executed either by the host e-mail program — or, in the case of an attachment, by the program associated with the attached file. Fortunately, BlackBerry's Messages doesn't support scripting languages. BlackBerry's viewer for such files doesn't support scripting either, so you won't be facing threats from e-mails having these attachments.

The security measures that RIM implemented on the BlackBerry platform have gained the trust of the U. S. government as well as many of the Forbes Top 500 enterprises in the financial and health industries.

Chapter 2

Navigating the BlackBerry Curve

*R*egardless of whether you previously owned a BlackBerry, you might have heard that the new BlackBerry Curve is totally different. You might be wondering how you spot a new BlackBerry Curve. Looks aren't deceiving in this case. From the outside, the new BlackBerry Curve 8500 is updated with an optical trackpad instead of a trackball — no more problems with the trackball getting stuck. The BlackBerry Curve 8500 design also has three media keys on the top. The BlackBerry Curve 8900 is slim and has a simple and elegant physical design. Bear with us, and you will be master of your BlackBerry Curve in no time.

Anatomy 101: The Body and Features of Your BlackBerry Curve

In this section and the following sections, we show you all the keys and features on your BlackBerry Curve. Figure 2-1 shows the primary ones for the Curve 8500 (see Figure 2-2 for the additional keys on the 8900), which are as follows:

✔ **Convenience keys:** With BlackBerry Curve, you have two convenience keys. By default, the convenience keys are preprogrammed to open an application.

In Chapter 3, we show you how to reprogram the convenience keys so that they display the programs you use the most.

🖝 **Display screen:** This screen is the graphical user interface (GUI) on your BlackBerry Curve.

🖝 **End key/Power key:** While on a phone call, use this key to end your call. If not on a phone call, press this key to jump straight back to the Home screen from wherever you are. Press and hold this key to turn your BlackBerry Curve on or off.

🖝 **Escape key:** This is the key to the right of the trackball or trackpad. Use this key to cancel a selection or return to a previous page within an application. If you hold this key down, it returns you to the Home screen from any program.

🖝 **Media keys (BlackBerry Curve 8500):** There are three media keys: Play/Pause key, Next Track key, Previous Track key. Play/Pause is used also to open Media Player (Chapter 14).

🖝 **Menu key:** Use this key to display the full menu of the application you're using.

🖝 **microSD slot:** The BlackBerry Curve has a microSD slot beneath the battery cover.

🖝 **Mute key:** This key mutes a call when on a call.

🖝 **Screen Lock key:** This key lets you quickly lock your screen before you slide your phone into your pocket.

🖝 **Send key:** Because your BlackBerry Curve can also function as a cellular phone, this key allows you to go straight to the Phone application, regardless of which application you are currently using. When you are already in the Phone application, the send key starts dialing the number you entered.

🖝 **Trackball or trackpad:** The Curve 8900 has a trackball; the 8500 has a trackpad. Navigate the display screen in four directions with the trackball or trackpad. When you press the trackball or trackpad, the short menu of the application you're using appears.

🖝 **QWERTY keyboard:** The keyboard is the input for your BlackBerry Curve — very straightforward.

Two types of contextual menus can appear on your BlackBerry Curve:

✔ **Full menu:** Lists all the options and features you can perform (see Figure 2-3, left). The full menu is accessed by pressing the menu key.

✔ **Short menu:** An abbreviated list of the full menu (see Figure 2-3, right). The short menu is accessed by pressing the trackball when you aren't prompted by a dialog box.

Left convenience   End/Power

Send   Display screen   Volume

Menu   Escape   Right convenience

Figure 2-1:
BlackBerry
Curve 8500.

Alt   Zero   Symbol   Delete

Left Shift   Right shift   Enter

Trackpad   Speakerphone

Screen lock   Mute

Trackball

Figure 2-2: BlackBerry Curve 8900.

Figure 2-3: Examples of a full menu and short menu in the Memo application.

New Appointment

Subject: Call Client

Select
Check Spelling
Clear Field
Save
Show Symbols
Switch Input Language
Switch Application
Close

09 9:00 AM
9 10:00 AM
Hour 0 Mins
anca (GMT)
Busy
15 Min.

New Appointment

Subject: Call Client
Location:

■All Day Event
Start: Mon, Aug 24, 2009 9:00 AM
End: Mon, Aug 24, 2009 10:00 AM
Duration: 1 Hour 0 Mins
Time Zone: Casablanca (GMT)
Show Time   Busy
Reminder: **Save**   15 Min.
■Conferen Full Menu

Display screen

When you first turn on your BlackBerry Curve, the display screen displays the *Home screen,* which is your introduction to the interface of your BlackBerry Curve. The different icons represent the different applications in your BlackBerry Curve. See Figure 2-4 for an example of what your Home screen might look like.

Figure 2-4:
Your
BlackBerry
Curve might
come with
a Home
screen like
this.

Depending on the theme you're using, your applications might be listed in text form rather than as icons. Remember that how your GUI looks depends on how you want it to look because the font and theme are customizable. For more on personalizing your BlackBerry Curve, see Chapter 3.

QWERTY keyboard

Unlike some PDA manufacturers — and they know who they are — RIM (Research In Motion) chose the same QWERTY keyboard you know and love from your personal computer as the BlackBerry Curve input method. That was a great decision because it means you don't have to master some new way of writing — graffiti or whatever — to get data into your Curve. All you have to do is type on a familiar keyboard — and you already know how to do that.

How you type on your BlackBerry Curve is up to you, but most people find that typing with two thumbs is the most efficient method.

Escape key

Simple yet useful, the escape key allows you to return to a previous screen or cancel a selection. The escape key is the arrow key to the right of the trackball.

Trackball and trackpad

You can perform two functions with the trackball or trackpad: navigating and pressing. When you navigate with your trackball or trackpad, you can move the cursor about the display screen in four directions. In a text-filled screen, such as the body of an e-mail, you can usually navigate through the text in four directions.

Depending on where you are on the BlackBerry Curve's screen, different situations determine what happens when you press the trackball or trackpad, also called the *trackball or trackpad click:*

- ✔ **Display a drop-down list:** When you're in a choice field, pressing the trackball or trackpad displays a drop-down list of choices for that field.

- ✔ **Confirm a choice:** The trackball or trackpad can also function as a confirmation key. For example, when you need to select a choice in a drop-down list, you can press the trackball or trackpad to confirm the highlighted choice.

- ✔ **Display a short menu:** When you're in a text-filled screen (an e-mail body or a Web page), pressing the trackball or trackpad displays a short menu (refer to Figure 2-3, right), which is just an abbreviated version of the full menu. You get the full menu by pressing the menu key.

Menu key

The menu key brings up the full menu for the application you're using. When on the Home screen, pressing the menu key displays a list of applications installed on your BlackBerry Curve. If you want to change the order of the applications in the list, see Chapter 3.

When you are on the Home screen, the behavior of the menu key depends on the BlackBerry Curve theme. The behavior just described is based on the default theme. See Chapter 3 for more on changing themes.

The microSD slot

Your BlackBerry Curve comes with 1GB of internal memory. If you're a music or video fan, you know that 1GB can't keep you entertained for a long commute. But no need to worry. The folks at RIM incorporated a microSD slot into your BlackBerry Curve so that you can add extended memory and store all the media files you want. The BlackBerry Curve supports up to a whopping 32GB microSD card.

You can purchase a microSD card separately for a relatively low price these days. At the time of this writing, a 16GB microSD card costs about $20, and a 32GB microSD costs about $40.

General Navigation Guidelines

In this section, we go over general shortcuts and navigation guidelines. On a Web page or an e-mail full of text, you can perform the tasks listed in Table 2-1.

Table 2-1	Curve Keyboard Shortcuts
Action	*To Do This*
Press the T key	Move to the top of the page
Press the B key	Move to the bottom of the page
Press the Space key	Move to the top of the next page
Press and hold the Shift key, and scroll the trackball horizontally	Select a line
Press and hold the Shift key, and scroll the trackball vertically	Select multiple lines
Press and hold the Shift key, and press the trackball	Copy selected text
Press and hold the Shift key, and press the Delete key	Cut selected text
Press and hold the Shift key, and press the trackball	Paste text
Press a letter key, and scroll the trackball	Insert an accented character
Press the Sym key, and press the letter below the symbol	Insert a symbol
Press Alt+Right Shift	Turn on caps lock
Press Alt+Left Shift	Turn on num lock

Switching applications

When you're navigating in an application, an option called Switch Application appears when you press the menu key. Switch Application (similar to Alt+Tab in Windows) lets you multitask between applications (see Figure 2-5).

Figure 2-5:
Switch
Application
menu.

The quickest way to get to Switch Application is to press and hold the menu key for 2 seconds.

Changing options

Throughout this book, you see examples of an options field being changed to a different value. The easiest way to change the value in a field is to first use the trackball or trackpad to highlight the field. Then press the trackball or trackpad to display a drop-down list of choices, such as the ones shown in Figure 2-6, and finally press the trackball or trackpad again to make your selection.

Date/Time	
Time Zone:	Casablanca (GMT)
(GMT) Casablanca, Monrovia, Reykjavik	
Time:	1:46 AM
Time Format:	24 hour
Date:	Mon, Aug 12 hour
Date/Time Source:	BlackBerry
Network Time:	4:46 AM
Network Date:	Mon, Aug 24, 2009

Figure 2-6:
An example
of an option
field's
drop-down
list.

General Keyboard Shortcuts

In many instances in this book, when you're asked to go to a BlackBerry Curve application (Profile, for example), you have to first highlight the application icon from the Home screen and then click the trackball or trackpad. You may be thinking, "Hey, there must be a shortcut for this," and you're right. This section and the ones that follow cover such general keyboard shortcuts, all in the name of making your life easier. (Shortcuts that are more application-specific are covered in the chapter dealing with the particular application.)

Before you get all excited about shortcuts, you need to take care of one bit of housekeeping. To use some of these general keyboard shortcuts, you first have to make sure that the Dial from Home Screen setting — buried deep within the Phone application — is turned off.

Inquiring minds want to know, so we'll tell you. The Dial from Home Screen option is designed for users who make frequent BlackBerry Curve phone calls. If you aren't a frequent phone user and want to access all applications with a press of a button, get ready to ditch Dial from Home Screen.

Here's how to turn off the Dial from Home Screen setting:

1. **From the BlackBerry Curve Home screen, highlight the Phone application and then press the trackball or trackpad.**

2. **Press the menu key and then select the Options menu.**

   A screen that lists a range of options appears.

3. **Select General Options.**

   The General Options screen appears.

4. **Highlight the Dial from Home Screen field and then select No.**

   Doing so shuts down the Dial from Home Screen option, enabling you to use Home-screen shortcuts.

5. **To confirm your changes, press the menu key and then select Save from the menu that appears.**

If you're a frequent phone user on your BlackBerry Curve, as opposed to an e-mail or Internet user, you may not want to turn off the Dial from Home Screen feature.

Using Home screen shortcuts

When you disable the Dial from Home Screen feature, you are free to use any Home screen shortcut. (The name for these shortcuts is actually a pretty good fit because you can use these shortcuts only while you are on the Home screen.)

Okay, here goes. To call up the application listed in the first column of Table 2-2, press the key listed in the table's second column.

Table 2-2	Home Screen Shortcuts
Application	*Shortcut Key*
Messages	M
Saved Messages	V
Compose	C
Search	S
Contacts	A
Tasks	T
Profile	F
Browser	B
Calendar	L
Calculator	U
MemoPad	D
Keyboard Lock	K
Phone	P

Other (non–Home screen) shortcuts

The following shortcuts can be used at any time, regardless of which screen you're in — or whether you have Dial from Home Screen enabled, for that matter:

 ✓ **Soft Device Reset** (also known as the *three-button salute*): Pressing **Alt+Shift+Del** forces a manual soft reset, which is just what you need when your BlackBerry Curve crashes or when you install an application and it needs a manual reset. You can do a hard reset by pulling out the battery from the back of the BlackBerry Curve. Without getting into the technical jargon, from a BlackBerry Curve user's perspective, a hard reset takes longer and is usually the last resort to solve any issues before contacting the help desk.

✔ **HelpME:** In the BlackBerry world, SOS is actually spelled **Alt+Shift+H**. Use it when you're on the phone with technical support. (It gives support personnel info such as your BlackBerry PIN, memory space, and version number so that they have information about your BlackBerry Curve when they try to troubleshoot your problems.)

The BlackBerry PIN isn't a security password; rather, it is a unique number that identifies your BlackBerry Curve, sort of like a serial number. But unlike a serial number, a BlackBerry can message another BlackBerry by using PIN-to-PIN messages (please see Chapter 9).

Chapter 3

Turning On Your BlackBerry Curve — and Keeping It Happy

. . . .

In This Chapter

▶ Putting your stamp on your BlackBerry Curve

▶ Watching your BlackBerry Curve's back

▶ Blocking spam e-mail and unwanted SMS messages

. . . .

Regardless of how long you've had your BlackBerry Curve — one week, one month, one year, or more — you'll want to have it around for as long as you possibly can. (Or at least until you have the bucks for that way-cool new model that's surely coming down the pike.) And for the duration that you *do* have your device, you'll want to trick it out so that it doesn't feel and sound exactly like the millions of other BlackBerry Curve devices out there. (C'mon, admit it — your BlackBerry Curve is definitely a fashion statement, so you'd better feel comfortable with what that statement is saying.)

In addition to customizing your BlackBerry Curve so that it expresses the inner you, you want to make sure that you keep your Curve in tip-top shape by watching out for such things as its battery life and information security. Luckily for you, this chapter puts all such worries to rest by filling you in on all you need to know to keep your BlackBerry Curve a finely tuned (and yet quirkily personal) little smartphone.

Making Your BlackBerry Curve Yours

BlackBerry smartphones are increasingly popular, so much so that close to 30 million BlackBerry smartphones are out there serving the needs of people like you. Because of this fact, we're certain that finding ways to distinguish your BlackBerry Curve from your colleagues' is high on your list of priorities.

Branding your BlackBerry Curve

Like any number of other electronic gadgets, your BlackBerry Curve comes to you off the shelf fitted with a collection of factory settings. This section helps you put your name on your BlackBerry Curve, figuratively and literally. You can start by branding your name on your BlackBerry Curve. Follow these steps:

1. **Press the menu key, and then highlight and select the Options (wrench) icon.**

2. **Select the Owner setting.**

   You see places to enter your owner information.

3. **Enter your name in the Name field and your contact information in the Information field.**

   The idea here is to phrase a message (like the one shown in Figure 3-1) that would make sense to any possible Good Samaritan who might find your lost BlackBerry Curve and want to get it back to you.

   If you lock or don't use your BlackBerry Curve for a while, the standby screen comes on, displaying the owner information that you entered. Read how to lock your BlackBerry Curve, either manually or by using an auto setting, in the later section "Keeping Your BlackBerry Curve Safe."

4. **Press the menu key and then select Save from the menu that appears.**

Figure 3-1:
List your
owner info
here.

Choosing a language, any language

Branding your BlackBerry Curve with your own John Hancock is a good start, but setting the language to your native tongue so that you don't need to hire a translator to use your Curve is equally important — and equally easy. You can also set your input method of choice here, which can affect whether AutoText shows up. Don't worry. We explain what that means in the next section.

Here's how you choose a language:

1. **Press the menu key and then select the Options (wrench) icon.**

2. **Select the Language setting.**

   Here, you can choose the language and input method of your choice.

3. **Select the Language field and then select your native tongue.**

   Depending on your network provider, as well as your region (North America, Europe, and so on), the language choices you have can vary. Most smartphones sold in North America default to English or English (U.S.).

   If your network provider supports it, you can install more languages in your BlackBerry Curve by using Application Loader in BlackBerry Desktop Manager. For more information on Application Loader, see Chapter 19.

4. **Press the menu key and then select Save from the menu that appears.**

Isn't it great when you can actually read what's onscreen? But don't think that you're finished quite yet. You still have some personalizing to do.

Typing with ease using AutoText

Even the most devoted BlackBerry Curve user has to admit that typing on a full keyboard is easier than thumb-typing on a BlackBerry Curve. In an attempt to even the score a bit, your BlackBerry Curve comes equipped with an AutoText feature, which is a kind of shorthand that can cut down on how much you have to type.

AutoText basically works with a pool of abbreviations that you set up. You then just type an abbreviation to get the word you associated with that abbreviation. For example, after setting up *b/c* as an AutoText word for *because,* any time you type **b/c**, you automatically get *because* onscreen.

Your BlackBerry Curve comes with a few default AutoText entries. Here are some useful ones:

✔ **mypin:** Displays your BlackBerry PIN

✔ **mynumber:** Displays your BlackBerry phone number

✔ **myver:** Displays your BlackBerry model number and OS version

The whole AutoText thing works best if you set up your own personal code, mapping your abbreviations to their meanings. (This is why we discuss AutoText as part of personalization.)

To set up your own code, do the following:

1. **Press the menu key and then select the Options (wrench) icon.**
2. **Select the AutoText option.**

   Here, you can choose to see (or search for) existing AutoText words or create new ones.

3. **Press the menu key and then select New.**

   The AutoText screen appears, as shown in Figure 3-2.

AutoText: New
Replace:
b/c
With:
because
Using: SmartCase
Language: All Locales

Figure 3-2:
Create
AutoText
here.

4. **In the Replace field, enter the characters that you want to replace (in this example, *b/c*). In the With field, type what replaces your characters (in this example, *because*).**
5. **In the Using field, choose between the SmartCase and Specified Case options.**

   • SmartCase capitalizes the first letter when the context calls for that, such as the first word in a sentence.

   • Specified Case replaces your AutoText with the exact text found in the With field.

   For example, say you have the AutoText *bbg* set up for the term *blackberryGoodies.com* and you want it to appear as is, in terms of letter cases (the first *b* isn't capitalized). If you use Specified Case, your AutoText always appears as *blackberryGoodies.com* no matter where it is in the sentence. If you instead were to choose SmartCase for this particular AutoText, it would be capitalized as the first word in a sentence, which isn't what you want.

6. **In the Language field, select All Locales from the list of options.**

   Our preference for this setting for any self-created AutoText is All Locales. What this means is that regardless of the language input method (for example, English UK, English U.S., or French), any self-created AutoText is available for you to use. So in the case of the AutoText *bbg* (*blackberryGoodies.com*), whether you are typing in French or Chinese, you can use this AutoText. On the other hand, if you select only the French input method for *bbg* as the Language field, you would be able to use this only if your input method is set to French in the Language option.

   You can choose the input method in the Language options. We go over choosing a language input method next.

7. **Press the menu key and then select Save from the menu that appears.**

If you specify a language input method other than All Locales, your input method setting in the Language option must match the Language field in AutoText to use your newly created AutoText. Follow these steps:

1. **Press the menu key and then select the Options (wrench) icon.**

2. **Scroll through the list of options until you find the Language setting and then select it.**

   Here, you can choose the language and input method.

3. **Select the Input Method field and then select the input method you need from the list.**

   For your new AutoText setting to work (assuming that you didn't choose All Locales as the language for your AutoText), this option needs to match the input method set in your Language option.

4. **Press the menu key and then choose Save.**

Getting your dates and times lined up

Having the correct date, time, and time zone is important when it comes to your BlackBerry Curve for, we hope, obvious reasons. Many of the fine features that make up the BlackBerry Curve core experience, as it were, depend on the time, date, and time zone being accurate.

Need an example? How about your BlackBerry Curve calendar events? Imagine, if you will, that you have a make-or-break meeting set for 9 a.m. (in your time zone) with a client in Paris, who is in who-knows-what time zone.

You definitely want to be on time for that appointment, but you probably won't be if you're planning on having your BlackBerry Curve remind you — that is, if you haven't set up the appropriate date, time, and time zone. Follow these steps to do that:

1. **Press the menu key and then select the Options (wrench) icon.**

2. **Select the Date/Time setting.**

   The Date/Time screen appears.

3. **For the Time Zone field, select a time zone.**

   The Date/Time screen confirms the time zone that you chose. Note that if you travel to a different time zone, you need to adjust this field because it does not adjust automatically.

4. **For the Time field, select the proper hour and minutes.**

   Here, you adjust the time to current hours and minutes.

5. **For the Date field, select the date.**

6. **For the Date/Time Source field, select Network.**

   This sets your date and time source to your service provider's server time (see Figure 3-3). By having this option set to Network, the time will always be accurate. However, if you are someone who always has the time set 10 minutes earlier than the actual time (so you can be on time for those important meetings), you would set the Date/Time Source field to BlackBerry.

7. **Press the menu key and then select Save from the menu that appears.**

   Doing so saves your date and time settings in perpetuity — a really long time, in other words.

Figure 3-3: Set the date and time of your BlackBerry Curve.

Date/Time	
Time Zone:	Eastern Time (-5)
(GMT-05:00) Eastern Time (US & Canada)	
Time:	7:50 AM
Time Format:	12 hour
Date:	Mon, Aug 24, 2009
Date/Time Source:	Network
Network Time:	2:50 PM
Network Date:	Mon, Aug 24, 2009

Customizing your screen's look and feel

Right up there with making sure that your date and time settings are accurate is getting the display font, font size, and screen contrast to your liking. Now we know that some of you don't give a hoot if your fonts are Batang or Bookman as long as you can read the text, but we also know that other folks won't stop configuring the fonts until they get them absolutely right. For all you tweakers out there, here's how you play around with your BlackBerry Curve's fonts:

1. **Press the menu key and then select the Options (wrench) icon.**

2. **Select the Screen/Keyboard setting.**

   The Screen/Keyboard screen appears with various customizable fields, as shown in Figure 3-4.

Figure 3-4:
The Screen/
Keyboard
screen,
waiting for
personaliza-
tion.

Screen/Keyboard	
Font Family:	BBAlpha Sans
Font Size:	9
Font Style:	Plain
The quick brown fox jumps over the lazy dog.	
Backlight Brightness:	100
Backlight Timeout:	45 Sec.
Automatically Dim Backlight:	On
LED Coverage Indicator:	Off
Key Tone:	Off
Key Rate:	Norm

3. **For the Font Family field, select a font from the drop-down list.**

   You can choose three to ten fonts, depending on your provider.

4. **For the Font Size field, select a font size.**

   One thing to keep in mind is that the smaller the font size, the more you can see onscreen; however, a smallish font is harder on the eyes.

   Note: As you scroll up and down the list of fonts and font sizes, notice that the text `The quick brown fox jumps over the lazy dog` below the Font Style setting takes on the look of the selected font and size so that you can preview what the particular text looks like. (In case you were wondering, this sentence uses every letter in the alphabet.)

5. **Press the menu key and then select Save from the menu that appears.**

Similar to setting Font Size, you can play with Font Style to set it to Bold, Italic, or Plain.

With fonts out of the way, it's time to change the brightness of your screen as well as a few other viewing options, including how to program the convenience key to exactly what is convenient to you:

1. **Press the menu key and then select the Options (wrench) icon.**

2. **Select the Screen/Keyboard setting.**

   The Screen/Keyboard screen appears with its various customizable fields (refer to Figure 3-4).

3. **For the Backlight Brightness field, select the desired brightness from the drop-down list.**

   You can choose 0 to 100, where 0 is the darkest and 100 is the brightest.

4. **For the Left Side Convenience Key Opens field, select from the drop-down an application for your left convenience key to open when you press it.**

5. **Repeat Step 4 for the Right Side Convenience Key Opens field.**

6. **For the Backlight Timeout field, select the time period for the backlight timeout.**

   You can choose 10 seconds up to 2 minutes. The lower this setting, the less time you'll have backlighting (after you press each key). However, a low setting helps you conserve battery life.

7. **Change the Automatically Dim Backlight field, if necessary.**

   When you're outdoors with a bright sun on your BlackBerry Curve, you'll probably have difficulty reading the screen. When the Automatically Dim Backlight feature is on (the default), it autoadjusts the backlight to be bright enough for you to read your BlackBerry Curve while outdoors.

8. **For the Horizontal Sensitivity field, select how sensitive you want the trackball or trackpad to be horizontally.**

   You can choose 20 to 100, where 20 is the least sensitive and 100 is the most sensitive.

9. **For the Vertical Sensitivity field, select how sensitive you want the trackball or trackpad to be vertically.**

   Again, 20 is the least sensitive and 100 is the most sensitive. Keep in mind that if your trackball or trackpad is too sensitive, it will be hard to control.

10. **To confirm your changes, press the menu key and then select Save.**

Choosing themes for your BlackBerry Curve

Your BlackBerry Curve is preloaded with different *themes,* which are pre-defined sets of looks (wallpaper, fonts, menu layout). You can download themes from BlackBerry Curve's mobile Web site.

Follow these steps to change your theme:

1. **Press the menu key and then select the Options (wrench) icon.**

2. **Select the Theme setting.**

   You see a list of available themes.

3. **Select the theme you want.**

   You see a preview of the theme you selected (see Figure 3-5).

4. **Press the menu key and then select Activate.**

   You should be able to see the change immediately.

It usually takes a while for a new theme to fully activate.

You can download other themes. Just remember that you have to use your BlackBerry Curve, not your PC, to access the following URL: `http://mobile.blackberry.com`.

Figure 3-5:
Preview of
currently
selected
theme.

Wallpapering your BlackBerry Curve

Like your desktop PC, the BlackBerry Curve Home screen can be personalized with wallpaper. You set an image to be your BlackBerry Curve Home screen background by using the BlackBerry Curve Media application. Follow these steps:

1. **Press the menu key and then select the Media icon.**

   The following categories are in Media: Music, Video, Ring Tones, Pictures, and Voice Notes.

2. **Select the Pictures category.**

   Doing so brings up four choices:

   - Camera: Turns on the BlackBerry camera.

   - All Pictures: Displays all the pictures stored on your BlackBerry.

   - Picture Folders: Displays the pictures stored on your BlackBerry, organized by folders.

   - Sample Pictures: Displays the pictures that came with your BlackBerry.

3. **Select the picture you want to use for your Home screen background.**

   The selected picture appears in full-screen view.

4. **Press the menu key and then select Set as Home Screen Image.**

   The picture is now your new Home screen wallpaper.

5. **Press and hold the escape key to return to the Home screen and see the result.**

You can download free wallpapers from the following Web sites (as long as you use your BlackBerry Curve, not your PC, to access the URLs):

- http://mobile.blackberry.com
- www.blackberrywallpapers.com
- www.crackberry.com/free-wallpapers

After you have your BlackBerry Curve's look and feel just the way you want, there's just one thing left to do before you can move on. You need to get your BlackBerry Curve to sound how you want it to.

Letting freedom ring

The whole appeal of the BlackBerry phenomenon is the idea that this little electronic device can make your life easier. One of the ways it accomplishes this is by acting as your personal reminder service — letting you know when an appointment is coming up, a phone call is coming in, an e-mail has arrived, and so on. Basically, your BlackBerry Curve is set to bark at you if it knows something it thinks you should know, too. Figure 3-6 lists the kinds of things your BlackBerry Curve considers bark-worthy, ranging from browser alerts to task deadlines.

Figure 3-6: Set attention-needy applications here.

Normal
BlackBerry Messenger Alert
BlackBerry Messenger New Message
Browser
Calendar
Level 1
Messages [Email]
Phone
SMS Text
Tasks

Different people react differently to different sounds. Some BlackBerry Curve barks would be greatly appreciated by certain segments of the population, whereas other segments might react to the same sound by pitching their BlackBerry Curve under the nearest bus. The folks at Research In Motion are well aware of this and have devised a great way for you to customize how you want your BlackBerry Curve to bark at you — they call it your *profile*.

You can jump right into things by using a predefined profile, or you can create your own profile. The upcoming sections take a look at both approaches.

Whether you create your own profile or customize a predefined profile, each profile is divided into several categories that represent the application for which you can define alerts.

In BlackBerry OS 4.6, the application to set your profiles is named Profiles and includes the following categorizations:

- **BlackBerry Messenger Alert:** Alerts you when BlackBerry Messenger has something to notify you regarding new contact notification.

- **BlackBerry Messenger New Message:** Alerts you when BlackBerry Messenger has a new message from a BlackBerry Messenger contact.

- **Browser:** Alerts you when you receive a new *channel push,* which is just a Web page sent to your BlackBerry Curve.

- **Calendar:** Alerts you when you have upcoming appointments.

- **Level 1:** Alerts you with a special tone when you have an urgent (as defined by your sender) e-mail. A BlackBerry PIN-to-PIN message can also be considered urgent. For more on PIN-to-PIN, see Chapter 9.

- **Messages [Email]:** Alerts you when a new e-mail message is in your inbox.

- **Phone:** Alerts you if you have an incoming call or a new voice mail.

- **SMS Text:** Alerts you when you have an SMS (Short Messaging Service) message.

- **Tasks:** Alerts you to an upcoming to-do deadline.

In BlackBerry OS 5.0, profiles can be found in the Sounds application, and Sound items are organized into the following categories:

- **Phone:** Alerts you if you have an incoming call or voice mail.

- **Messages:** Alerts you if you have an incoming e-mail, SMS, MMS, or BlackBerry PIN message. Also, you can set different alerts for each individual e-mail account.

- **Instant Messages:** Alerts you if you have any BlackBerry Messenger Alerts; if you have third-party instant messaging installed (such as Google Talk), you can set the alerts here as well.

- **Reminders:** Alerts you if you have set up calendar reminders, tasks reminders, or e-mail follow-up flags (see Chapter 8).

- **Other:** This category is a notification setting for third-party applications such as Facebook a well as the Browser application.

You can personalize all the listed applications according to how you want to be alerted. Because how you customize them is similar, we use one application, Messages, as an example in the text that follows.

After this, we go over creating a profile from scratch. You may be wondering why you need to create a profile if you can personalize the predefined ones. If your needs are different from the predefined settings, creating a profile is the way to go.

Using factory settings

If you're okay with customizing a predefined, factory-loaded profile, just do the following if you have OS 4.6:

1. **From the BlackBerry Curve Home screen, select the Profile application.**

   A pop-up screen appears, listing different profiles (Quiet, Vibrate, Normal).

2. **Select Advanced, which appears at the end of the list.**

   A screen appears, listing different profiles.

3. **Highlight the Normal profile in the list, press the menu key, and then select Edit.**

   The Normal screen appears, listing the applications with alert capabilities mentioned in the preceding section (refer to Figure 3-6).

4. **Select the Messages [Email] application.**

   You're faced with the Messages for Normal profile, which is divided into an Out of Holster section and an In Holster section, as shown in Figure 3-7. A *holster* (in this context) is simply the belt clip or case that houses your BlackBerry Curve while you aren't using it. BlackBerry Curve is smart enough to know when it is in a holster. With RIM's BlackBerry holster, a magnet built into the holster autoswitches the Curve to In Holster mode within the selected profile.

5. **For the Out of Holster field, select a tone from the drop-down list of alert options.**

   Doing so enables sound in Out of Holster mode.

Figure 3-7: Choose a tone to alert you when your BlackBerry Curve is out of its holster.

Messages [Email] in Normal	
Out of Holster:	None
Ring Tone:	BBPro_Sanguine
Volume:	Mute
Number of Beeps:	1
Repeat Notification:	LED Flashing
Number of Vibrations:	2
In Holster:	Vibrate
Ring Tone:	BBPro_Sanguine
Volume:	Mute
Number of Beeps:	1
Repeat Notification:	LED Flashing

6. **For the Ring Tone field, select the tune you want from the drop-down list.**

   As you scroll through the tunes and pause, your BlackBerry Curve plays the tune so that you know what it sounds like before you change it.

7. **Press the menu key and then select Save.**

As you may have guessed from how Messages in the Normal profile is divided, your BlackBerry Curve can notify you in different ways based on whether your BlackBerry Curve is in plain view (Out of Holster) or tucked away next to your belt (In Holster). To set up a different sound for In Holster mode, just put the necessary info in the fields for the In Holster section — and be sure to choose a different tune this time. (Choosing the same tune kind of defeats the purpose, doesn't it?)

If you're like us and get more than 200 e-mails daily, you probably don't want your BlackBerry Curve sounding off 200 times a day. You can set up your Curve so that it notifies you only if an e-mail has been marked urgent, requiring your immediate attention. You can do this by setting the notification for your Messages application to None for both In Holster and Out of Holster. Then, in the Level 1 option (refer to Figure 3-6), you can set your desired notification for both In Holster and Out of Holster. That way, you conveniently filter any unnecessary e-mail notifications, leaving just the urgent stuff to sound off to you.

For BlackBerry OS 5.0, follow these steps to customize alerts for your BlackBerry:

1. **From the BlackBerry Curve Home screen, select the Sounds application.**

   A pop-up screen appears, listing different profiles (Silent, Vibrate, Normal, Loud, Medium, Phone Calls Only, All Alerts Off).

2. **Select Edit Profiles, which appears at the end of the list.**

   A screen appears, listing different profiles.

3. **Highlight the Normal profile in the list, press the menu key, and then select Edit.**

   The Normal screen appears, listing the applications with alert capabilities mentioned in the preceding section (refer to Figure 3-6).

4. **Expand the Messages heading by pressing the trackball or trackpad once, and select any of the e-mail accounts you have.**

   A screen appears with options to set the ring tone, LED, and vibration.

5. **For Ring Tone, you can set the following options:**

   • Ring Tone: The ring tone you want.

   • Volume: How loud you want the ring tone, from Silent to 10 (the loudest).

- Count: The number of times the ring tone repeats, from 1 to 3.

- Play Sound: Whether the ring tone will play while your BlackBerry Curve is in or out of the holster or whether it will always play.

6. **For LED, set it On or Off.**

7. **For vibration, set it to be On, Off, or Custom.**

   If you choose Custom, you have the following options:

   - Length: How long each vibration lasts: Short, Medium, or Long.

   - Count: The number of times the vibration occurs; you can choose 1, 2, 3, 5, or 10.

   - Vibrate: Whether the vibration will occur while your BlackBerry is in or out of holster or will always vibrate.

8. **Press the menu key and then select Save.**

Creating your own profile

You need to know which applications on your BlackBerry Curve have alert capabilities because then you can personalize each "Hey, you!" to your liking. You can have your BlackBerry Curve so personalized that you can tell whether you have a phone call or an incoming message just by how your BlackBerry Curve sounds.

If you're already familiar with the different applications and are clear how you want each one to alert you, go on and create your own profile. As we mention earlier, you can achieve the same result by personalizing the predefined profiles that come with your BlackBerry Curve. But if you like to keep the predefined profiles the way they are, create a new profile by following the steps for your OS version.

If you have OS 4.6, follow these steps to create a new profile:

1. **From the BlackBerry Curve Home screen, select the Profile application.**

   A pop-up screen appears, listing different profiles (Quiet, Vibrate, Normal).

2. **Select Advanced, which appears at the end of the list.**

   A screen appears, listing different profiles.

3. **Press the menu key and then select New.**

   A new Profile screen appears, as shown in Figure 3-8, prompting you to name your profile.

Name: MyOwnProfile
BlackBerry Messenger Alert
BlackBerry Messenger New Message
Browser
Calendar
Level 1
Messages [Email]
Phone
SMS Text
Tasks

Figure 3-8:
Create your
own profile
from this
menu in
OS 4.6.

4. **In the Name field, enter a name for your profile.**

   For this example, just type **MyOwnProfile**.

5. **Configure your new profile.**

   To customize each of the nine applications, refer to the OS 4.6 part of the preceding section, "Using factory settings," Steps 3–7.

6. **Press the menu key and then select Save.**

   Your newly created profile appears in the Profile screen.

7. **Select My Profile.**

   You can start to use your newly created profile.

If you have OS 5.0, follow these steps to create a new profile:

1. **From the BlackBerry Curve Home screen, select the Sound application.**

   A pop-up screen appears, listing different profiles.

2. **Select Edit Profiles, which appears at the end of the list.**

   A screen appears, with a line Add Custom Profile and also a list of profiles.

3. **Select Add Custom Profile.**

   A New Custom Profile screen appears, prompting you to name your profile.

4. **In the Name field, enter a name for your profile.**

   For this example, just type **MyOwnProfile**.

5. **Configure your new profile.**

To customize each of the categories of applications, refer to the OS 5.0 part of the preceding section, "Using factory settings," Steps 3–7.

6. **Press the menu key and then select Save.**

   Your newly created profile appears in the Profile screen.

7. **Select My Profile.**

   You can start to use your newly created profile.

You can switch between your current profile and the Quiet profile by pressing and holding the # key.

Regardless of whether the ring tone is for an incoming call or an incoming e-mail, you can download more ring tones to personalize your BlackBerry Curve. Also, you can use any MP3 file in your Media application as your personalized ring tone. Follow these steps:

1. **From the Home screen, press the menu key and then select the Media application.**

2. **In Media, select the Music category.**

   Doing so brings up various music classifications such as Artist, Album, and Genres.

3. **Highlight the music file you want to use for your ring tone.**

4. **Press the menu key and then select Set as Phone Tune.**

   This sets the music file as your new phone tune.

5. **Press and hold the escape key to return to the Home screen.**

Keeping Your BlackBerry Curve Safe

The folks at RIM take security seriously, and so should you. Always set up a password on your BlackBerry Curve. If your BlackBerry Curve hasn't prompted you to set up a password, you should do so immediately. Here's how:

1. **From the BlackBerry Curve Home screen, select the Options (wrench) icon.**

2. **Select the Password option.**

3. **Highlight the Password field and then select Enabled.**

All this does for now is enable the Password feature. You won't be prompted to type a password until you save the changes you just made.

4. Click the Set Password button.

At this time, you should be prompted to enter a new password, as shown in Figure 3-9.

If you have set a password before, the button will be called Change Password.

Figure 3-9:
It's time to enter a new password.

5. Type a password and then type it again for verification.

From this point on, whenever you lock your BlackBerry Curve and want to use it again, you have to type the password. How do you lock your BlackBerry Curve? Good question. Keep reading.

When you set your password on a BlackBerry Curve, you must make sure that you know what letters your password uses and not just which keys you pressed. You need the same password if you link your BlackBerry Curve with Desktop Manager for synchronization. For more on Desktop Manager, read Chapters 16, 17, and 18.

Setting up your password is a good first step, but just having a password won't help much if you don't take the further step of locking your BlackBerry Curve when you aren't using it. (You don't want people at the office or at the table next to you at the coffee shop checking out your e-mails or phone history when you take a bathroom break, do you?) So how do you lock your BlackBerry Curve? Let us count the ways . . . we came up with two.

You can go the Autolock after Timeout (also known as Security Timeout) route by following these steps:

1. **Press the menu key and then select the Options (wrench) icon.**

2. **Select the Password option.**

   The Password screen appears.

3. **Highlight the Security Timeout field and then select the desired minutes.**

   The preset times range from 1 minute to 1 hour.

4. **Press the menu key and then select Save.**

 If you're more the hands-on kind of person, you can go the Manual Lockout route by scrolling to the keyboard Lock icon on your Home screen and pressing the trackball. (Pressing K while on the Home screen does the same thing. Make sure to turn off the Dial from Home Screen option. See Chapter 2 for more info on using Home screen shortcuts.)

As a shortcut, to lock your BlackBerry Curve, just press and hold the asterisk (*) key.

No matter what route you take to lock your BlackBerry Curve, you use your (newly created) password to unlock it when you get back from wherever you've been.

Blocking That Spam

With your BlackBerry Curve, you can block certain e-mails, SMS numbers, or BlackBerry PINs from getting to your inbox. It's like having your own spam blocker on your Curve!

To set up your personal spam blocker, follow these steps:

1. **From the Home screen, select the Options (wrench) icon.**

2. **Select the Security option.**

3. **Select the Firewall option.**

   This opens the Firewall screen.

4. **Highlight the Status field and select Enable.**

   This enables the spam blocker.

5. **Under Block Incoming Message, make sure what you want to block is selected:**

    • SMS: Blocks SMS messages.

    • PIN: Blocks BlackBerry PIN messages.

    • BlackBerry Internet Service: Blocks e-mail messages (for example, the e-mail account that you set up from Google or Yahoo! Mail).

    • Enterprise Email: Blocks enterprise e-mail (if you're in a corporate e-mail network).

6. **In the Except Messages From area, select the desired options:**

    • Contact: Blocks everything except the e-mails and phone numbers in your Contacts.

    • Specific Address: Blocks everything specified by you (you can set up the list described in Steps 7 and 8).

7. **Press the menu key and then select Configure Exception.**

    This opens the Firewall exception screen.

8. **Press the menu key and then select the desired options:**

    • Add Email: Specify the e-mail you want to block by selecting this check box.

    • Add PIN: Specify the BlackBerry PIN you want to block by selecting this check box.

    • Add Phone Number: Specify the SMS number you want to block by selecting this check box.

Part II
Organizing with Curve

The 5th Wave   By Rich Tennant

"Well, here's what happened—I forgot to put it on my 'To Do' list."

In this part . . .

Find out how to use your BlackBerry Curve to its fullest to get — and remain — organized. Peruse the chapters here to find out how to use Contacts, keep appointments, set alarms, use the timer and Bedside mode with the Clock application, and keep your passwords safe and easy to retrieve.

Chapter 4

Remembering and Locating Your Acquaintances

Address books were around long before the BlackBerry was conceived. And BlackBerry Contacts serves the same function as any address book: a place where you record and organize information about people. However, Contacts also affords you a central place to reach your contacts in myriad ways: by landline phone; cellphone; e-mail; or the speedy messaging of PIN, SMS, MMS, or BlackBerry Messenger.

Most likely, in your busy lifestyle, you can benefit from using your BlackBerry Contacts if any of the following fits:

✔ You travel.

✔ You meet clients frequently.

✔ You spend a lot of time on the phone.

✔ You ask people for their phone number or e-mail address more than once.

✔ You carry around a paper day planner.

✔ Your wallet is full of important business cards, with phone numbers written on the backs, that you can never find.

If you're one of those stubborn folks who insist they don't need an address book — "I'm doing just fine without one, thank you very much!" — think of it this way: You've probably been using a virtual address book all the time, the one buried in your cellphone. That address book probably isn't even a very good one! Read this chapter to see how to transfer all that good contact info from an old phone into your new BlackBerry–based Contacts.

Accessing Contacts

The Contacts icon looks like an old-fashioned address book. (Remember those?) You can see it highlighted in Figure 4-1. Opening Contacts couldn't be simpler: Select the Contacts icon from the Home screen.

Figure 4-1:
The
Contacts
icon.

You can also access Contacts from Phone, Messages, BlackBerry Messenger, and Calendar. For example, say you're in Calendar and you want to invite people to one of your meetings. Look no further — Contacts is in the menu, ready to lend a helping hand.

Another way to get to Contacts is by pressing A while on the Home screen. Go to Chapter 2 for more on Home-screen shortcuts.

Working with Contacts

Getting a new gizmo is always exciting because you just know that your newest toy is chock-full of features you're dying to try out. We bet you feel that way about your BlackBerry Curve. The first thing you'll want to do is try to call or e-mail someone, right? But wait a sec. You don't have any contact information yet, which means you have to type in someone's e-mail address each time you send an e-mail — what a hassle.

It's time to get with the plan. Most of us humans — social creatures that we are — maintain a list of contacts somewhere, such as in e-mail program, on an old cellphone, or on a piece of paper kept tucked away in a wallet. We're pretty sure that you have some kind of list somewhere. The trick is getting that list into your BlackBerry Curve so that you can access your info more efficiently. The good news for you is that getting contact info into your BlackBerry Curve isn't hard.

Often, the simplest way to get contact information into your BlackBerry Curve is to enter it manually. However, if you've invested a lot of time and energy in maintaining some type of Contacts application on your desktop computer, you may want to hot-sync that data into your Curve. For more on synchronizing data, check Chapter 16.

Creating a contact

Imagine that you just ran into Jane Doe, an old high school friend whom you haven't seen in years. Jane is about to give you her number, but you don't have a pen or pencil handy to write down her information. Are you then forced to chant her phone number to yourself until you can scare up a writing implement? Not if you have your handy BlackBerry Curve with you.

With BlackBerry in hand, follow these steps to create a new contact:

1. **On the BlackBerry Home screen, select the Contacts application.**

   As we mention earlier, you also can access Contacts from different applications. For example, see Chapter 9 to find out how to access Contacts from Messages.

2. **In Contacts, highlight Add Contact and then press the trackball or trackpad.**

   The New Contact screen appears, as shown in Figure 4-2.

3. **Enter the contact information in the appropriate fields.**

   Use your BlackBerry Curve keyboard to enter this information. Scroll down to see additional fields.

   When entering an e-mail address, press the Space key to insert an at symbol (@) or a period (.). BlackBerry is smart enough to figure out that you need an @ or a period.

New Contact

Title:
First: |
Last:
Picture:

Company:
Job Title:

Email:

Figure 4-2:
Create a
new contact
here.

We don't think you can overdo it when entering a person's contact information. Enter as much info as you possibly can. Maybe the benefit won't be obvious now, but when your memory fails you or your boss needs a critical piece of info that you happen to have, you'll thank us for this advice.

4. **(Optional) For those contacts who have more than one e-mail address — say, work and home — just create another new, blank Email field for the same contact.**

    a. Press the menu key.

    b. Select Add Email Address.

   You can have up to three e-mail addresses per contact.

5. **Press the trackball or trackpad, and then select Save.**

   Your new contact is added to the list, as shown in Figure 4-3.

Find: |

Add Contact:

Jane Doe

Figure 4-3:
The
Contacts
screen after
adding a
contact.

Here's something slick to know when you're entering phone information for a contact: BlackBerry Curve can also dial an extra number after the initial phone number. That extra number can be someone's extension, or a participant code on a conference number, or simply your voice mail PIN. When you're entering the contact's phone number, type the primary phone number, press the Alt key and press X, and then add the extension number. Say you enter 11112345678X1111; when you tell your Curve to call that number, it will dial 11112345678 first. Then you'll see a prompt asking you to continue or skip dialing the extension.

The menu is always available through the menu key, but just for convenience, we prefer to use the trackball or trackpad, which displays a shortened menu list based on where you are.

Adding notes

The Notes field on the New Contact screen (you may need to scroll down a bit to see it) is useful for adding a unique description about your contact. For example, use the field to hold info to jog or refresh your memory with tidbits such as *Knows somebody at ABC Corporation* or *Can provide introduction to a Broadway agent.* Or perhaps your note is something personal, such as *Likes golf; has 2 children: boy, 7, & girl, 3; husband's name is Ray.* It's up to you. Again, the more useful the information, the better it will serve you.

Customizing with your own fields

Perhaps you'd like to add contact information that doesn't fit into any of the available fields. Although you can't really create additional fields from scratch, you can commandeer one of the User fields for your own purposes.

The User fields are located at the bottom of the screen, so you have to scroll down to see them. Basically, you can use these fields any way you want (which is great), and you can even change the field's name. (Face it, *User field* isn't that helpful as a descriptive title.) For example, you can rename User fields to capture titles that follow a name (such as MD, PhD, and so on). Or how about profession, birthdate, hobbies, school, or nickname? You decide what information is important to you.

Changing the field name for this particular contact changes it for all your contacts.

To rename a User field, follow these steps:

1. **Scroll to the bottom of the screen to navigate to one of the User fields.**

2. **Press the menu key and then select Change Field Name.**

    The Change Field Name selection on the menu appears only if the cursor is in a User field.

3. **Use the keyboard to enter the new User field name.**

4. **Press the trackball, trackpad, or enter key to save.**

   You're all set.

Adding a picture for a contact

Like most phones, your BlackBerry Curve can display a picture of the caller. Here's how to add a photo for a contact:

1. **Have access to a digital picture of the person.**

   See Chapter 13 for more about taking photos with your BlackBerry Curve.

2. **Get the photo to your BlackBerry Curve.**

   You can send it via e-mail, copy it to the microSD card, or copy it to the built-in memory of Curve. If you don't know how to use the microSD, Chapter 16 is your gateway to media satisfaction.

3. **From the Home screen, select the Contacts icon.**

4. **Highlight a contact.**

5. **Press the menu key and then select Add Picture (see Figure 4-4).**

New Contact

Title:
First:
Last:
Picture:

Figure 4-4:
Add a
picture
here.

Cor   Save
Job   Add Custom Ring Tone
Em   **Add Picture**
Wo   Full Menu

6. **Use the trackball or trackpad to navigate to the drive and folder that contains the picture.**

   You can use multiple locations for storing media files, such as pictures. Chapter 15 gives you the scoop.

7. **Select the picture.**

   The picture you choose is displayed in full onscreen with a rectangle on it.

8. **Slide the trackball or trackpad to position the rectangle on the face.**

Contacts uses a tiny image, just enough to show the face of a person. The rectangle you see here indicates how the application crops the image.

9. **Press the trackball or trackpad and then select Crop and Save.**

   You're all set. Just save this contact to keep your changes.

10. **Press the menu key and then select Save.**

Assigning a tone

Oh, no, your ringing Curve has woken you. Ring tones help you decide whether to ignore the call or get up. We hope, you can easily switch to Sleep mode if you decide to ignore the call.

If you have OS 4.6 (perhaps BlackBerry Handheld Software v4.6), follow these steps to assign a ring tone to one of your contacts:

1. **While editing a contact, press the trackball or trackpad and then select Add Custom Ring Tone from the menu (refer to Figure 4-4).**

2. **Press the trackball or trackpad.**

   A screen similar to Figure 4-4 gives you an option to customize the ring tone settings. From this screen, you can select a ring tone; set the volume; and control whether to make the LED blink, the phone vibrate, and the settings work while you're on a call.

3. **Select the ring tone you want.**

4. **Press the menu key and then select Save.**

If you have OS 5.0 (possibly BlackBerry Handheld Software v5.0), follow these steps to assign a ring tone to one of your contacts:

1. **While editing a contact, scroll to the Ring Tones/Alerts section.**

   Under the Ring Tones/Alerts section, you should see Phone and Messages. You can customize the ring tone when you receive a call and when you have a new message, such as an e-mail or an SMS.

2. **Select Phone and customize the ring tone on the screen that follows.**

   You see and can change the following options:

   - Ring Tone: You select a ring tone from a list of tones here.

   - Volume: Allows you to control the volume. The default is set to use the Active Profile settings. Other values are 1 to 10; 10 is the loudest.

   - Play Sound: Lets you control in what state to play the tone. Values are Active Profile, In Holster, Out of Holster, and Always; the default is set to Active Profile.

   - LED: Allows you to use LED to indicate a call.

- Vibration: Allows you to enable vibration as a way of notification. Choices are Active Profile, Off, On, and Custom. The default is Active Profile. Choosing Custom allows you to control how long you want the vibration to last.

  - Vibrate with Ring Tone: Allows you to choose between vibrating and playing the tone. Choices are Active Profile, On, and Off. The default value is Active Profile.

3. **Press the escape key.**

   You're back to the Edit Contact screen.

4. **Select Messages.**

   You are presented with the Messages screen, allowing you to customize the ring tone when you receive a message. You can do all the customizations listed in Step 2 plus the following:

   - Notify Me During Calls: Allows you to toggle notification while you are actively on a call. Your choices are Yes or No, and the default is No.

5. **Press the escape key.**

6. **Press the menu key and then select Save.**

Spend a little bit of time adding your own contact record(s). We recommend adding at least one record for your business contact info and one for your personal contact info. This saves you from having to type your own contact information every time you want to give it to someone. You can share your contact record by sending it as an attachment to an e-mail. (See the later section "Sharing a Contact.")

Adding contacts from other BlackBerry applications

When you get an e-mail message or a call, that person's contact information is in Messages or Phone. It's just logical to add the information. You may have noticed that Phone lists only outgoing numbers. That's half of what you need. You can access incoming phone calls in Messages:

1. **On the BlackBerry Home screen, select Messages.**

2. **In Messages, press the menu key and then select View Folder.**

3. **Select Phone Call Logs.**

A phone log entry stays only as long as you have free space on your BlackBerry Curve. When BlackBerry runs out of space (which could take years, depending on how you use it), it deletes read e-mails and phone logs, starting from the oldest.

You can view your device memory information by going to Options from the Home screen and selecting Memory. The next screen shows you two types of memory: application memory and media card. Pay close attention to application memory. This is where your applications are installed, including data from out-of-the-box applications such as Contacts, Messages, and Calendar. Your Curve has 128MB total application memory, and you should see how much is free from this screen.

Creating a contact from an existing e-mail address or phone number in Messages is easy:

1. **On the BlackBerry Home screen, select Messages.**

2. **In Messages, select the e-mail address or the phone number.**

3. **Select Add to Contacts.**

   A New Contact screen appears, filled with that particular piece of information.

4. **Enter the rest of the information you know.**

5. **Press the menu key and then select Save.**

The best solution for capturing contact information from e-mail is an application called gwabbit. The app has the intelligence of detecting contact information and gives you a quick and easy way to add it to Contacts. You can purchase gwabbit for $9.99 a year and download the app from their Web site at www.gwabbit.com.

Viewing a contact

Okay, you just entered your friend Jane's name into your BlackBerry, but you have this nagging thought that you typed the wrong phone number. You want to quickly view Jane's information. Here's how you do it:

1. **On the BlackBerry Home screen, select Contacts.**

2. **In Contacts, scroll to and highlight the contact name you want and then press the trackball or trackpad.**

   Pressing the trackball, trackpad, or enter key while a name is highlighted is the same as opening the menu and choosing View — just faster.

   View mode displays only information that's been filled in, as shown in Figure 4-5. It doesn't bother showing blank fields.

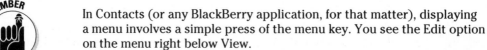

Jane Doe

Email: jane.doe@blackberryfordu
mmies.com

Work: 212-111-2222

Figure 4-5:
View mode
for a
contact.

Editing a contact

Change is an inevitable part of life. Given that fact, your contact information is sure to change as well. To keep current the information you diligently put in Contacts, you have to do some updating now and then. To update a contact, follow these steps:

1. **On the BlackBerry Home screen, select Contacts.**

2. **In Contacts, scroll to and highlight a contact name, press the menu key, and then select Edit.**

   The Edit Contact screen for that contact makes an appearance.

   In Contacts (or any BlackBerry application, for that matter), displaying a menu involves a simple press of the menu key. You see the Edit option on the menu right below View.

3. **Scroll through the various fields of the Edit Contact screen, editing the contact information as you see fit.**

   If you want to edit only a few words or letters in a field (instead of replacing all the text), slide the trackball or trackpad while pressing and holding the Alt key (located to the left of the Z key) to position your cursor precisely on the text you want to change. Then make your desired changes.

4. **Press the menu key and then select Save.**

   The edit you made for this contact is saved.

When you're editing information, and you want to replace the entry with a new one, it's much faster to first clear the contents, especially if you have a lot of old data. When you are in an editable field (as opposed to a selectable field), just press the menu key and then select Clear Field. This feature is available in all text-entry fields and for most BlackBerry applications.

Deleting a contact

It's time to get rid of somebody's contact information in your Contacts. Maybe it's a case of duplication or a bit of bad blood. Either way, BlackBerry Curve makes it easy to delete a contact.

1. **On the BlackBerry Home screen, select Contacts.**

2. **In Contacts, scroll to and highlight a contact name you want to delete, press the menu key, and then select Delete.**

   A confirmation screen appears, as shown in Figure 4-6.

Figure 4-6:
The con-
firmation
screen
when you're
about to
delete a
contact.

3. **Select Delete.**

   The contact you selected is deleted and disappears from your Contacts list.

Dealing with the confirmation screen can be a pain if you want to delete several contacts in a row. If you are 100 percent sure that you want to ditch a number of contacts, you can suspend the Confirmation feature by setting the Confirm Delete option to No on the Contacts Options screen. See the "Setting preferences" section, later in this chapter, for more on Contacts Options.

Copying Contacts from Desktop Applications

Most people use desktop applications to maintain their contacts — you know, Microsoft Outlook, IBM Lotus Notes, or Novell GroupWise. And a word to the wise: You don't want to maintain two address books. That's a recipe for disaster. Luckily for you, RIM (Research In Motion) makes it easy to get your various contacts — BlackBerry, desktop, laptop, whatever — in sync.

Your BlackBerry Curve comes with a collection of programs called BlackBerry Desktop Manager, one of which is Synchronize. You can use Synchronize to

- Sync between your device and the PC software for managing contacts such as Outlook.

- Set up and configure the behavior of the program, including how the fields in the desktop version of Contacts map to the Contacts fields in your BlackBerry.

Chapter 16 shows how to use Synchronize.

Looking for Someone?

Somehow — usually through a combination of typing skills and the shuttling of data between various electronic devices — you've created a nice, long list of contacts in Contacts. Nice enough, we suppose, but useless unless you can find the phone number of Rufus T. Firefly at the drop of a hat.

That's where the Find screen comes in. In fact, the first thing you see in Contacts when you open it is the Find screen, as shown in Figure 4-7.

Find:
Add Contact:
Daniel
Dante Sarigumba
Dean Sarigumba
Drew Sarigumba

Figure 4-7: Your search starts here.

You can conveniently search through your contacts by following these steps:

1. **In the Find field, enter the starting letters of the name you want to search for.**

Your search criterion is the name of the person. You could enter the last name or first name or both, although the list is usually sorted by first name and then last name. As you type the letters, the list shrinks based on the matches. Figure 4-8 illustrates how this works.

2. **Using the trackball or trackpad, scroll to and highlight the name from the list of matches.**

   If you have a long list in Contacts, and you want to scroll down a page at a time, just hold down the Alt key (it's located to the left of the Z key) and scroll. You get where you need to go a lot faster.

3. **Press the menu key and select from the possible actions listed on the menu that appears.**

   After you find the person you want, you can select among these options, as shown in Figure 4-9:

   • Activity Log: Opens a screen listing e-mails, calls, and SMS messages you've made to the contact.

   • View Work Map: Appears only if you have filled in the work address information. This allows you to map the location using Maps.

   • Email: Starts a new e-mail message. See Chapter 8 for more information about e-mail.

   • PIN: Starts a new PIN-to-PIN message, which is a messaging feature unique to BlackBerry. With PIN-to-PIN, you can send a quick message to someone with a BlackBerry. See Chapter 9 for more details about PIN-to-PIN messaging.

- Call: Uses Phone to dial the number.

- SMS: Starts a new SMS message. SMS stands for Short Messaging Service, which is used in cellphones. See Chapter 9 for more details about SMS.

- SIM Phone Book: This menu option enables you to view contacts saved on the SIM card. For more information on how to use this option, see the "Transferring Contacts" section, later in this chapter.

- MMS: Starts a new MMS message. MMS is short for Multimedia Messaging Service, an evolution from SMS that supports voice and video clips. See Chapter 9 for more details about MMS.

  The MMS item appears in the menu only if you have filled in the contact's Mobile field.

- Send as Attachment: Starts a new e-mail message with the contact as an attachment. See Chapter 8 for more information.

- Invite to Messenger Contact: This menu option, which is near the top of the menu list (so you don't see it in Figure 4-9), allows you to add this contact to your contacts list in BlackBerry Messenger. (Note that this option appears only if you have BlackBerry Messenger installed.)

You can attach a contact, a security certificate or a file. Those three choices are in the menu displayed after pressing the menu key.

The Add Custom Ring Tone you see in Figure 4-9 was described previously, in the "Assigning a tone" section.

If you have a finger-fumble and press a letter key in error, press the escape key once to return to the original list (the one showing all your contacts), or press the trackball or trackpad once and then select View All.

Figure 4-9:
Action
options for
the selected
contact.

Activity Log
View Work Map
Email Dante Sarigumba
PIN Dante Sarigumba
Call Dante Sarigumba
SMS Dante Sarigumba
MMS Dante Sarigumba
SIM Phone Book
Send As Attachment
Add Custom Ring Tone

You aren't hallucinating: Sometimes `Email <contact name>` or `Call <contact name>` appears on the menu, and sometimes it doesn't. Contacts knows when to show those menu options. If a contact has a phone number, `Call <contact name>` and `SMS <contact name>` show up, and the same is true for e-mail and the personal identification number (PIN). In fact, this list of actions is a convenient way to find out whether you have particular information — a phone number or an e-mail address — for a particular contact.

In a corporate environment, your BlackBerry Enterprise server administrator may disable PIN-to-PIN messaging because it doesn't go to the corporate e-mail servers and, therefore, can't be monitored. If this is the case, the menu option `PIN<contact name>` won't appear, even though you entered PIN information for your contacts. Note that you'll still be able to receive a PIN-to-PIN message, but you won't be able to send one.

Organizing Your Contacts

You've been diligent by adding your contacts to Contacts, and your list has been growing at a pretty good clip. It now has all the contact information for your business colleagues, clients, and (of course) family and friends. In fact, Contacts has grown so much that it holds hundreds of contacts, and it's taking more time to find someone.

Imagine that you just saw an old acquaintance, and you want to greet the person by name. You know that if you saw the name, you'd recognize it. The trouble is that your list has 300-plus names, which would take you a long time to scroll through — so long, in fact, that this acquaintance would surely come right up to you in the meantime, forcing you to hide the fact that you can't remember his name. (How embarrassing.) In this scenario, the tried-and-true Find feature wouldn't be much help. What you need is a smaller pool of names to search.

This isn't rocket science. You'll want to do one of the following:

- ✔ **Organize your contacts into groups.** Using groups (as every kindergarten teacher could tell you) is a way to arrange something (in your case, contacts) to make them more manageable. How you arrange your groups is up to you. You should base the principle on whatever makes sense to you and fits the group you set up. For example, you can place all your customer contacts in a Clients group and family members in a Family group.

- ✔ **Set up your contacts so that you can filter them.** Use the Filter feature in combination with BlackBerry's Categories. (Using *Categories,* you can label your contacts to make it easy to filter them.) The Filter feature can narrow the Contacts list to such an extent that you only have to scroll down and find your contact — no need to type search keywords, in other words.

Whether you use the Group or Filter feature is up to you. You find out how to use both methods in the next sections of this chapter.

Creating a group

A BlackBerry *group* in Contacts — as opposed to any other kind of group you can imagine — is just a simple filter or category. In other words, using a group just arranges your contacts into subsets without affecting the contact entries themselves. In Contacts, a group shows up in the contacts list just like any other contact. The only wrinkle here is that when you select the group, the contacts associated with that group — and only the contacts associated with that group — appear onscreen.

Need some help visualizing how this works? Go ahead and create a group, following these steps:

1. **On the BlackBerry Home screen, select Contacts.**

2. **In Contacts, press the menu key and then select New Group.**

   A screen similar to that shown in Figure 4-10 appears. The top portion of the screen is where you type the group name, and the bottom portion is where you add your list of group members.

New Group: |

BlackBerry Group Contact

* No Contacts *

Figure 4-10:
An empty
screen
ready for
creating a
group.

3. **Type the name of the group in the New Group field.**

   You can name it anything. For this example, let's name it *Poker Buddies*.

4. **Press the trackball or trackpad and then select Add Member.**

   The main Contacts list shows up in all its glory, ready to be pilfered.

5. **Select the contact you want to add to your new group list, press the trackball or trackpad, and then select Continue from the menu that appears.**

   Everybody knows a Rob Kao, so select him. Doing so places Rob Kao in your Poker Buddies group list, as shown in Figure 4-11.

   You can't add a contact to a group if that contact doesn't have at least an e-mail address or a phone number. (BlackBerry Curve is very strict on this point.) If you need to skirt this roadblock, edit that contact's information and put in a fake (and clearly inactive) e-mail address, such as `notareal@emailaddress.no`.

New Group: Poker Buddies
BlackBerry Group Contact
Rob Kao (Email)

Figure 4-11:
Your new
group
has one
member.

6. **Repeat Steps 4 and 5 to add more contacts to your list.**

   After you're satisfied, save your group in the next step.

7. **Press the trackball or trackpad and then select Save Group from the menu that appears.**

   Your Poker Buddies group is duly saved, and you can now see Poker Buddies in your main Contacts list.

Using the Filter feature on your contacts

Are you a left-brainer or a right-brainer? Yankees fan or Red Sox fan? Innie or Outie? Dividing up the world into categories is something everyone does (no divisions there), so it should come as no surprise that BlackBerry divides your contacts into distinct categories as well.

By default, two categories are set for you on the BlackBerry Curve:

✔ Business

✔ Personal

Why stop at two? BlackBerry makes it easy to create more categories. In this section, you first find out how to categorize a contact and then you see how to filter your Contacts list. Finally, you find out how to create categories.

Categorizing your contacts

Whether you're creating a contact or editing one, you can categorize a particular contact as long as you're in Edit mode.

If the trick is getting into Edit mode, it's a pretty simple trick. Here's how it's done:

1. **On the BlackBerry Home screen, select Contacts.**

2. **In Contacts, highlight the contact, press the menu key, and then select Edit.**

   Contacts is now in Edit mode for this particular contact, which is exactly where you want to be.

3. **Press the menu key and then select Categories.**

   A Categories list appears, as shown in Figure 4-12. By default, you see only the Business and the Personal categories.

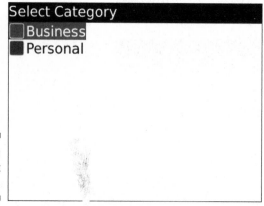

Figure 4-12:
Default
categories.

4. **Press the trackball, trackpad, or Space key to select the check box next to Personal.**

5. **Press the menu key and then select Save.**

   You are brought back to the Edit screen for this particular contact.

6. **Press the trackball or trackpad and then select Save (again) from the menu that appears.**

Filtering your contacts

You now have one — count 'em, one — contact with Personal as its category, which means you can filter your Contacts list by using a category. Here's how:

1. **On the BlackBerry Home screen, select Contacts.**

2. **Press the menu key and then select Filter.**

   Your Categories list appears.

   If you haven't added any categories in the meantime, you see only the default Business and Personal categories.

3. **Select the Personal check box.**

   Your Contacts list shrinks to just the contacts assigned to the Personal category, as shown in Figure 4-13.

Find:

Personal

Add Contact:

Dante Sarigumba

Figure 4-13:
The
Contacts list
after a filter
is applied.

Rob Kao

As you add contacts to a category, you can use Find. Enter the first few letters of the name to further narrow the contact search. If you need a refresher on how Find works, see the "Looking for Someone?" section, earlier in this chapter.

Adding a category

Whoever thought the default categories (Business and Personal) were enough for the complexities of the real world probably didn't know many people. BlackBerry makes it easy to add categories, so you can divide your world as much as you like:

1. **On the BlackBerry Home screen, select Contacts.**

2. **In Contacts, press the menu key and then select Filter.**

   You get a view of the default categories (refer to Figure 4-12).

3. **Press the menu key (again) and then select New.**

   A pop-up screen asks you to name the new category.

4. **Type the name of the category in the Name field and then press Enter.**

   The category is automatically saved. The Filter screen lists all the categories, including the one you just created. Just press the escape key to get back to the Contacts main screen.

Setting preferences

Vanilla, anyone? Some days you'll wish that your Contacts list were sorted differently. For example, there's the day when you need to find the guy who works for ABC Company but has a foreign name that you can hardly pronounce, let alone spell. What's a body to do?

You're in luck. Contacts Options navigates some out-of-the-ordinary situations. Figure 4-14 shows the Contacts Options screen. Despite its simplicity, it provides you with four important options that change Contacts behavior:

- ✔ **Sort By:** Changes how the list is sorted. You can use First Name, Last Name, or Company. Use the Space key to toggle among the choices. Remember that guy from ABC Company? You can use the Sort By option to sort by company. By doing that, all contacts from ABC Company are listed next to one another, and with any luck, the guy's name will jump out at you.

- ✔ **Separators:** Changes the dividers in the Contacts list. It's purely an aesthetic change, but check it out — you may like the stripes.

- ✔ **Allow Duplicate Names:** Self-explanatory. If you turn this on, you can have multiple people who happen to share the same name in your Contacts. If you disable this option, you get a warning when you try to add a name that matches one already on your list. Maybe you're just tired and are mistakenly trying to add the same person twice to your list. Then again, sometimes people just have the same name. We recommend keeping the default value of Yes, allowing you to have contacts with the same names.

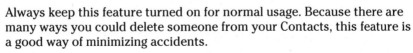

✔ **Confirm Delete:** Displays a confirmation screen for all contact deletions.

Always keep this feature turned on for normal usage. Because there are many ways you could delete someone from your Contacts, this feature is a good way of minimizing accidents.

How do you change any of these options? The fields behave like any other on a BlackBerry application. Simply highlight the field and then press the trackball or trackpad to bring up a menu from which you can select the possible Options values. For example, Figure 4-15 shows the possible Sort By fields.

Contacts Options

Views

| Sort By: | First Name |
| Separators: | Lines |

Actions

| Allow Duplicate Names: | Yes |
| Confirm Delete: | Yes |

Figure 4-14: Choose your sort type here.

Contacts Options

Views

Sort By:	First Name
Separators:	Last Name
	Company

Actions

| Allow Duplicate Names: | Yes |
| Confirm Delete: | Yes |

Figure 4-15: The Sort By field options.

Sharing a Contact

Suppose you want to share your contact information with a friend who also has a BlackBerry. A *vCard* — virtual (business) card — is your answer and can make your life a lot easier. In BlackBerry land, a vCard is a contact in Contacts that you send to someone as an attachment to an e-mail.

At the receiving end, the BlackBerry Curve (being the smart device that it is) recognizes the attachment and informs the BlackBerry owner that he or she has the option of saving it, making it available for his or her viewing pleasure in Contacts.

Sending a vCard

Because a vCard is nothing more than a Contacts contact attached to an e-mail, sending a vCard is a piece of cake. (Of course, you do need to make sure that your recipient has a BlackBerry device to receive the information.)

Here's how you go about sending a vCard:

1. **On the BlackBerry Home screen, select the Messages application.**

2. **In Messages, press the menu key and then select Compose Email.**

   A screen where you can compose a new e-mail appears.

3. **In the To field, start typing the name of the person to whom you want to send this vCard.**

4. **When you see the name in the drop-down list, highlight it and then press the trackball or trackpad.**

   You see an e-mail screen with the name you just selected as the To recipient.

5. **Type the subject and message.**

6. **Press the menu key and then select Attach Contact.**

   Contacts opens.

7. **Highlight the name of the person whose contact information you want to have attached and then press the trackball or trackpad.**

   The e-mail composition screen reappears, and an icon that looks like a book indicates that the e-mail now contains your attachment. Now all you have to do is send your e-mail.

8. **Press the trackball or trackpad and then select Send from the menu that appears.**

   You just shared the specified contact information. (Don't you feel right neighborly now?)

Receiving a vCard

If you get an e-mail with a contact attachment, here's how you save it to your Contacts:

1. **On the BlackBerry Home screen, select Messages.**

2. **Select the e-mail that contains the vCard.**

   The e-mail with the vCard attachment opens.

3. **Scroll down to the attachment. When the cursor is hovering over the attachment, press the trackball or trackpad and then select View Attachment from the menu that appears.**

   The vCard makes an appearance onscreen. Now save the contact in Contacts.

4. **Press the menu key and then select Add to Contacts.**

   The vCard is saved and is available in Contacts.

Transferring Contacts

Are you switching to BlackBerry Curve from an old AT&T or Cingular cell-phone? You've probably accumulated contacts on that phone by painstakingly typing them. Good news! Maybe you don't have to type them into BlackBerry Curve!

The trick is to use the old phone's *SIM card* (see Figure 4-16) as an external storage device, such as a flash drive. The SIM card is an electronic chip that can store information, including your phone numbers and contacts.

Figure 4-16:
Transfer
contacts
with a SIM
card.

This should work on almost any GSM-compatible phone. The big U.S. GSM carriers are AT&T (including old Cingular phones) and T-Mobile; in Canada, Rogers. To find whether you have a GSM phone, look for the SIM card. Take the battery out of your cellphone; behind the battery, you should see a SIM card. If you don't see a SIM card, you don't have a GSM phone.

Copying contacts from a GSM phone

The process for copying contacts on a BlackBerry Curve is pretty straightforward, but the steps for retrieving them depend on your old phone.

For the purpose of showing you what's what, we use a Nokia 6300 phone as an example. You will probably need the manual for your old phone because it's likely that the exact steps aren't the same.

To copy contacts from an old GSM cellphone to a BlackBerry Curve, follow these steps:

1. **Take out the SIM card out of your BlackBerry Curve, and put it in the old cellphone.**

   Moving a SIM card is no big deal. The SIM card is usually behind the battery, so you have to remove the back cover of the device to get to it:

   • On the Curve, there's a lock at the bottom of the back of the device. Just press this with your thumb to unlock the cover. You can pull the cover out starting from where the lock is located. You should be able to gently pry the BlackBerry Curve battery out with your fingernail.

   • Follow the instructions from the old cellphone's manual to open it and remove the old SIM card, and then insert the BlackBerry Curve SIM card into the old cellphone. Put the battery back in the old cellphone, and switch it on.

2. **Use the old cellphone's menu to copy the old contacts list to the SIM card.**

The contacts list may be called something like *Contacts* or *Names.* You'll probably need the old cellphone's manual to work through the process. The sidebar "Copying the contacts list" shows how it works on a Nokia 6300.

If your old cellphone phone doesn't recognize your BlackBerry SIM card, perhaps the phone is *locked.* Phone providers can "lock" phones to their network, making the phones unusable in other networks. If this is the case, call your phone provider, and ask for instructions to unlock your phone.

3. Put the SIM card back into your BlackBerry.

Reinserting the SIM card and battery resets your BlackBerry.

Don't forget to put the old SIM card back into the old phone!

4. On the BlackBerry Home screen, select Contacts.

5. In Contacts, press the menu key and then select SIM Phone Book.

It might take some time to load the contacts from your SIM card; how long depends on how many contacts you've saved to the card. (You'll see a progress bar on the screen.) After the contacts are loaded, they are listed on the screen, and you can start browsing or copying them to your Contacts list.

The SIM Phone Book menu item is located toward the bottom of the menu, as shown in Figure 4-17. You need to scroll down to see it.

Figure 4-17:
The Contacts menu, showing the SIM Phone Book option.

6. Copy each contact you want on your new BlackBerry Curve.

To do so, highlight the contact, press the menu key and select Add to Contacts. Repeat this step for each contact you want to copy. (It's still a lot better than actually *typing* each contact on your BlackBerry.)

Copying the contacts list

The steps for copying the contacts list depend on your old phone. You probably need the owner's manual for your own phone, but here's how it works on a Nokia 6300:

1. **Select Names by pressing the top of the rightmost top button.**

   On this phone, Names is the equivalent of Contacts. The phone displays a list of contacts.

2. **Select Options by pressing the leftmost top button.**

   The Names menu appears, as shown in the figure.

3. **On the Names menu, select Mark All.**

4. **Select Options by pressing the leftmost top button.**

   The Names menu appears.

5. **Select Copy Marked.**

   A menu displays two options: From Phone to SIM Card and From SIM Card to Phone.

6. **Select From Phone to SIM Card.**

7. **Select All and then select Keep Original from the next menu.**

   A confirmation screen appears.

8. **Select OK to confirm the copy.**

The Nokia 6300 phone starts copying the contents of the Phone Book to the SIM card. While it's making the copy, the screen displays a bar that moves back and forth. If you have many contacts on your phone, this process can take some time, so be patient. When the contacts are loaded onto the SIM card, the screen displays the number of contacts that were copied.

When the contacts are copied, you can switch the SIM card back to the BlackBerry Curve.

SIM cards have a limited capacity. If one or two old contacts don't fit on your SIM card, just type them into your BlackBerry Curve. But if you need to move many more contacts, you can clear and refill the SIM card as many times as needed to move all your old contacts:

1. **On your Curve, launch Contacts.**

2. **Press the menu key and then select SIM Phone Book.**

   On this screen, you should see the already-copied contacts in your SIM card. Deleting the contact here deletes it only from the SIM card, not from the Contacts application. There's no facility to delete all at once — only one at a time.

3. **Press the Del key to delete a contact and then select Delete on the confirmation screen.**

   This is the best time to disable the confirmation screen and speed up the deletion. If you need a refresher on how to do it, check the "Setting Preferences" section, earlier in this chapter.

4. **Swap the BlackBerry SIM card back into the old cellphone.**

5. **Use the old cellphone's menu to copy individual contacts that didn't fit when you copied "all" contacts.**

   Put the BlackBerry SIM card back in the BlackBerry Curve, and follow Steps 4–6 of the preceding instructions to copy the extra contacts from the SIM card to BlackBerry Contacts.

Copying a BlackBerry Curve contact

Someday, you may want to copy your carefully constructed BlackBerry Contacts list to another cellphone. It's possible, with a little help from two BlackBerry experts.

This is one of the most difficult tricks unless someone shows you how.

So here's how to copy each contact you want to move:

1. **View the contact information.**

   Follow the steps in the "Viewing a contact" section, earlier in this chapter.

2. **On the view screen, scroll to a Phone Number field, press the menu key, and then select Copy to SIM Phone Book.**

   The Copy to SIM Phone Book feature (see Figure 4-18) shows up only when you position the cursor in a Phone Number field.

3. **On the Phone Book entry screen, press the trackball or trackpad, and then select Save.**

   The screen immediately returns to the View contact screen. You can repeat these steps to copy more contacts from the BlackBerry Curve.

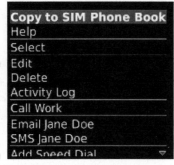

Figure 4-18:
Copy
BlackBerry
info to a
cellphone.

When all the contacts you want are on the BlackBerry SIM card, insert the SIM card into the other phone, and follow its instructions to copy contacts from the SIM card.

If your other phone doesn't recognize your BlackBerry SIM card, perhaps the phone is locked. Phone providers lock the phones to their network, making the phones unusable in other networks, all the time. If this is the case, call your phone provider, and ask for instructions on how to unlock your phone.

Searching for Someone Outside Your Contacts

Does your employer provide your BlackBerry Curve? Do you use Outlook or Lotus Notes on your desktop machine at work? If you answer yes to both questions, this is for you.

BlackBerry Contacts allows you to search for people in your organization, basically using any of the following software, which contains employee databases:

✔ Microsoft Exchange (for Outlook)

✔ IBM Domino (for Lotus Notes)

✔ Novell GroupWise

Exchange, Domino, and GroupWise serve the same purposes:

✔ Facilitate e-mail delivery in a corporate environment

✔ Enable access to a database of names:

• Global Address Lists (GALs) in Exchange

• Notes Address Books in Domino

• GroupWise Address Books in GroupWise

To search for someone in your organization through a database of names, simply follow these steps:

1. **On the BlackBerry Home screen, select Contacts.**

2. **Press the menu key and then select Lookup.**

   Some corporations may not enable the Lookup feature. Please check with your IT department for more information.

3. **Type the name you're searching for and then press the trackball or trackpad.**

   You could enter the beginning characters of a person's last or first name. You are searching your company's database, not Contacts, so this step may take some time.

   For big organizations, we recommend being more precise when searching. For example, searching for *Dan* yields more hits than searching for *Daniel.* The more precise your search criteria, the fewer hits you'll get and the faster the search will be.

   While the search is in progress, you see the word `Lookup` and the criteria you put in. For example, if you enter **Daniel,** the top row reads `Lookup: Daniel.` After the search is finished, BlackBerry displays the number of hits, or matches — for example, `20 matches: Daniel.`

4. **Select the number of matches.**

   The matches appear. A header at the top of this screen details the matches displayed in the current screen as well as the total hits. For example, if the header reads something like `Lookup Daniel (20 of 130 matches)`, 130 people in your organization have the name *Daniel,* and BlackBerry is displaying the first 20. You have the option of fetching more by pressing the trackball or trackpad and then choosing Get More Results from the menu that appears.

   You can add the listed name(s) to your Contacts by using the Add command (for the currently highlighted name) or the Add All command for all the names in the list. (As always, press the trackball or trackpad to call up the menu that contains these options.)

5. **Select the person whose information you want to review.**

   The person's contact information is displayed on a read-only screen (you can read but not change it). You may see the person's title; e-mail address; work, mobile, and fax numbers; and snail-mail address at work. Any of that information gives you confirmation about the person you're looking for. Of course, what shows up depends on the availability of this information in your company's database.

Synchronizing Facebook Contacts

Do you network like a social butterfly? You must be using one of the popular social networking BlackBerry applications, such as MySpace or Facebook. You must have tons of friends from these networking sites and want to copy their contact information to your Curve. There are ways to achieve this, and individual networking sites will have their own unique way. But if you're in Facebook, you're lucky.

With the latest Facebook application (version 1.6 as of this writing), it's much easier to get Facebook contacts to your Curve. The Facebook app also allows you to synchronize information between your Curve and your friend's information in Facebook.

Adding a Facebook friend's info to Contacts

Pulling down your friend's information from Facebook is quite easy:

1. **Select the Facebook icon from the Home screen.**

   The Facebook application is filed under the Downloads folder.

2. **Press the menu key and then press F.**

   Your friends list shows up in the screen similar to the one on the left in Figure 4-19.

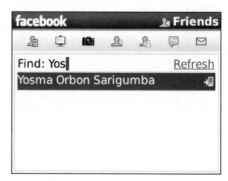

Figure 4-19: Select Facebook friends to add to Contacts here.

3. **In the Find field, start typing your friend's name.**

   This narrows the list, as shown on the right in Figure 4-19.

4. **Highlight the friend you want to add to Contacts, press the menu key, and select Connect to BlackBerry Contact.**

   A dialog box appears, as shown in Figure 4-20, allowing you to choose whether to connect this Facebook friend to an existing contact or add the friend as a new contact to your Curve. In this case, you want to add.

   If the same person exists in your Curve and in Facebook, you can simply link the contact here. Also, see the next section to get an automatic update on your BlackBerry whenever your friend changes his or her profile in Facebook.

Figure 4-20: Connect a Facebook friend to an existing contact or add a new contact here.

facebook   👥 Friends

facebook

This friend is not currently connected with your BlackBerry Contact list. Select the BlackBerry contact you want to connect this friend to.

Select Contact | New Contact

Aian Arcilla

The term *connect* in the Facebook application means telling the app which contact is associated with a Facebook friend. After the app records this linkage, it knows which contact to update when information in Facebook changes.

5. **Select New Contact.**

   A progress screen appears momentarily, telling you that it's getting the contact information from Facebook. When it's finished, a new contact is added to your Curve with the contact info shown on the screen.

6. **Press the escape key.**

   The Facebook app displays a prompt, asking you whether to ask for a phone number. This is a default behavior even if the phone number is already in your BlackBerry.

7. **Select either Yes or No in the prompt to request for phone number.**

   You're back to the previous Facebook screen, and an Address Book icon has been added to the right of your friend's name, indicating that this friend is now connected, or linked, to a BlackBerry contact, as shown in Figure 4-21.

Automatic syncing between Facebook profiles and Contacts

When running the Facebook application for the first time, you're asked to enable synchronization. Here are Facebook and BlackBerry connections you can choose among:

Figure 4-21:
The Address
Book icon
shows
that your
Facebook
friend is
connected
to a
BlackBerry
contact.

Figure 4-21: The Address Book icon shows that your Facebook friend is connected to a BlackBerry contact.

✔ **BlackBerry Message application:** When enabled, you'll see new Facebook notifications in your Messages application.

✔ **BlackBerry Calendar application:** When enabled, a calendar item is automatically created in your Curve whenever you have a new Facebook event.

✔ **BlackBerry Contacts application:** When enabled, your Curve contacts are periodically updated with the latest Facebook information, including the profile pictures. For this to happen, your Curve contacts also will be sent to Facebook.

If you opted out of these options the first time you ran Facebook, you can still enable them from the Facebook Options screen. The following steps enable Contacts synchronization:

1. **Select the Facebook icon from the Home screen.**

   The Facebook application is filed under the Downloads folder.

2. **Press the menu key and then select Options.**

The Options screen appears. A lot of information and text are on this screen, and you have to scroll down to see all the options. Feel free to check other options, but for synchronizing contacts, refer to the first two pages of the screen, which should look like the one shown in Figure 4-22.

3. **Add a check mark to the BlackBerry Contacts application.**

   There's explanatory text right below this check box. If you scroll down, you should see another check box, which allows you to synchronize Facebook profile photos with Contacts photos.

4. **Add a check mark to the option titled Update Existing Photos in Your BlackBerry Contacts List with Facebook Friend Profile Photos (Figure 4-22, right).**

5. **Press the escape key, and select Yes on the Save Changes prompt.**

   Your Contacts will now be periodically updated with Facebook friends.

Figure 4-22:
Enable
Facebook
friends
synchroni-
zation with
Facebook
Options.

facebook ✍ Options

You are currently logged in as Dante Sarigumba.

Logout

Run Setup Wizard

Connect your Facebook account with:
☑ BlackBerry Calendar application ?
☑ BlackBerry Message application ?
☑ BlackBerry Contacts application ?

facebook ✍ Options

information about you and your Facebook Friends will also be periodically sent from Facebook to your BlackBerry Contact list and Calendar, and you acknowledge that access to this data (e.g. by applications) will no longer be subject to you and your Facebook Friends privacy settings once stored on your BlackBerry device.)

☑ Update existing photos in your BlackBerry contacts list with Facebook friend profile photos

Chapter 5

Never Miss Another Appointment

*T*o some folks, the key to being organized and productive is mastering time management and using their time wisely (and we aren't just talking about reading this book while you're commuting to work). Many have discovered that there is no better way to organize their time than to use a calendar — a daily planner tool. Some prefer digital to paper, so they use a planner software program on their PC, whether installed on their hard drive or accessed through an Internet portal (such as Yahoo!). The smartest of the bunch, of course, use their BlackBerry handheld because it has the whole planner thing covered in handy form with its Calendar application.

In this chapter, we show you how to keep your life (personal and work) in order by managing your appointments with your BlackBerry Calendar. What's great about managing your time on a BlackBerry instead of on your PC is that your BlackBerry is always with you to remind you. Just remember that you won't have any more excuses for forgetting that important quarterly meeting or Bertha's birthday bash.

Accessing BlackBerry Calendar

 BlackBerry Calendar is one of the BlackBerry core applications, like Contacts or Phone (read more about the others in Chapter 2), so it's easy to get to. From the Home screen, press the menu key and then select Calendar. Voilà! You have Calendar.

Choosing Your Calendar View

The first time you open Calendar, you'll likely see Day view, the default setting, as shown in Figure 5-1. However, you can change the Calendar view to a different one that works better for your needs:

- ✔ **Day view:** Gives you a summary of your appointments for the day. By default, it lists all your appointments from 9 a.m. to 5 p.m.

- ✔ **Week view:** Shows you a seven-day summary of your appointments. In this view, you can see how busy you are in a particular week.

- ✔ **Month view:** Shows you every day of the month. You can't tell how many appointments are in a day, but you can see on which days you have appointments.

- ✔ **Agenda view:** A bit different from the other views. It isn't a time-based view like the others; it basically lists your upcoming appointments. In the list, you can see details of the appointments, such as where and when.

Aug 19, 2009   7:48p ⟨M T W T F S S⟩
9:00a
10:00a
11:00a Business Meeting (At YUL   🔔
airport)
12:00p
1:00p
2:00p
3:00p
4:00p

Figure 5-1:
Day view in Calendar.

Different views (such as Week view, shown in Figure 5-2) offer you a different focus on your schedule. Select the view you want based on your scheduling needs and preferences. If your life is a little more complicated, you can switch between views for a full grasp of your schedule.

Figure 5-2:
Change your
Calendar
view to fit
your life.

To switch between different Calendar views, simply follow these steps:

1. **From the Home screen, press the menu key and then select Calendar.**

   Doing so calls up the Calendar application in its default view — Day view.

2. **Press the menu key and then select the view of your choice from the menu that appears (shown in Figure 5-3).**

   As we mention earlier, depending on your current calendar view, you can switch among Day, Week, Month, and Agenda views.

Figure 5-3:
Choose your
Calendar
view here.

Moving between Time Frames

Depending on what view of Calendar you're in, you can easily move to the preceding or next day, week, month, or year. For example, if you're in Month view, you can move forward to the next month. Likewise, you can also move back to the preceding month. In fact, if you like to look at things in the long term, you can jump ahead (or back) a year at a time. (See Figure 5-4.)

Figure 5-4:
Move
among
months or
years in
Month view.

Aug 19 2009	Week 34	7:54p
Go To Date...	s t	
Prev Month		
Next Month	F	S	S
Prev Year	31	1	2
Next Year		
New Alarm	7	8	9
New	14	15	16
View Day	21	22	23
View Week	28	29	30
View Agenda		
Options	4	5	6

You have similar flexibility when it comes to the other Calendar views. See Table 5-1 for a summary of what's available.

Table 5-1	Moving between Views
Calendar View	*Move Between*
Day	Days and weeks
Week	Weeks
Month	Months and years
Agenda	Days

You can always go to today's date regardless of what Calendar view you're in. Just press the menu key and then select Today from the menu that appears.

Furthermore, you can jump to any date you choose by pressing the menu key and then selecting Go to Date. Doing so calls up a handy little dialog box that lets you choose the date you want. To change the date, select the desired day, month, and year, as shown in Figure 5-5.

Figure 5-5:
Go to any
date you
want.

Customizing Your Calendar

To change the initial (default) view in your Calendar — from Day view to Month view, for example — Calendar Options is the answer. To get to Calendar Options, open Calendar, press the menu key, and select Options from the menu that appears. You see choices similar to the ones shown in Table 5-2.

Table 5-2	Calendar Options
Option	*Description*
Formatting	
First Day of Week	The day that first appears in your Week view.
Start of Day	The time of day that defines your start of day in Day view. The default is 9 a.m. If you change this to 8 a.m., for example, your Day view starts at 8 a.m. instead of 9 a.m.
End of Day	The time of the day that defines the end of day in Day view. The default is 5 p.m. If you change this to 6 p.m., for example, your Day view ends at 6 p.m. instead of 5 p.m.
Views	
Initial View	Specifies the Calendar view that you first see when opening Calendar.
Show Free Time in Agenda View	If Yes, this field allows an appointment-free day's date to appear in Agenda view. If No, Agenda view doesn't show the date of days on which you don't have an appointment.

(continued)

Table 5-2 *(continued)*

Option	Description
Show End Time in Agenda View	If Yes, this field shows the end time of each appointment in Agenda view. If No, Agenda view shows only the start time of each appointment.
Actions	
Snooze	The snooze time when a reminder appears. The default is 5 minutes.
Default Reminder	How far in advance your BlackBerry notifies you before your appointment time. The default is 15 minutes.
Enable Quick Entry	Available only in Day view. Allows you to make a new appointment by typing characters. This way, you don't need to press the trackball or trackpad and select New. *Note:* If you enable this, Day view shortcuts described in this book's online Cheat Sheet don't apply.
Keep Appointments	This is the number of days your BlackBerry Curve will save your calendar item. We recommend that you keep it on Never.
Show Tasks	A scheduled task will be shown on your calendar just like a Calendar event. (A scheduled task is a task with a due date.)
Show Alarms	You can see alarms in your calendar if you set this option to Yes.

All Things Appointments: Adding, Opening, and Deleting

After you master navigating the different Calendar views (and that should take you all of about two minutes) and you have Calendar customized to your heart's content (another three minutes, tops), it's time (pun intended) to set up, review, and delete appointments. We also show you how to set up a meeting with clients or colleagues.

Creating an appointment

Setting up a new appointment is easy. You need only one piece of information: when your appointment occurs. Of course, you can easily add related information about the appointment, such as the meeting's purpose, its location, and whatever additional notes are helpful.

Managing multiple calendars

Like your e-mail accounts, you may have multiple calendars. For example, say you have a calendar from your day job and a calendar from your personal life or softball club. Whatever the reason, your BlackBerry Curve has a great way for you to manage multiple calendars.

From Calendar Options, you see a screen similar to the following figure. The colored squares represent different calendars to give you a better view of which event belongs to which calendar. For example, you can assign red to your day job calendar and green to your softball club calendar. When two events conflict (share the same time slot), you can better prioritize with the color.

To change the color of each calendar, follow these steps:

1. **Open Calendar.**

2. **Press the menu key and select Options Menu.**

   This opens a screen similar to the following figure.

Calendar Options
General Options
Conference Call Options
Calendars

- dante.sarigumba@gmail.com
- dante@sarigumba.com
- dantesarigumba@yahoo.com
- dante_rs@tmo.blackberry.net
- dsarigumba@smrtguard.com
- ☐ Facebook

3. **Select a calendar of your choice.**

   The calendar properties screen opens.

4. **Highlight the colored square and then select the desired color. (You can choose among six colors.)**

   If you have more than one e-mail address "hooked" into your BlackBerry, you will see them here.

5. **Press the menu key and tap the Save button.**

In addition to setting a standard one-time, limited-duration meeting, you can set all-day appointments, recurring meetings, and reminders. Sweet!

Creating a one-time appointment

To add a new one-time appointment, follow these steps:

1. **Open Calendar.**

2. **Press the menu key and then select New.**

   The New Appointment screen appears.

3. **Fill in the key appointment information.**

   Type all the information regarding your appointment in the appropriate spaces. You should at least enter the time and the subject of your appointment. See Figure 5-6.

4. Press the menu key and then select Save.

This saves your newly created appointment.

New Appointment

Subject: Birthday Party

Location: Dante's House

☐ All Day Event
Start: Thu, Aug 20, 2009 1:00 PM
End: Thu, Aug 20, 2009 2:00 PM
Duration: 1 Hour 0 Mins
Time Zone: Casablanca (GMT)
Show Time As: Busy
Reminder: 15 Min.
■ Conference Call

Figure 5-6:
Set an
appointment
here.

Your new appointment is now in Calendar and viewable from any Calendar view.

You can have more than one appointment in the same time slot. Your BlackBerry Calendar allows conflicts in your schedule because it lets you make the hard decision about which appointment to forgo.

Creating an all-day appointment

If your appointment is an all-day event — for example, if you're in corporate training or have an all-day doctor's appointment — select the All Day Event check box on the New Appointment screen, as shown in Figure 5-7. You can do so by scrolling to the check box and pressing the trackball or trackpad. When this check box is selected, you can't specify the time of your appointment — just the start date and end date (simply because it doesn't make sense to specify a time for an all-day event).

New Appointment

Subject: BlackBerry Conference
Location: Hotel

☑ All Day Event
Start:	Mon, Nov 9, 2009
End:	Mon, Nov 9, 2009
Duration:	1 Day
Time Zone:	Casablanca (GMT)
Show Time As:	Free
Reminder:	15 Min.

■ Conference Call

Figure 5-7:
Set an
all-day
event here.

Setting your appointment reminder time

Any appointment you enter in Calendar can be associated with a reminder alert — either a vibration or a beep, depending on how you set things up in your profile. (For more on profiles, see Chapter 3.) You can also choose to have no reminder for an appointment. From the New Appointment screen, simply scroll to the Reminder field and select a reminder time anywhere from None to 1 Week before your appointment time.

The native Profile application is simply another useful BlackBerry application that allows you to customize how your BlackBerry alerts you when an event occurs. Examples of events are an e-mail, a phone call, or a reminder for an appointment.

By default, whatever reminder alert you set goes off 15 minutes before the event. However, you don't have to stick with the default. You can choose your own default reminder time. Here's how:

1. **Open Calendar.**

2. **Press the menu key and then select Options.**

    Doing so calls up the Calendar Options screen.

3. **Select Default Reminder.**

4. **Choose a default reminder time anywhere from None to 1 Week before your appointment.**

So from now on, any new appointment has a default reminder time of what you just set up. Assuming that you have a reminder time other than None, the next time you have an appointment coming up, you see a dialog box like the one shown in Figure 5-8, reminding you of the appointment.

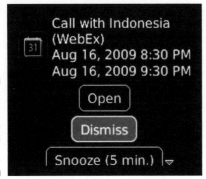

Figure 5-8:
You get a
reminder
dialog box if
you want.

Creating a recurring appointment

You can set up recurring appointments based on daily, weekly, monthly, or yearly recurrences. Everyone has some appointment that repeats, such as birthdays or anniversaries (or taking out the trash every Thursday at 7:30 a.m. — ugh).

For all recurrence types, you can define an Every field. For example, say you have an appointment that recurs every nine days. Just set the Recurrence field to Daily and the Every field to 9, as shown in Figure 5-9.

New Appointment	
End:	Tue, Aug 18, 2009 6:00 PM
Duration:	1 Hour 0 Mins
Time Zone:	Casablanca (GMT)
Show Time As:	Busy
Reminder:	15 Min.
■ Conference Call	
Recurrence:	Daily
Every:	9
End:	Never
Occurs every 9 days.	
■ Mark as Private	

Figure 5-9:
An appoint-
ment
recurring
every nine
days.

Depending on what you select in the Recurrence field, you have the option to fill in other fields. If you enter Weekly in the Recurrence field, for example, you have the option of filling in the Day of the Week field. (It basically allows you to select the day of the week on which your appointment recurs.)

If you enter Monthly or Yearly in the Recurrence field, the Relative Date check box is available. With this check box selected, you can ensure that your appointment recurs relative to today's date. For example, if you choose the following, your appointment occurs every two months on the third Sunday until July 31, 2012:

> **Start:** Sunday, June 21, 2009 at 12 p.m.
>
> **End:** Sunday, June 21, 2009 at 1 p.m.
>
> **Recurrence:** Monthly
>
> **Every:** 2
>
> **Relative Date:** Selected
>
> **End:** Saturday, July 31, 2012

On the other hand, if all options in this example remain the same except that Relative Date isn't selected, your appointment occurs every two months, on the 21st of the month, until July 31, 2012.

If all this "relative" talk has you dizzy, don't worry: The majority of your appointments won't be as complicated as this.

Opening an appointment

After you set an appointment, you can view it in a couple of ways:

✔ If you set up reminders for your appointment and the little Reminder dialog box appears onscreen at the designated time before your appointment, you can view your appointment by clicking the box's Open button. In the same dialog, you can Snooze the reminder (refer to Figure 5-8).

✔ In Calendar, go to the exact time of your appointment and view it there.

While looking at an appointment, you can make changes (a new appointment time and new appointment location) and then save them.

Appointments versus Meetings

Technically, any event in your Calendar counts as an appointment, whether it's a reminder for your best friend's birthday or a reminder of a doctor's appointment for a checkup. However, when you invite people to an appointment or you get invited to one, regardless of whether it's a face-to-face meeting or a phone conference, that appointment becomes a *meeting*.

Sending a meeting request

Sending a meeting request to others is similar to creating a Calendar appointment. Follow these steps:

1. **Open Calendar.**

2. **Press the menu key and then select New.**

3. **Fill in the key appointment information (subject, location, and time).**

4. **Press the menu key and then select Invite Attendee.**

   You're taken to Contacts to select your meeting attendee.

5. **Select your contact via Contacts:**

   • If your contact is in Contacts: Highlight the contact you want and then press the trackball or trackpad.

   • If you don't yet have contacts or if the one you want isn't in Contacts: Select the Use Once option to enter the appropriate e-mail address and then press the enter key to finish and return to Calendar.

   After returning from Contacts, you see the attendees in your Calendar meeting notice.

6. **Press the menu key and then select Save.**

   An e-mail is sent to your meeting attendees, inviting them to your meeting.

Responding to a meeting request

Whether for work or a casual social event, you've likely received a meeting request by e-mail, asking you to respond to the meeting by choosing one of three options: Accept, Tentative, or Decline. (If it's from your boss for an all-staff meeting, and you just can't afford to decline again because it's so close to Christmas bonus time, that's an Accept.)

You can accept any meeting request from your managers or colleagues on your BlackBerry just as you would on your desktop PC. In the PC world, you respond to an e-mail request for a meeting by clicking the appropriate button in your e-mail client (Microsoft Outlook, for the vast majority of you). In the BlackBerry world, a meeting request also comes in the form of an e-mail; after reading the e-mail, just choose Accept, Tentative, or Decline in the Messages application. Your response is sent back in an e-mail. We go into more detail about the Messages application in Chapter 9.

After you respond to the meeting request, the meeting is added to your Calendar automatically. If you have a change of heart later, you can change your response (yes, you can later decline that useless meeting after all) in Calendar, and the declined event disappears from your Calendar.

Setting your meeting dial-in number

You may have colleagues and friends all over the country or even on another continent. Group phone meetings may require a

- ✔ Dial-in number
- ✔ Moderator code (if you are the moderator)
- ✔ Participation code

To set your phone conference dial-in details, follow these steps:

1. **Open Calendar.**

2. **Press the menu key and then select Options menu item.**

3. **Select Conference Call Options.**

   A screen similar to Figure 5-10 appears.

4. **Enter the appropriate numbers.**

5. **Press the menu key and select Save.**

   Your conference call number is saved.

Figure 5-10:
Setting up
conference
call dial-in
details.

> **Conference Call Options** [123]
>
> **Moderator**
> Phone: ➕14087926300
> Access Code: 12345432
> **Participant**
> Phone:
> Access Code: 12345432

The next time you create a new appointment, if you tap the Conference Call check box in the Appointment Screen, you see the conference number, as shown in Figure 5-11.

Figure 5-11: Conference call information displayed in the Appointment screen.

Appointment Details	123
Reminder:	15 Min.

☑ Conference Call
Moderator
 Phone: +14087926300
 Access Code: 12345432
Participant
 Phone:
 Access Code: 12345432

Recurrence:	None

No Recurrence.

■ Mark as Private

Chapter 6

Setting Alarms and Keeping Your Passwords

* *

* *

*I*n this chapter, we introduce you to the Clock application, which not only tells you the time, but also allows you to set alarms and a timer. In addition, you can use the application as a stopwatch. And in keeping with one of the key themes of this book — making your life easier — the Clock app has a feature called Bedside mode that turns your Curve into a quiet bedside companion.

To add to the theme of making your life a little easier, we make sure that you get the scoop on keeping your passwords in a single location safely by using the Password Keeper application.

Accessing Clock

Clock can be found right on the Home screen, as you can see on the left side of Figure 6-1. Just look for the icon of an alarm clock. Once you find the Clock icon, simply select it, and you should see a screen similar to the one on the right side of Figure 6-1.

Figure 6-1:
Launch
Clock (left)
and view
your clock
(right).

If you've changed themes, different icons might be displayed (refer to Chapter 3 for more on themes). Just remember that the Clock application is always located on the Home screen.

Customizing Your Clock

If the default analog clock doesn't fit your taste, you can change it. Customizing your clock is easy and doesn't take much time.

You customize the clock in the Options screen. Follow these steps:

1. **Select Clock from the Home screen.**

   The Clock application opens.

2. **Press the menu key and then select Options.**

   The Clock Options screen appears, as shown on the left side of Figure 6-2, ready and willing to be customized.

Figure 6-2:
Customize
your clock
here.

Clock Options	
Clock	
Clock Face:	Analog
Home Time Zone:	Casablanca (GMT)
When Charging:	Display Clock
Set Time	
Alarm	
Alert Type:	Tone
Alarm Tune:	Alarm_Antelope
Volume:	Medium

Clock Options	
Snooze Time:	5 Min
Number of Vibrations:	1
Bedside Mode	
Disable LED:	Yes
Disable Radio:	No
Dim Screen:	Yes
Stopwatch	
Stopwatch Face:	Analog
Countdown Timer	

3. **Move to each field and choose the option you want.**

Each of these fields is described shortly.

4. **Press the escape key and then select Save from the prompt.**

The Clock Options screen is divided into five sections, as follows:

✔ **Clock section:** This is where you choose the type of clock, time zone, and time.

- Clock Face: Allows you to set the type of clock. The options are Analog (the default; refer to the right side of Figure 6-1), Digital, Flip Clock, and LCD Digital. Digital looks like the clock shown on left side of Figure 6-3, and Flip Clock is shown on the right side of Figure 6-3.

- Home Time Zone: Select your time zone from the list.

- When Charging: Allows you to control the behavior of the clock when you connect your Curve to the charger. Possible choices are Do Nothing, Display Clock (the default), and Enter Bedside Mode.

- Set Time: Click this button, and you see a Date/Time screen that displays the current time in edit mode, allowing you to change the time. You can also change the time zone, as well decide whether to synchronize your BlackBerry time to the network carriers' time.

✔ **Alarm section:** Navigate here if you want to customize the behavior of the alarm:

- **Alert Type:** Choose the type of notification. The options are Tone (the default), Vibrate, and Tone + Vibrate.

- **Alarm Tune:** Choose from a list of ring tones you want to play. This setting applies only if you have Tone or Tone + Vibrate selected for the Alert Type. The default tone is Alarm_Antelope.

Figure 6-3: Digital (left) and Flip (right) clocks.

- **Volume:** You can set the volume of the tone to Low, Medium (the default), High, or Escalating. Escalating means that the tone starts from Low and gradually goes to High.

- **Snooze Time:** Just like with your ordinary alarm clock, you have the option to hit the snooze. You can choose 30, 15, 10, or 5 (the default) minutes, 1 minute, or None.

- **Number of Vibrations:** The default is 1, which is a quick vibration of your Curve as your alarm. Choices are to repeat the vibration either 2 or 3 times.

✔ **Bedside Mode section:** This section allows you to set the behavior of your Curve when it is in Bedside mode:

- **Disable LED:** Allows you to disable LED notifications during Bedside mode. Choices are Yes (the default) and No.

- **Disable Radio:** Allows you to disable the radio during Bedside mode. Choices are Yes and No (the default).

  Disabling the radio means that all communication-related applications — such as e-mail, SMS, BlackBerry Messenger, instant messaging clients, and Phone — cannot receive incoming signals.

- **Dim Screen:** Choose the Yes (the default) or No option to control the dimming of the screen when in Bedside mode.

✔ **Stopwatch section:** A section to change the face of the stopwatch:

- **Stopwatch Face:** Choose between an Analog (the default) and a Digital stopwatch.

✔ **Countdown Timer section:** Navigate here if you want to customize the behavior of the timer:

- **Timer Face:** Your choices are Analog (the default) and Digital.

- **Timer Tune:** Choose from a list of ring tones you want to play when the timer reaches the time you set.

- **Volume:** You can either select Mute or set the volume of the tone to Low, Medium (the default), High, or Escalating. Escalating means that the tone starts Low and gradually goes to High.

- **Vibrate:** Choose Yes if you want the Curve to vibrate when the timer reaches the time set; otherwise, choose No (the default).

Setting a Wake-Up Alarm

The Clock application is also your bedside alarm clock. You can set it to wake you up once or on a regular basis.

Here's how you tell your wake-up buddy to do the work for you:

1. **Select Clock from the Home screen.**

   The Clock appears.

2. **Press the menu key and then select Set Alarm.**

   A time field appears on the bottom of the screen, as shown in Figure 6-4. The time defaults to the previous set alarm time or, if you haven't used the alarm before, the current time. If the default time isn't your intended alarm time, proceed to Step 3 to change the time.

Figure 6-4: Set your alarm time here.

3. **Scroll sideways to select the specific portion of the time that you want to change, and enter the values.**

   Any highlighted portion of the time is editable. You can change the hours; minutes; AM/PM; and whether the alarm is ON, OFF, or only WEEKDAYS. Setting a value doesn't create an entry in Calendar or Tasks. You can either enter the value or scroll up or down to choose among possible values.

4. **Press the trackball or trackpad to accept all your changes.**

Setting and Exiting Bedside Mode

You can use a setting in the Clock application called Bedside mode to minimize disturbances by your Curve. With Bedside mode, you can dim the screen, disable the LED, and even turn off the radio, all of which pretty much make your Curve behave like a brick. Bear in mind that when you turn off the radio, you won't get incoming phone calls or any type of messaging. If you want a refresher on how to set these options, see "Customizing Your Clock," previously in this chapter.

To set your BlackBerry Curve in Bedside mode:

1. **Select Clock from the Home screen.**

2. **Press the menu key and then select Enter Bedside Mode (see Figure 6-5, left).**

   That's it. Your Curve should now behave like a good bedside companion.

Figure 6-5:
Enter and
exit Bedside
mode here.

 Buy a charging pod from shop.blackberry.com or shop.crackberry.com. Then you can put your Curve on a bedside table in an upright position while the charging pod is adding juice to your device. Make sure that the Clock setting (not just the Curve) is in Bedside mode when charging. (To do so, select Clock from the Home screen. Press the menu key and then select Options. Under the Clock section, change When Charging to Enter Bedside Mode.)

To exit from Bedside mode:

1. **Select Clock from the Home screen.**

2. **Press the menu key and then select Exit Bedside Mode, as shown on the right side of Figure 6-5.**

Using Stopwatch

In case you ever need a stopwatch, you need look no further than your BlackBerry Curve. Here's how to run the stopwatch:

1. **Select Clock from the Home screen.**

2. **Press the menu key and then select Stopwatch.**

   You see a screen similar to Figure 6-6. There are two buttons on this screen:

- Stopwatch button: Select this button to start and stop the stopwatch.

- Lap button: The image on this button looks like a circular arrow. This button is useful when someone is doing multiple laps in a swimming pool or on a track field and you want to record how long each lap takes. Select this to record the completion of a single lap; the lap and the lap time will be listed on the screen. Lap is labeled as Lap 1 for the first lap, Lap 2 for the second lap, and so on.

Figure 6-6:
Start (left) and stop (right) your stopwatch.

3. **To start the stopwatch, select the Stopwatch button.**

4. **To stop the stopwatch, select the Stopwatch button again.**

Using Timer

Have you overcooked something? Not if you have a good timer to warn you:

1. **Select Clock from the Home screen.**

2. **Press the menu key and then select Timer.**

   A screen similar to the left side of Figure 6-7 appears. The left button with the stopwatch image is the start and pause button. You can use the right one with the circular arrow image to stop and reset the timer. The default time for your timer is based on what you set earlier. If you haven't set a time, proceed to the next step.

3. **Press the menu key and then select Set Timer.**

   A screen similar to the right side of Figure 6-7 appears.

4. **Enter the time.**

   You can enter the time based on hours, minutes, and seconds by using the numeric keys. Enter the time from left to right. For example, if you want to set the timer for 5 minutes and 20 seconds, just press 5, 2, and 0 in succession.

Figure 6-7:
Start and set the time of the timer.

5. Select Start.

Your timer starts ticking. Once it reaches the time, it will notify you.

You can customize the type of timer notification to a tone, a vibration, or both. To do so, select Clock from the Home screen. Press the menu key and then select Options. Under the Countdown Timer section, make your selections.

Using Password Keeper

Suppose that you're in front of an Internet browser, trying to access an online account. For the life of you, you just can't remember the account password. It's your third login attempt, and if you fail this time, your account will be locked. Then you have to call the customer hotline and wait hours before you can speak to a representative. Argghh! We've all done it. Luckily, BlackBerry Curve gives you an application to avoid this headache.

Password Keeper is the simple yet practical BlackBerry Curve application that makes your life that much easier. Password Keeper is filed in Applications (as shown in Figure 6-8).

Setting a password for Password Keeper

The first time you access Password Keeper, you're prompted to enter a password. *Be sure to remember the password you choose,* because this is the password to all your passwords. Forgetting this password is like forgetting the combination of your safe. There is no way to retrieve a forgotten Password Keeper password. You are prompted to enter this master password every time you access the application.

Trust us — one password is much easier to remember than many passwords.

Figure 6-8:
Password
Keeper
in the
Applications
folder.

Creating credentials

Okay, so you're ready to fire up your handy-dandy Password Keeper application. Now, what kinds of things does it expect you to do for it to work its magic? Obviously, you'll need to collect the pertinent info for all your various password-protected accounts so that you can store them in the protected environs of Password Keeper. So when creating a new password entry, be sure you have the following information (see Figure 6-9):

- ✔ **Title:** This one's straightforward. Just come up with a name to describe the password-protected account — My Favorite Shopping Site, for example.
- ✔ **Username:** This is where you enter the username for the account.
- ✔ **Password:** Enter the password for the account here.
- ✔ **Website:** Put the Web-site address (its URL) here.
- ✔ **Notes:** Not exactly crucial, but the Notes field does give you a bit of room to add a comment or two.

The only required field is Title, but a title alone usually isn't of much use to you. We suggest that you fill in as much other information here as possible, *but at the same time, be discreet about those locations where you use your username and password* — so don't put anything in the Website field or use My eBay Account as a title. That way, in the unlikely case that someone gains access to your password to Password Keeper, the intruder will have a hard time figuring out where exactly to use your credentials.

```
New Password
Title:
|
Username:

Password:

Website:
http://
Notes:
```

Figure 6-9:
Set your
password
here.

Generating random passwords

If you're the kind of person who uses one password for everything but knows deep in your heart that this is just plain wrong, wrong, wrong, random password generation is for you. When creating a new password for yet another online account (or when changing your password for an online account you already have), fire up Password Keeper, press the trackball or trackpad, and then select Random Password from the menu that appears, as shown in Figure 6-10. Voilà! A new password is automatically generated for you.

Using random password generation makes sense in conjunction with Password Keeper because you don't have to remember the randomly generated password that Password Keeper came up with for any of your online accounts — that's Password Keeper's job.

Using your password

The whole point of Password Keeper is to let your BlackBerry Curve's electronic brain do your password remembering for you. So imagine this scenario: You can no longer live without owning a personal copy of the *A Chipmunk Christmas* CD, so you surf on over to your favorite online music store and attempt to log in. You draw a blank on your password, but instead of seething, you take out your Curve, open Password Keeper, and do a find.

Type the first letters of your account title in the Find field to search for the title of your password. After you find (and highlight) the title, you press the trackball or trackpad, and the screen for your account appears, conveniently listing the password. All you have to do now is enter the password in the login screen for the online music store, and Alvin, Simon, and Theodore will soon be wending their way to your address, ready to sing "Chipmunk Jingle Bells."

Yes, you *can* copy and paste your password from Password Keeper to another application — BlackBerry Browser, for instance. Just highlight the password name, press the trackball or trackpad, and select Copy to Clipboard from the menu that appears. Then navigate to where you want to enter the password, press the trackball or trackpad, and select Paste from the menu. Keep in mind that for the copy-and-paste function to work for passwords from Password Keeper, you need to enable the Allow Clipboard Copy option in Password Keeper options (see the upcoming Table 6-1). You can copy and paste only one password at a time.

After you paste your password in another application, clear the Clipboard by pressing the trackball or trackpad and choosing Clear Clipboard. The Clipboard keeps your last copied password until you clear it.

Figure 6-10:
Generate
a random
password.

Password Keeper options

Password Keeper's Options menu, accessible by pressing the menu key while in Password Keeper, allows you to control how Password Keeper behaves. For example, you can set what characters can make up a randomly generated password. Table 6-1 describes all the options in Password Keeper.

Changing your password to Password Keeper

If you want to change your master password to Password Keeper — the password for opening Password Keeper itself — follow these steps:

1. **Select Password Keeper.**

   The initial login screen for the Password Keeper application appears.

2. **Enter your old password to access Password Keeper.**

3. **In Password Keeper, press the menu key and then select Change Password.**

   Doing so calls up the Password Keeper screen that allows you to enter your new password, as shown in Figure 6-11.

4. **Enter a new password, confirm it by entering it again, and then use your trackball or trackpad to click OK.**

Table 6-1	Password Keeper Options
Option Name	*Description*
Random Password Length	Select a number between 4 and 16 for the length of your randomly generated password.
Random Includes Alpha	If True, a randomly generated password includes alphabetic characters.
Random Includes Numbers	If True, a randomly generated password includes numbers.
Random Includes Symbols	If True, a randomly generated password includes symbols.
Confirm Delete	If True, all deletions are prompted with a confirmation screen.
Password Attempts	Select 1 to 20 attempts to successfully enter the password to Password Keeper.
Allow Clipboard Copy	If True, you can copy and paste passwords from Password Keeper.
Show Password	If True, the password is displayed; otherwise, asterisks take the place of the password characters.

Figure 6-11:
Change your
Password
Keeper
password
here.

Chapter 7

Calling Your Favorite Person

. . . .

In This Chapter

▶ Accessing the BlackBerry Phone application

▶ Making calls and receiving them

▶ Managing your calls with call forwarding and more

▶ Customizing your BlackBerry Phone setup

▶ Conferencing with more than one person

▶ Talking hands-free on your BlackBerry phone

▶ Multitasking with your BlackBerry phone

. . . .

*T*he BlackBerry phone operates no differently from any other phone you've used. So why bother with this chapter? Although your BlackBerry phone operates like any other phone, it has capabilities that far outreach those of your run-of-the-mill cellphone. For example, when was the last time your phone was connected to your to-do list? Have you ever received an e-mail and placed a call directly from that e-mail? We didn't think so. But with your BlackBerry, you can do all these things and more.

In this chapter, we first cover phone basics and then show you some of the neat ways the BlackBerry Phone application intertwines with other BlackBerry applications and functions.

Using the BlackBerry Phone Application

Accessing the Phone application from the BlackBerry is a snap. You can press the green Send button located right below the display screen to get into the Phone application.

You can get to the Phone application also by pressing any of the numeric keys. To do this, however, you have to make sure that the Dial from Home

Screen option is enabled in Phone Options. If you're a frequent phone user, we recommend that you enable this option.

To enable dialing from the Home screen, follow these steps:

1. **From your BlackBerry Curve, press the green send key.**

   Phone opens, showing the dial screen as well as your call history list.

2. **Press the menu key and then select the Options (wrench) icon.**

3. **Select General Options.**

4. **Highlight the Dial from Home Screen option, press the trackball or trackpad, and then select Yes from the drop-down list.**

   This enables you to make a phone call by pressing the numeric keys from the Home screen.

5. **Press the menu key and then select Save.**

Making and Receiving Calls

The folks at RIM have created an intuitive user interface to all the essential Phone features, including making and receiving calls.

Making a call

To make a call, start from the Home screen, and type the phone number you want to dial. As soon as you start typing numbers, the Phone application opens. When you finish typing the destination number, press the green send key.

Calling from Contacts

Because you can't possibly remember the phone numbers of all your friends and colleagues, calling from Contacts is convenient and useful. To call from Contacts, follow these steps:

1. **Open the Phone application.**

2. **Press the menu key.**

   The Phone menu appears, as shown in Figure 7-1.

3. **Select Call from Contacts.**

   Contacts opens. From here, you can search as usual for the contact you'd like to call.

4. **From Contacts, highlight your call recipient and then select Call.**

   This makes the call. Note that if your contact has more than one number, the BlackBerry Curve is smart enough to list all available numbers (through a pop-up dialog box).

Help

Call From Contacts
Call Voice Mail

Email Rob Kao

Call Rob Kao

SMS Rob Kao

View History

Add Speed Dial

Delete

View Speed Dial List

Dialing letters

One of the nice features of BlackBerry Phone is that you can dial letters, and BlackBerry will figure out the corresponding number. For example, to dial 1-800-11-LEARN, do the following on your BlackBerry:

1. **From the Home screen or the Phone application, dial 1-8-0-0-1-1.**

   As you type the first number, the Phone application opens (if it isn't open already) and displays the numbers you dialed.

2. **Press and hold the Alt key, and then dial (press) L-E-A-R-N.**

   The letters appear onscreen as you type.

3. **Press the green send key.**

   The call is initiated.

Receiving a call

Receiving a call on your BlackBerry is even easier than making a call. You can receive calls in a couple of ways. One is by using your BlackBerry's automated answering feature, and the other is by answering manually.

Automated answering is triggered whenever you take your BlackBerry out of your holster; in other words, just taking out the BlackBerry forces it to automatically pick up any call, so you can start talking right away. However, you don't have time to see who is calling you (on your Caller ID). ***Note:*** To disable autoanswering, be sure that your BlackBerry isn't in its holster when an incoming call arrives.

What's the advantage of disabling autoanswering? Well, manual answering prompts you to answer a call or ignore a call when you receive an incoming call (see Figure 7-2). This way, you can see on your Caller ID who is calling you before you decide to pick up or ignore the call.

However, if you want to turn on autoanswer, you can do this in Phone Options:

1. **Open the Phone application.**

2. **Press the menu key.**

   The Phone menu appears (refer to Figure 7-1).

3. **Select Options.**

   The Phone Options screen appears, listing the categories of options.

4. **Select General Options.**

   This opens the General Options screen.

5. **In the Auto Answer Calls field, select Out of Holster.**

6. **Press the menu key and then select Save.**

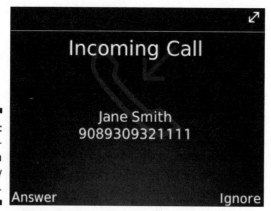

Figure 7-2:
An incoming call on a BlackBerry Curve.

Handling missed calls

So you missed a call from that important client. What made it worse is that you didn't notice the missed call because you didn't see the little Missed Call icon. That happened because you pay attention only to what is in your e-mail message box. What can you do to make sure that you return that call?

You can make missed calls appear in your e-mail message box so that you are sure to return your missed calls (if you choose to, that is).

To have your missed calls appear in your inbox, follow these steps:

1. **Open the Phone application.**

2. **Press the menu key.**

   The Phone menu appears (refer to Figure 7-1).

3. **Select Options.**

   The Phone Options screen appears, listing the different categories of options.

4. **Select Call Logging.**

   This opens the Call Logging screen.

5. **Highlight the Missed Calls option, and press the trackball or trackpad.**

   You can also select All Calls, which means that incoming and outgoing calls will be displayed in your e-mail inbox.

6. **Press the menu key and then select Save.**

Phone Options while on a Call

When you're on the phone, situations might arise in which you'd want to mute your conversation, place a call on hold, or change the call volume. No problem. BlackBerry Curve makes such adjustments easy.

Muting your call

You may want to use the Mute feature while on a conference call (see the upcoming section "Arranging Conference Calls") when you don't need to speak but do need to hear what is being discussed. Maybe you're on the bus or have kids in the background, making your surroundings noisy. By using Mute, these background noises are filtered out from the conference call.

To mute your call, follow these steps:

1. **While in a conversation, press the menu key.**

   The Phone menu appears in all its glory.

2. **Select Mute.**

   You hear a tone, indicating that your call is being muted.

Follow these steps to unmute your call:

1. **While a call is on mute, press the menu key.**

   The Phone menu makes another appearance.

2. **Select Turn Mute Off.**

   You hear a tone, indicating that your call is now unmuted.

Placing your call on hold

Unlike muting a call, placing a call on hold prohibits both you and your caller from hearing each other. To put a conversation on hold, follow these steps:

1. **While in a conversation, press the menu key.**

   The Phone menu appears yet again.

2. **Select Hold.**

   Your call is now on hold.

Follow these steps to unhold your call:

1. **While a call is on hold, press the menu key.**

   A new menu appears.

2. **Select Resume.**

   You can continue your conversation.

Adjusting the call volume

Adjusting the call volume, a simple yet important action on your BlackBerry phone, can be performed by simply pressing the volume up or volume down key on the side of your BlackBerry.

Customizing Your BlackBerry Phone

Would you like to change some things about how the BlackBerry phone works? In the following sections, we go through some settings that can make you the master of your BlackBerry phone.

Setting up your voice mail number

This section shows you how to set up your voice mail access number. Unfortunately, the instructions for setting up your voice mailbox vary, depending on your service provider. However, most service providers are more than happy to walk you through the steps to get your mailbox set up in a jiffy.

To set up your voice mail access number, follow these steps:

1. **Open the Phone application.**

2. **Press the menu key and then select Options.**

   A list of phone options appears.

3. **Select Voice Mail.**

   This opens the voice mail configuration screen.

4. **Scroll to the Access Number field, and enter your voice mail access number.**

   If this field is empty, and you don't know the voice mail access number, contact your service provider.

5. **Press the menu key and then select Save.**

Using call forwarding

On the BlackBerry Curve, you have two types of call forwarding:

- **Forward all calls:** Any calls to your BlackBerry Curve are forwarded to the number you designate. Another name for this feature is *unconditional forwarding*.

- **Forward unanswered calls:** Calls that meet different types of conditions are forwarded to different numbers as follows:

  - If busy: You don't have call waiting turned on, and you're on the phone.

  - If no answer: You don't hear your phone ring or somehow are unable to pick up your phone (perhaps you're in a meeting).

  - If unreachable: You're out of network coverage and cannot receive any signals.

Out of the box, your BlackBerry forwards any unanswered calls, regardless of conditions, to your voice mail number by default. However, you can add new numbers to forward a call to.

You need to be within network coverage before can you change your call forwarding option. After you're within network coverage, you can change your call forwarding settings by doing the following:

1. **Open the Phone application, press the menu key, and select Options.**

   A list of phone options appears.

2. **Select Call Forwarding.**

   Your BlackBerry now attempts to connect to the server. If it's successful, you'll see the Call Forwarding screen.

   If you don't see the Call Forwarding screen, wait until you have network coverage and try again.

3. **From the Call Forwarding screen, press the menu key and then select Edit Numbers.**

   A list of numbers appears. If this is the first time you're setting call forwarding, most likely only your voice mail number is in this list.

4. **To add a new forwarding number, press the menu key and then select New Number.**

   A pop-up menu appears, prompting you to enter the new forwarding number.

5. **In the pop-up window, enter the number you want to forward to and then press the trackball or trackpad.**

   The new number you entered now appears on the call forward number list. You can add this new number to any call forwarding types or conditions.

6. **Press the escape key.**

   You are returned to the Call Forwarding screen.

7. **Select the If Unreachable field.**

   A drop-down list appears, listing numbers from the call forwarding number list, including the one you just added.

8. **Select the number you want to forward to.**

   Doing so places the selected number into the If Unreachable field. You can see this on the Call Forwarding screen.

9. **Confirm your changes by pressing the menu key and then selecting Save.**

Configuring speed dial

Speed dial is a convenient feature on any phone. And after you get used to having it on a phone system, it's hard not to use it on other phones, including your BlackBerry phone.

Viewing your speed dial list

To view your speed dial list, follow these steps:

1. **Open the Phone application.**

2. **Press the menu key and then select View Speed Dial List.**

   This displays a list of speed dial entries, as shown in Figure 7-3. If you haven't set up any speed dials, this list will be empty.

   Note that the A and Q keys have already been assigned. The A key locks the screen, and the Q key changes profile settings to vibrate.

Figure 7-3: The speed dial list on a BlackBerry Curve.

> Speed Dial Numbers
>
> P
> Q Change profile to Vibrate
> R Rob Kao (W) 2122221212
> S
> T
> U
> V
> W Voice Mail 5198884369
> X
> Y
> Z

Adding a number to speed dial

Setting up speed dial numbers is as easy as using them. It takes a few seconds to set them up, but you benefit every time you use this feature.

To assign a number to a speed dial slot, follow these steps:

1. **Open the Phone application.**

2. **Press the menu key, select Options, and then select View Speed Dial List.**

   This displays your list of speed dial numbers.

3. **Scroll to an empty speed dial slot, press the menu key, and then select New Speed Dial.**

   BlackBerry Contacts appears so that you can select a contact's phone number. Note that the phone number you are assigning is associated with the letters on the left side of the screen.

4. **From the contacts list, select a contact.**

   If more than one number is associated with the selected contact, you're prompted to select which number to add to the speed dial list. The number appears in the speed dial list.

Using speed dial

After you have a few speed dial entries set up, you can start using them. To do so, while on the Home screen or in the Phone application, press a speed dial key. The call is initiated to the number associated with that particular speed dial key.

Arranging Conference Calls

To have two or more people on the phone with you — the infamous conference call — do the following:

1. **Use the Phone application to place a call to the first participant.**

2. **While the first participant is on the phone with you, press the menu key and then select New Call.**

   This automatically places the first call on hold and brings up a New Call screen, as shown in Figure 7-4, prompting you to place another call.

Figure 7-4:
A meeting participant is on hold.

3. **Place a call to the second participant by dialing a number, pressing the menu key, and then selecting Call.**

   You can dial the number by using the number pad, or you can select a frequently dialed number from your call log. To place a call from your Contacts, press the menu key from the New Call screen and then select Call from Contacts. Your BlackBerry then prompts you to select a contact to dial.

   The call to the second meeting participant is just like any other phone call (except that the first participant is still on the other line).

4. **While the second participant is on the phone with you, press the menu key and then select Join Conference, as shown in Figure 7-5.**

   This reconnects the first participant with you. Now you can talk to both participants at the same time.

Figure 7-5:
Join two other people in a conference call.

Another name for having two people on the phone with you is *three-way calling,* which isn't a new concept. If you want to chat with four people or even ten people on the phone at the same time, you certainly can. Simply repeat Steps 2 through 4 until all the participants are on the phone.

Talking privately to a conference participant

During a conference call, you may want to talk to one participant privately. This is called *splitting* your conference call. Here's how you do it:

1. **While on a conference call, press the menu key and then select Split Call.**

   A pop-up screen appears, listing all the participants of the conference call.

2. **From the pop-up screen, select the participant with whom you want to speak privately, as shown in Figure 7-6.**

   This action places all other participants on hold and connects you to the participant you selected. On the display screen, you can see to whom you are connected — this confirms that you selected the right person to chat with privately.

Figure 7-6:
Split your
conference
call.

3. **To talk to all participants again, press the menu key and then select Join Conference.**

   Doing so brings you back to the conference call with everyone else.

Alternating between phone conversations

Whether you're in a private conversation during a conference call or you're talking to someone while you have someone else on hold, you can switch between the two conversations by swapping them. Follow these steps:

1. **While talking to someone with another person on hold, press the menu key and then select Swap.**

   Doing so switches you from the person with whom you're currently talking to the person who was on hold.

2. **Repeat Step 1 to go back to the original conversation.**

Dropping that meeting-hugger

If you've been on conference calls, you can identify those chatty "meeting-huggers" who have to say something about everything. Don't you wish that you could drop them off the call? Well, with your BlackBerry, you can (as long as you are the meeting moderator or the person who initiated the call). Follow these steps to perform the drop-kick:

1. **While on a conference call, press the menu key and then select Drop Call.**

   A pop-up screen appears, listing all conference call participants.

2. **Select the meeting-hugger you want to drop.**

   That person is disconnected.

3. **Everyone else now can continue the conversation as usual.**

Communicating Hands-Free

More and more places prohibit the use of mobile phones without a hands-free headset. Here are the hands-free options for your BlackBerry.

Using the speaker phone

The Speaker Phone function is useful under certain situations, such as when you're in a room full of people who want to join your phone conversation. Or you might be all by your lonesome in your office but are stuck rooting through your files — hard to do with a BlackBerry scrunched up against your ear. (We call such moments *multitasking* — a concept so important that we devote an entire upcoming section to it.)

To switch to the speaker phone while you're on a phone call, press the menu key and then select Activate Speaker Phone. You can also use the Speaker key (the same as the $ key) to turn on the speaker phone.

Pairing your BlackBerry with a Bluetooth headset

Because BlackBerry smartphones come with a wired hands-free headset, you can start using yours by simply plugging it into the headset jack on the left side of the BlackBerry. You adjust the volume of the headset by pressing up or down on the volume keys, the same way you would adjust the call volume without the headset.

Using the wired hands-free headset can help you avoid being a police target, but if you're multitasking on your BlackBerry, the wired headset can get in the way and become inconvenient.

This is where the whole Bluetooth wireless thing comes in. You can purchase a BlackBerry Bluetooth headset to go with your Bluetooth-enabled BlackBerry.

After you purchase a BlackBerry-compatible Bluetooth headset, you can pair it with your BlackBerry. Think of *pairing* a Bluetooth headset with your BlackBerry as registering the headset with your BlackBerry so that it recognizes the headset.

First things first: You need to prep your headset for pairing. Now, each headset manufacturer has a different take on this, so you'll need to consult your headset documentation for details. With that out of the way, continue with the pairing as follows:

1. **From the Home screen, press the menu key and then select Bluetooth.**

2. **Press the menu key to display the Bluetooth menu.**

   You see the Enable Bluetooth option. If you see the Disable Bluetooth option instead, you can skip to Step 4.

3. **From the menu, select Enable Bluetooth.**

   This enables Bluetooth on your BlackBerry.

4. **Press the menu key to display the Bluetooth menu and then select Add Device.**

   You see the Searching for Devices progress bar, um, progressing, as shown in Figure 7-7. When your BlackBerry discovers the headset, a Select Device dialog box appears with the name of the headset.

5. **From the Select Device dialog box, select the Bluetooth headset.**

   A dialog box appears to prompt you for a passkey code to the headset.

Figure 7-7:
Searching
for a
headset.

6. **Enter the passkey, and press the trackball or trackpad.**

   Normally, the passkey code is 0000, but refer to your headset documentation. After you successfully enter the passkey code, you see your headset listed in the Bluetooth setting.

7. **Press the menu key to display the Bluetooth menu and then select Connect.**

   Your BlackBerry now attempts to connect to the Bluetooth headset.

8. **When you see a screen similar to Figure 7-8, you can start using your Bluetooth headset.**

Figure 7-8: Now you can use your Bluetooth headset.

Using voice dialing

With your headset and the Voice Dialing application, you can truly be hands-free from your BlackBerry. You may be thinking, how do I activate the Voice Dialing application without touching my BlackBerry? Good question. The majority of hands-free headsets (Bluetooth or not) come with a multipurpose button.

Usually, a multipurpose button on a hands-free headset can mute, end, and initiate a call. Refer to the operating manual of your hands-free headset for more info.

After your headset is active, press its multipurpose button to activate the Voice Dialing application. You will be greeted with a voice stating, "Say a command." At this point, simply say, "Call," and state the name of a person or say the number. (For example, say, "Call President Obama" or "Call 555-2468.") The Voice Dialing application is good at recognizing the name of the person and the numbers you dictate. However, we strongly suggest that you try out the voice dialing feature before you need it.

Multitasking while on the Phone

One of the great things about the BlackBerry Curve is that you can use it for other tasks while you're on the phone. For example, you can take notes or make a to-do list. Or you can look up a phone number in BlackBerry Contacts that your caller is requesting. You can even compose an e-mail and receive e-mails while on a call!

When multitasking, you really need to be using a hands-free headset or a speaker phone. Otherwise, your face would be stuck to your BlackBerry, and you couldn't engage in your conversation and multitask at the same time.

Accessing applications while on the phone

After you have donned your hands-free headset or have turned on a speaker phone, you can start multitasking by doing the following:

You can turn on the speaker phone by pressing the Speaker key (the same as the $ key).

1. **While in a conversation, from the Phone application, press the menu key and then select the Home screen.**

   (Alternatively, you can simply press the escape key while in the Phone application to return to the Home screen.) This returns you to the Home screen without terminating your phone conversation.

2. **From the Home screen, you can start multitasking.**

While on the phone and multitasking, however, you can still access the Phone menu from other applications. For example, from your to-do list, you can end a call or put a call on hold.

Taking notes while on the phone

To take notes of your call, follow these steps:

1. **During a phone conversation, press the menu key and then select Notes.**

   This displays the Notes screen.

2. **Type notes for the conversation, as shown in Figure 7-9.**

   When the call ends, the notes are automatically saved for you.

Figure 7-9:
Take notes
while on a
phone call.

Accessing phone notes

From the call history list (see Figure 7-10), you can access notes that you've made during a call or a conference call. In addition, you can edit notes and add new notes.

Figure 7-10:
Call history,
where you
can see
conversation
notes.

Forwarding phone notes

You can forward your phone notes just like any e-mail. While on the Call History screen (refer to Figure 7-10), press the menu key and then select Forward.

You can add notes not only while you're on the phone but also afterward. While you are viewing a call history, press the menu key. Then select Add Notes if you have no notes for the call, or select Edit Notes if you already have notes for the call.

Part III
Getting Online with Your Curve

It's an e-mail from my mother. She wants me to know how happy she is for us.

In this part . . .

Here's the good stuff: using your BlackBerry for e-mail (Chapter 8), text messaging (Chapter 9), messaging using the BlackBerry Messenger (Chapter 10) and going online and Web surfing (Chapter 11).

Chapter 8

You've Got (Lots of) E-Mail

Your BlackBerry Curve brings a fresh new face to the convenience and ease of use that you associate with e-mail. You can "hook" as many as ten e-mail accounts (from your work e-mail to personal e-mail from providers such as Yahoo! and AOL) to your Curve. You can set up an e-mail signature, configure e-mail filters, and search for e-mails.

In this chapter, you find answers on how to use and manage the e-mail capabilities of your Curve to their full potential. From setup to sorts, it's all covered here.

Getting Up and Running with E-Mail

Regardless of your network service provider (such as T-Mobile, or Rogers, or Vodafone), you can set up your Curve to receive mail from at least one of your e-mail accounts. Thus, with whatever address you use to send and receive e-mail from your PC (Yahoo!, Gmail, and so on), you can hook up your Curve to use that same e-mail address. Instead of checking your Gmail from your desktop, for example, you can now get it on your Curve.

Most network service providers allow you to connect as many as ten e-mail accounts to your Curve. This provides you with the convenience of one central point from which you can get all your e-mail, without having to log on to multiple e-mail accounts. Such convenience!

In an enterprise environment — depending on your company policy — you might not be able to access the BlackBerry Internet Service site to link your personal e-mail accounts to your Curve. If you work for a Fortune 500 company, most likely you can't access BlackBerry Internet Service. However, you can still configure e-mail settings (such as the BlackBerry e-mail filter and BlackBerry e-mail reconciliation) to make your e-mail experience that much better. (See the upcoming section "Enabling Wireless Reconciliation.") If you're an enterprise user, skip to the parts where you see the Enterprise icon to configure your e-mail settings. If you haven't set up e-mail on your company-owned Curve, see the upcoming section "Setting up e-mail in an enterprise environment."

Using the BlackBerry Internet Service client

You can pull together all your e-mail accounts into one by using the BlackBerry Internet Service client (formerly known as the BlackBerry Web client). The BlackBerry Internet Service client allows you to do the following:

- **Manage multiple e-mail accounts:** As we mention earlier, you can combine as many as ten of your e-mail accounts onto your Curve. See the next section for details.

- **Use wireless e-mail reconciliation:** No more trying to match your Curve e-mail against e-mail in your combined account(s). Just turn on wireless e-mail reconciliation, and you're good to go. For more on this, see the upcoming section "Enabling Wireless Reconciliation."

- **Create e-mail filters:** You can filter e-mails on your Curve so that you get only those messages that you truly care about. See the "Filtering your e-mail" section, near the end of this chapter.

Think of the BlackBerry Internet Service client as an online e-mail account manager, but one that doesn't keep your e-mails. Instead, it routes the e-mails from your other accounts to your Curve (because it's directly connected to your Curve).

Combining your e-mail accounts into one

To start *aggregating,* or combining, e-mail accounts (such as Gmail) onto your Curve, you must first run a setup program from the BlackBerry Internet Service client. You can access the Service client from your Curve or from your desktop computer.

To access the BlackBerry Internet Service client from your PC, you need the URL that is specific to your network service. Contact your network service provider (T-Mobile, Verizon, and so on) directly to get that information.

After you've logged on to the BlackBerry Internet Service client, you should see a screen similar to Figure 8-1. If your network provider has activated your account, you should see one e-mail address — the default address of your account.

You will see a set of options on the left navigation bar. The Email Accounts option allows you to add, edit, and delete e-mail accounts. In addition, for each e-mail address, you can set up filters and an e-mail signature.

Figure 8-1:
Set up
an e-mail
account
here.

As we mention previously, your Curve already has a default e-mail address that you can use to receive and send e-mail. If you don't have any other e-mail account that you want to meld into your BlackBerry e-mail account, simply skip to the upcoming "Configuring Your E-Mail Signature" section.

Adding an e-mail account

To add an e-mail account to your BlackBerry account, follow these steps from your desktop PC:

1. **From the BlackBerry Internet Service client (refer to Figure 8-1), click the Set Up Account button.**

2. **On the e-mail account screen, enter the e-mail address and logon credentials for that e-mail address:**

   • E-mail address: The address from which you want to receive e-mail (for example, `myid@yahoo.com`)

   • Account logon: The one you use to log on to this e-mail account

   • Password: The one you use with the logon

3. **Click Next.**

   You're finished. It's that easy!

You can also manage your accounts from your Curve. From the Home screen, press the menu key and select Set Up Internet E-Mail. The rest is pretty much the same on the Curve as it is on a PC.

With your BlackBerry Curve, you can create and set up the BlackBerry Internet Service account as you would on your PC. Although you could do this even before OS 5.0, the new interface has made setting up a BlackBerry Internet Service account much easier.

To add an e-mail account to your BlackBerry account from your BlackBerry, follow these steps:

1. **From your BlackBerry Home screen, select Setup Folder.**

2. **Select the Person E-mail Setup icon.**

   You are prompted with a login screen similar to Figure 8-2. If you haven't created your account, you see a Create button to create your BlackBerry Internet Service account username and a password for you to log in.

Figure 8-2:
BlackBerry
Internet
Service
setup on
BlackBerry
OS 5.0.

3. **After you log in, click Add.**

   A screen with different e-mail domains (such as Yahoo! and Google) appears, as shown in Figure 8-3.

Figure 8-3:
Select
an e-mail
domain.

4. **Select an e-mail domain.**

5. **Enter the e-mail address and password, and then select Next.**

   You see a setup confirmation screen.

If you have OS 4.6, follow these steps to add e-mail accounts to your BlackBerry:

1. **From your BlackBerry Home screen, select Setup Folder.**

2. **Select the Person E-mail Setup icon.**

You are prompted with a login screen. If you haven't created your account, you see a Create New Account link to create your BlackBerry Internet Service account username and a password for you to log in.

3. After you log in, click the Add My Existing E-mail Account link.

A screen with a different text field appears. This is where you can enter an e-mail address and the password associated with that e-mail account.

4. Enter the e-mail address and password, and click Next.

You see a setup confirmation screen.

Setting up e-mail in an enterprise environment

This section is for you if your Curve can't receive and send e-mail yet — such as when you first get your Curve or you swap an old model for a new one.

If your e-mail function works properly on your Curve, you can skip this section.

Follow these steps to activate your BlackBerry Curve for enterprise use:

1. From the Home screen, press the menu key and then select Enterprise Activation.

The Enterprise Activation screen opens, with two fields for you to fill in:

- Your corporate e-mail address: For example, *myaccount@abc Company.com*

- Your password: From your IT department

2. Type your corporate e-mail account along with the appropriate password.

If you don't know this information, contact your corporate system administrator.

3. Press the menu key and then select Activate.

Your Curve attempts to activate itself with your corporation.

Some corporations don't allow any employee-purchased BlackBerry smartphones to be activated with corporate e-mail. Check with your system administrator for corporate BlackBerry policies.

Getting e-mail in an enterprise environment using Desktop Redirector

If you are a sole proprietor or consultant who works in a corporation that runs Exchange or Lotus, and you would like to get enterprise e-mails on your Curve, this section is for you.

Typically, to get enterprise e-mail, your Curve would have to be configured with the BlackBerry Enterprise Server. Expect this if your employer hands you a Curve. However, if you work for a company as a contractor, you probably won't be getting a BlackBerry from that company. When you want to get enterprise e-mail so that you don't fall behind, you need Desktop Redirector so that you can get company e-mail on your personal BlackBerry.

To start using Desktop Redirector, you first need to install BlackBerry Desktop Manager; see Chapter 16 for details about how to do this. After you install Desktop Manager with Redirector, make sure that Redirector starts every time you boot your PC.

Depending on the corporate security policy, some corporations allow Desktop Redirector, and some do not. Before you start using Desktop Redirector, contact the IT department in the company you work for.

Here are just a few caveats when using Desktop Redirector:

✔ You can get enterprise e-mail as long as your PC is turned on and has an Internet connection.

✔ When someone sends you an attachment, you can't retrieve it from your Curve. Unfortunately, that is the limitation for Desktop Redirector.

✔ When someone sends you a meeting notice, you can't accept or reject it.

Configuring Your E-Mail Signature

If you're tired of writing *Regards, John Smith* over and over to close an e-mail, set an e-mail signature. By default, your e-mail signature is something like "Sent via My BlackBerry," which can be cool in the first week, showing off to people that you are à la mode with your BlackBerry. But sooner or later, you may not want people to know that you are out and about while answering e-mail. Or you may want something more personal.

Follow these steps to configure your e-mail signature by using the BlackBerry Internet Service client:

1. **Log on to the client on your PC.**

2. **In the BlackBerry Internet Service client (refer to Figure 8-1), click the Edit icon for the desired e-mail account.**

   The edit screen appears, as shown in Figure 8-4.

Figure 8-4:
The e-mail account edit screen.

3. **In the Signature field, type the desired text for your e-mail signature.**

4. **Click Save.**

Enabling Wireless Reconciliation

With wireless reconciliation, you don't need to delete the same e-mail in two places (on your computer and on your Curve). The two e-mail inboxes reconcile with each other — hence, the term *wireless reconciliation*. Convenient, huh?

Enabling wireless e-mail synchronization

You can start wireless e-mail synchronization by configuring your Curve. Follow these steps:

1. **From the Home screen, press the menu key and then select Messages.**

   This opens the Messages application. You see the message list.

2. **In the message list, press the menu key and then select Options.**

   The Options screen appears, with two option types: General Options and E-mail Reconciliation.

3. **Select E-mail Reconciliation.**

   This opens the E-mail Reconciliation screen, which has the following options:

   - Delete On: Configures how BlackBerry handles your e-mail deletion.

   - Wireless Reconciliation: Turns on or off the wireless sync function.

   - On Conflict: Controls how BlackBerry handles any inconsistencies between e-mail on your Curve and the BlackBerry Internet Service client.

     With this option, you can choose who "wins": your Curve or the BlackBerry Internet Service client.

4. **Select Delete On and then select one of the following from the drop-down list:**

   - Handheld: A delete on your Curve takes effect only on your Curve.

   - Mailbox & Handheld: A delete on your Curve takes effect on both your Curve and your inbox on the BlackBerry Internet Service client.

   - Prompt: This option prompts your Curve to ask you at the time of deletion where the deletion takes effect.

5. **Select Wireless Reconciliation and then select On from the drop-down list.**

6. **Select On Conflict, and make a selection from the drop-down list.**

   If you choose Handheld Wins, the e-mail messages in your e-mail account will match the ones on the handheld.

Next, you need to configure BlackBerry Internet Service to ensure that Synchronize Deleted Items is selected:

1. **Log on to the client on your PC.**

2. **In the BlackBerry Internet Service client (refer to Figure 8-1), click the Edit icon for the desired e-mail account.**

   The edit screen appears (refer to Figure 8-4).

3. **In the Synchronize Deleted Items field, make sure the check box is selected.**

4. **Click Save.**

Unfortunately, some e-mail accounts might not work well with the e-mail reconciliation feature of the BlackBerry, so you still may have to delete an e-mail twice.

Permanently deleting e-mail from your Curve

When deleting e-mail on your Curve, the same message in that e-mail account is placed in the Deleted folder. You can set up your Curve to permanently delete e-mail, but use this option with caution because after that e-mail is gone, it's truly gone.

To permanently delete e-mail on your BlackBerry Internet Service client from your Curve, follow these steps:

1. **Open the Messages application.**

2. **In the message list, press the menu key and then select Options.**

3. **On the Options screen, select E-mail Reconciliation.**

4. **On the E-mail Reconciliation screen, press the menu key and then select Purge Deleted Items.**

   You see all your e-mail accounts.

5. **Choose the e-mail account from which you want to purge deleted items.**

   A screen appears, warning you that you are about to purge deleted e-mails on your Service client.

6. **Select Yes.**

   Deleted e-mails in the selected e-mail account are purged.

Unfortunately, some e-mail accounts may not work with the Purge Deleted Items feature.

Working with E-Mail

From the Messages application, you send and receive your e-mails and also configure wireless e-mail reconciliation with your e-mail account(s). See the preceding section for information on e-mail reconciliation.

To access Messages, press the menu key from the Home screen and then select Messages. The first thing you see after opening Messages is the message list. Your message list can contain e-mail, voice mail messages, missed-phone-call notices, Short Messaging Service (SMS) messages, and even saved Web pages.

Receiving e-mails

Whether you're concerned about security or speed of delivery, with BlackBerry's up-to-date secured network, you're in good hands when receiving e-mail on your Curve.

And whether you've aggregated accounts or just use the plain-vanilla BlackBerry e-mail account, you receive your e-mail the same way. When you receive an e-mail message, your Curve notifies you by displaying a numeral next to a mail icon (an envelope) at the top of the screen. This number represents how many new (unread) e-mails you have (see Figure 8-5). A red asterisk next to the envelope indicates that you have new mail and that you haven't opened the Messages application yet. Your Curve can also notify you of new e-mail by vibration, a sound alert, or both. You can customize this from the Profile application, detailed in Chapter 3.

Figure 8-5:
You've
got (333)
e-mails!

Retrieving e-mail

Retrieving your e-mail is simple. Follow these steps:

1. **From the Home screen, press the menu key and then select Messages.**

2. **In the message list, scroll to any e-mail, and press the trackball or trackpad.**

   You can tell whether an e-mail is unopened by the small, unopened envelope icon on the left side of the e-mail. A read e-mail bears an opened envelope icon, a sent e-mail has a check mark as its icon, and a document icon represents a draft e-mail.

3. **After you finish reading the message, press the escape key to return to the message list.**

Sorting the message list

Your Curve mail lists messages in order by the date and time they were received, but you can sort by different criteria. For example, to see only incoming e-mail, press Alt+I. (For more predefined hot keys, see the upcoming section "Reusing saved searches.")

Sorting and searching are closely related on your Curve. In a sense, searching is really sorting your e-mail based on your search criteria. You can search your e-mail by the name of the sender or by keywords. Or you could run a search as broad as looking through all the e-mail that has been sent to you. See the later section "Searching through Messages Like a Pro" for more on searching and sorting.

Saving a message to the saved folder

You can save any important e-mail in a folder so that you can find it without sorting through tons of e-mail. To do so, simply scroll to the e-mail you want to save, press the menu key, and then select Save from the menu. A pop-up message confirms that your e-mail has been saved. Your saved e-mail remains in the message list.

To retrieve or view a saved e-mail, follow these steps:

1. **Open the Messages application.**

2. **In the message list, press the menu key and then select View Saved Messages.**

   You see the list of messages you saved.

3. **Select the message you want and then press the trackball or trackpad to open it.**

Viewing attachments

Your Curve is so versatile that you can view most e-mail attachments just like you can on a desktop PC. And we're talking sizable attachments, too, such as JPEGs (photos), Word docs, PowerPoint slides, and Excel spreadsheets. Table 8-1 shows a list of supported attachments viewable from your BlackBerry.

If you are using BlackBerry Desktop Redirector to get your e-mail onto your Curve, you won't get attachments on your Curve.

Table 8-1	BlackBerry-Supported Attachments
Supported Attachment Extension	*Description*
.bmp	BMP image file format
.doc/.docx	MS Word document
.dot	MS Word document template
.gif	GIF image file format
.htm	HTML Web page
.html	HTML Web page
.jpg	JPEG image file format
.pdf	Adobe PDF document
.png	PNG image file format
.ppt/.pptx	MS PowerPoint document
.tif	TIFF image file format
.txt	Text file
.wpd	Corel WordPerfect document
.xls/xlsx	MS Excel document
.zip	Compressed file format

To tell whether an e-mail has an attachment, look for the standard paper-clip icon next to your e-mail in the message list.

You retrieve all the different types of attachments the same way. This makes retrieving attachments an easy task. To open an attachment, follow along:

1. **While reading an e-mail, press the menu key and then select Open Attachment.**

You see a screen that contains the name of the file, a Table of Contents option, and a Full Contents option. For Word documents, you can see different headings in outline form in the Table of Contents option. For picture files, such as JPEGs, you can go straight to the Full Contents option to see the graphic.

For all supported file types, you see Table of Contents and Full Contents as options. Depending on the file type, use your judgment on when you should use the Table of Contents option.

 2. **Scroll to Full Contents, press the menu key, and then select Retrieve.**

Your Curve attempts to contact the BlackBerry Internet Service client to retrieve your attachment. This retrieves only part of your attachment. As you peruse a document, your Curve retrieves more as you scroll through the attachment.

Editing attachments

Your Curve comes with Documents To Go, which means that out of the box, you not only can view, but also edit Word and PowerPoint documents. You can even save the documents to your Curve and transfer them later to your PC.

As an example, imagine editing a Word document that you received as an attachment to an e-mail:

 1. **Open the e-mail.**

 2. **In the message list, open an e-mail with a Word document attached.**

This opens the e-mail for you to read. Notice the little paper clip, indicating that it has an attachment.

 3. **Press the menu key and then select Open Attachment.**

You're prompted with a pop-up that asks whether you want to view the Word document or edit with Documents To Go.

 4. **Select Edit with Documents To Go.**

Here, you can view and edit a document.

 5. **Press the menu key and then select Edit Mode.**

In Edit mode, you can edit your document.

 6. **When you are finished editing and viewing, you can either save the document on your Curve or e-mail it:**

 • To e-mail the edited document, press the menu key and then select Send via E-mail.

You see an e-mail message with the Word document. Follow the steps described in the next section to send this e-mail attachment as you would any other e-mail.

 • To save the document, press the menu key and then select Save.

TIP

If you want to save the attachment to your Curve, you have to navigate its folder structure. For documents, the default save location usually is the Documents folder.

Sending e-mail

The first thing you probably want to do when you get your BlackBerry to write an e-mail to let your friends know that you just got a BlackBerry. Follow these steps to send an e-mail message:

1. **Open the Messages application.**

2. **In the message list, press the menu key, and select Compose E-mail.**

   You are prompted with a blank e-mail that you need to fill out, just like you would do on your PC.

3. **In the To field, type the recipient's name or e-mail address.**

   As you type, you see a list of contacts from your Contacts that match the name or address you're typing. You can make a selection from this list.

4. **Enter a subject in the Subject field, and type your message in the Body field.**

5. **When you're finished, press the menu key and then select Send.**

   Your message has wings.

Forwarding e-mail

When you need to share an important e-mail with a colleague or a friend, you can forward that e-mail. Simply do the following:

1. **Open the e-mail.**

   For information on opening e-mail, see "Retrieving e-mail," previously in this chapter.

2. **Press the menu key and then select Forward.**

3. **Type the recipient's name or e-mail address in the To field and then add a message if needed.**

   When you start typing your recipient's name, a drop-down list of your contacts appears, and you can choose the recipient from it.

4. **Press the menu key and then select Send.**

   Your message is on its way to your recipient.

Sending e-mail to more than one person

When you need to send an e-mail to more than one person, just keep adding recipient names as needed. You can also add recipient names to receive a Cc (carbon copy) or Bcc (blind carbon copy). Here's how:

1. **Open the e-mail.**

   For information on opening e-mail, see the previous section "Retrieving e-mail."

2. **Press the menu key and then select Compose E-mail.**

3. **Specify the To field for the e-mail recipient and then press the Return key.**

   Another To field is added automatically below the first. The Cc field works the same way.

4. **To add a Bcc recipient, press the menu key and then select Add Bcc.**

   You see a Bcc field. You can specify a Bcc recipient the same way you do To and Cc recipients.

Whether you're composing a new e-mail, replying, or forwarding an e-mail, you add new Cc and Bcc fields the same way.

Attaching a file to your e-mail

Many people are surprised that you can attach any document on your Curve or on the microSD card. You can attach Word, Excel, and PowerPoint documents as well as pictures, music, and videos. To send an e-mail with a file attached, follow these steps:

1. **Open the Messages application.**

2. **In the message list, press the menu key and then select Compose E-mail.**

   You are prompted with a blank e-mail that you can fill out as you would on your PC. Enter the recipient's name in the To field and then enter the subject and body of the message.

3. **Press the menu key and then select Attach File.**

   You're prompted with a list of your folders. Think of these as the folders on your PC.

4. **Navigate to the file of your choice, and press the trackball or trackpad.**

   After you select a file, you see the file in the e-mail message.

5. **When you're finished, press the menu key and then select Send.**

   Your message and attached file wing their way to the recipient.

Spell-checking your outgoing messages

Whether you're composing an e-mail message or an SMS text message, you can always check your spelling with the built-in spell checker. Simply press the menu key and then select Check Spelling. When your Curve finds an error, the spell checker makes a suggestion, as shown in Figure 8-6. To skip the spell check for that word and go on to the next word, press the escape key. If you want to skip spell-checking for an e-mail, simply press and hold the escape key.

Title: Checking the spell checker

When you miss spellt a word

> spell
> spells
> spelt

Figure 8-6:
The BlackBerry spell checker in action.

Your Curve, just like Microsoft Word, underlines a misspelled word.

By default, the spell checker doesn't kick in before you send your message, but you can configure it to check spelling before you send an e-mail. Follow these steps:

1. **Open the Messages application.**

2. **Press the menu key and then select Options.**

3. **Select the Spell Check option.**

4. **Select the Spell Check E-mail before Sending check box.**

5. **Press the menu key and then select Save.**

The underline feature is a default setting called Check Spelling as You Type. To turn off this feature, disable the Spell Check option in Message Options.

Deleting e-mail

If you want to really clean up your old e-mails, and you don't want to scroll through tons of messages, you can do the following:

1. **Open the Messages application.**

2. **From the message list, highlight a horizontal date mark, press the menu key, and then choose Delete Prior.**

   The *date mark* is simply a horizontal bar with dates. Just like you can highlight e-mails in the message list, you can highlight the date mark. You are prompted to confirm the deletion.

   Before you take the plunge, remember that going ahead will *delete all the e-mails before the particular date mark.* You cannot retrieve deleted items from your BlackBerry.

3. **Select Delete to confirm your deletion.**

   All your e-mails before the date mark are history.

Filtering your e-mail

Most of us get e-mail that isn't urgent or doesn't concern us. Instead of receiving these e-mails on your Curve — and wasting both time and effort to check them — you can filter them out. While in the BlackBerry Internet Service client, set up filters to make your BlackBerry mailbox receive only the e-mails that you care about. (Don't worry; you'll still receive all your e-mails on your main computer.)

To create a simple filter that treats messages as urgent and forwards them to your Curve, follow these steps. In this example, we're setting a filter to mark work-related messages as urgent.

1. **From your PC, log on to the BlackBerry Internet Service client (refer to Figure 8-1).**

2. **Click the Filter icon for the desired e-mail account.**

   The Filter screen that appears shows a list of filters that have been created. Figure 8-7 doesn't have any filters yet.

3. **Click the Add a filter link.**

   The Add Filter screen appears, as shown in Figure 8-8.

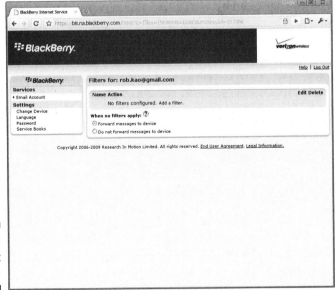

Figure 8-7:
Filter list
screen.

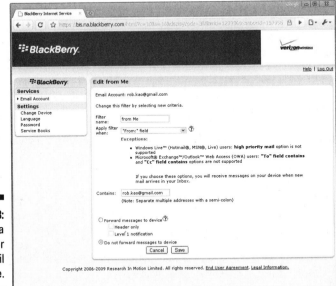

Figure 8-8:
Create a
filter for
your e-mail
here.

4. **Enter a name in the Filter Name text box.**

   The filter name can be anything you like. We're using "from Me".

5. **From the Apply Filter When drop-down list, choose the condition to place on the filter:**

   - A High-Priority Mail Arrives: The filter applies only to urgent e-mail.

   - Subject Field Contains: The Contains field is enabled (you can type text in it). You can specify what keywords the filter will look for in the subject field. Separate entries with a semicolon (;).

   - From Field Contains: The Contains field is enabled (you can type text in it). You can type full addresses or part of an address. For example, you can type **rob@robkao.com** or just **kao**. Separate entries with a semicolon (;).

   - To Field Contains: Similar to From Field Contains, enter e-mail address(es).

   - CC Field Contains: Similar to From Field Contains, enter e-mail address(es).

   If you need more conditions, just add filters. Each filter can have one condition.

   For this example, we select From Field Contains.

6. **Specify the text in the Contains field.**

   See the details in Step 5 for what to enter in the Contains field. Continuing this example, type the domain of your work e-mail address. For example, if your work e-mail address is *myName*@XYZCo.com, enter **XYZCo.com**.

7. **Select one of the following options:**

   Forward Messages to Device: Select this radio button, and you can then select either or both check boxes below it:

   - Header Only: You want only the header of the e-mails that meet the condition(s) you set in Steps 3, 4, and 5 to be sent to you. (A *header* doesn't contain the body of the e-mail — just who sent it, the subject, and the time it was sent.) Choose this check box if you get automated alerts, where receiving only the subject is sufficient.

   - Level 1 Notification: Level 1 Notification is another way of saying *urgent e-mail.* When you receive a Level 1 e-mail, it appears in bold in Messages.

   Do Not Forward Messages to Device: Any e-mail that meets the conditions you set in Steps 3, 4, and 5 aren't sent to your BlackBerry.

8. **Confirm your filter by clicking the Save button.**

   You return to the Filter screen, where you can see your newly created filter in the list.

If you have a hard time setting the criteria for a filter, just make a best guess and then check it by having a friend send you a test e-mail. If the test e-mail isn't filtered correctly, set the conditions until you get them right.

Searching through Messages Like a Pro

Searching is a function you probably won't use every day, but when you run a search, you usually need the information fast. Take a few minutes here to familiarize yourself with general searching.

The BlackBerry Messages application provides three ways to search through your messages. Two of the three ways are specific, and one is a broad search:

- **Search by sender or recipient:** Specific. This method assumes that you already know the sender or recipient.
- **Search by subject:** Specific. This approach assumes that you already know the subject.
- **General search:** Broad. You don't have a specific assumption.

You can search through anything listed in the messages list. This means that you can search through SMS and voice mail as well as e-mail.

Searching by sender or recipient

Search by sender or recipient when you're looking for a specific message from a specific person. For example, suppose that your brother constantly sends you e-mail (which means your message list has many entries from him). You're trying to locate a message he sent you approximately two weeks ago regarding a fishing-trip location. You scrolled down the message list, but you just can't seem to find that message. Or maybe you want to find a message you sent to Sue but can't lay your hands on it.

To find a message when you know the sender or recipient, follow these steps:

1. **Open the Messages application.**

2. **In the message list, highlight a message that you sent to or received from that particular person.**

   The choice you get in the next step depends on whether you highlighted a sent message or a received message.

3. **Press the menu key and then select one of these options:**

   • To search for a message *from* someone specific: Because that certain someone sent you the message, choose Search Sender.

   • To search for a message *to* someone specific: Because you sent that certain someone the message, choose Search Recipient.

   This starts the search. Any results appear onscreen.

Searching by subject

Search by subject when you're looking for an e-mail titled by a specific subject that you already know. As is the case when running a search by sender or recipient, first scroll to an e-mail that bears the same subject you're searching for. Then follow these steps:

1. **Open the Messages application.**

2. **In the message list, highlight an e-mail titled by the specific subject you're searching for.**

3. **Press the menu key and then select Search Subject.**

   The search starts, and the results appear onscreen.

Running a general search

A general search is a broad search from which you can perform keyword searches of your messages. To run a general search, follow these steps:

1. **Open the Messages application.**

2. **In the message list, press the menu key and then select Search.**

3. **In the Search screen that appears, fill in your search criteria (see Figure 8-9).**

```
Search
Name:
  In                    Any Address Field
Subject: Urgent
Message:
  Include Encrypted Messages:      Yes
Service:                    All Services
Folder:                      All Folders
Show:              Sent and Received
Type:                               All
```

Figure 8-9: The Search screen in Messages.

The search criteria for a general search follow:

- Name: This is the name of the sender or recipient to search by.

- In: This is related to the Name criterion. Use this drop-down list to indicate where the name may appear, such as in the To or Cc field. From the drop-down list, your choices are From, To, Cc, Bcc, and any address field.

- Subject: This is where you type some or all keywords that appear in the subject.

- Message: Here, you enter keywords that appear in the message.

- Service: If you set up your BlackBerry to receive e-mail from more than one e-mail account, you can specify which e-mail account to search.

- Folder: This is the folder in which you want to perform the search. Generally, you should select All Folders.

- Show: This drop-down list specifies how the search result will appear — namely, whether you want to see only e-mails that you sent or e-mails that you received. From the drop-down list, your choices are Sent and Received, Received Only, Sent Only, Saved Only, Draft Only, and Unopened Only.

- Type: This drop-down list specifies the type of message that you're trying to search for: e-mail, SMS, or voice mail. From the drop-down list, your choices are All, E-mail, E-mail with Attachments, PIN, SMS, Phone, and Voice Mail.

From the Search screen shown in Figure 8-9, you can have multiple search criteria or just a single one. It's up to you.

4. **Press the menu key and then select Search to launch your search.**

   The search results appear onscreen.

You can narrow the search results by performing a second search on the initial results. For example, you can search by sender and then narrow those hits (results) by performing a second search by subject.

You can also search by sender or recipient when you're looking for a specific message from a specific person. Scroll to an e-mail that bears the specific sender or recipient. Press the menu key and then select Search Sender or Search Recipient. If the e-mail that you highlighted is an incoming e-mail, you'll see Search Sender. If the e-mail is outgoing, you'll see Search Recipient.

Saving search results

If you find yourself searching with the same criteria over and over, you may want to save the search and then reuse it. Here's how:

1. **Follow Steps 1–3 in the preceding section for an outgoing e-mail search.**

2. **Press the menu key and then select Save.**

   The Save Search screen appears, from which you can name your search and assign it a shortcut key (see Figure 8-10).

Figure 8-10:
Name your
search, and
assign it a
shortcut
key.

```
Save Search
Title: Urgent Subject
Shortcut Key (Alt +):                    u
Name:
   In                    Any Address Field
Subject: Urgent
Message:
   Include Encrypted Messages:       Yes
Service:                       All Services
Folder:                         All Folders
Show:                   Sent and Received
Type:                                  All
```

3. **In the Title field, enter a name.**

   The title is the name of your search, which appears on the Search Results screen.

4. **Scroll to the Shortcut Key field, press the trackball or trackpad, and select a letter from the drop-down list.**

   You can choose among ten letters.

5. **Confirm your saved search by pressing the menu key and then selecting Save.**

Reusing saved searches

Right out of the box, your BlackBerry comes with five saved search results. Any new saved result will make your search that much more robust.

Follow these steps to see all saved search results:

1. **Open the Messages application.**

2. **In the message list, press the menu key and then select Search.**

3. **Press the menu key and then select Recall.**

   The recall screen opens, and you can see the five preloaded search shortcuts, as well as any searches you saved, as shown in Figure 8-11.

Figure 8-11: The Recall screen, showing default search hot keys.

To reuse one of the saved search results, simply select a desired search from the list, press the menu key, and select Search.

If you have multiple e-mail accounts set up, you can set up a search shortcut so that you view only one specific account. For example, say you have both your personal e-mail and your small-business e-mail accounts set up on your BlackBerry. In the Message application, you see e-mails from both, which can be overwhelming at times. From the general Search screen (refer to Figure 8-9), set the Service drop-down list to the one you want, and follow the preceding steps to save the search and assign a shortcut key. The next time you want to see only a certain account, you can get to it in an instant!

Follow Up Your E-Mail

With OS 5.0, your can automatically add reminders to any e-mail that you want to follow up. This is similar to the follow-up flag in Microsoft Outlook. Why would you want to do this on your BlackBerry? If you get a flurry of e-mail in the morning and read through them before replying, sometimes you'll forget which ones need a response. This is one example where a follow-up flag would help.

To add a follow-up flag:

1. **Open the Messages application.**

2. **Highlight the e-mail in need of a follow up, and press the menu key.**

3. **Select Flag for Follow Up.**

   You see a red flag next to your message.

4. **While the flagged e-mail is still highlighted, press the menu key again.**

5. **Select Flag Properties.**

   You can select the following:

   - Request: This is the type of follow up. You can choose from Call, Review, Forward, and more.

   - Color: Yup, you guessed it. This is the color of the flag.

   - Status: You can choose whether the status is completed or not.

   - Due: This is the due date for this follow up. When the due date arrives, you get a pop-up reminder, similar to a calendar reminder.

Long Live E-Mail

No closet has unlimited space, and your BlackBerry e-mail storage has limits, too. You've likely pondered how long your e-mails are kept in your BlackBerry. (The default is 30 days. Pshew.) You can choose several options: from 15 days to forever (well, for as long as your BlackBerry has enough space for them).

Because any message you save is kept for as long as you want, a good way to make sure that you don't lose an important message is to save it.

To change how long your e-mails live on your BlackBerry, follow these steps:

1. **Open the Messages application.**

2. **Press the menu key and then select Options.**

3. **Select General Options.**

4. **Scroll to the Keep Messages option and then press the trackball or trackpad.**

5. **From the drop-down list that appears, choose the time frame that you want and then press the trackball or trackpad:**

   • Forever: If you choose Forever, you'll seldom need to worry about your e-mails being automatically deleted. On the downside, though, your BlackBerry will eventually run out of memory. At that point, you must manually delete some e-mails to free space to accept new e-mails.

   A good way to archive your e-mail is to back up your e-mails by using BlackBerry Desktop Manager. See Chapter 18 for more on backing up your BlackBerry on your PC.

   • Time option: If you choose a time option, any message older than that time frame is automatically deleted from your BlackBerry the next time you reboot your BlackBerry. However, the message will be deleted only on your BlackBerry — even if you turn on e-mail reconciliation — because these deletions are only on the device.

6. **Confirm your changes by pressing the menu key and then selecting Save.**

Chapter 9

Too Cool for E-Mail

In This Chapter

▶ Sending PIN-to-PIN messages

▶ Using SMS and MMS

▶ Setting up and using IM

▶ Figuring out messaging etiquette

*Y*our BlackBerry is primarily a communication tool, with e-mail messages and phone conversations as the major drivers. It's a wonderful technology, but sometimes, another means of communication is more appropriate. For instance, e-mail isn't the tool of choice for instant messaging — most people would find that method slow and cumbersome. Nor is e-mail the best tool to use when you want to alert someone to something.

Your BlackBerry offers some less-obvious ways to communicate — ways that may serve as the perfect fit for a special situation. In this chapter, you get the scoop on PIN-to-PIN messaging and text messaging (also known as *Short Messaging Service,* or *SMS*). We also give you tips on how to turn your BlackBerry into a lean (and not-so-mean) instant messaging (IM) machine.

Sending and Receiving PIN-to-PIN Messages

PIN-to-PIN messaging is based on the technology that underpins two-way pager systems. Unlike sending a standard e-mail, when you send a BlackBerry PIN-to-PIN message, the message doesn't venture outside the RIM infrastructure in search of an e-mail server and (eventually) an e-mail inbox. Instead, it stays solidly in the RIM world, where it is shunted through the recipient's network provider until it ends up on the recipient's BlackBerry.

So when you use PIN-to-PIN messaging, that's another way of saying *sending a message from one BlackBerry to another BlackBerry.*

A little bit of RIM history

Sometime during the last millennium, Research In Motion (RIM) wasn't even in the phone business. Before BlackBerry became all the rage with smartphone features, RIM was doing a tidy little business with its wireless e-mail.

Back then, RIM's primitive wireless e-mail service was served by network service providers on a radio bandwidth: DataTAC and Mobitex networks. These were separate from a typical cellphone infrastructure's bandwidth.

RIM devices at that time already had PIN-to-PIN messaging. This type of messaging is akin to a pager, where a message doesn't live in a mailbox but is sent directly to the BlackBerry with no delay. (No one wants a paging system that moves at turtle speed when you can get one that moves like a jackrabbit, right?)

Several interesting facts followed from RIM's initial decision. Of note, most cellphone users in New York City were left without service during the 9/11 disaster. The entire cellphone infrastructure in New York and surrounding areas was overwhelmed when faced with too many people trying to use the bandwidth available. However, one communication device continued to work during that stressful time: RIM's PIN-to-PIN messaging kept the information flow going.

PIN stands for personal identification number (familiar to anyone who's ever used an ATM) and refers to a system for uniquely identifying your device.

Here's the neat part. According to RIM (Research In Motion), the message isn't saved anywhere in this universe *except* on the one device that sends the PIN message and the other device that receives it. Compare that with an e-mail, which is saved in at least four separate locations (the mail client and e-mail servers of both sender and recipient), not to mention all the system's redundancies and the backups employed by the server. Think of it this way: If you whisper a little secret in someone's ear, only you and that special someone know what was said. In a way, PIN-to-PIN messaging is the same thing, with one BlackBerry whispering to another BlackBerry. Now, that's discreet.

If you tend to read the financial newspapers — especially the ones that cover corporate lawsuits extensively — you'll know that there's no such thing as privacy in e-mail. PIN-to-PIN messaging, in theory at least, is as good as the old Code of Silence. Now, is such privacy really an advantage? You can argue both sides of the issue, depending on what you want to use PIN-to-PIN messaging for.

Basically, if you like the idea that your communications can be kept discreet, PIN-to-PIN messaging has great curb appeal. If you don't care about privacy issues, you still may be impressed by PIN-to-PIN messaging's zippy nature. (It really is the Ferrari of wireless communication — way faster than e-mail.)

The Code of Silence in an enterprise environment has always been a thorny issue in companies that have strict regulatory requirements. As expected, RIM addressed this issue with a new feature in later operating systems allowing BlackBerry Enterprise Server administrators to flip a flag, forcing the device to forward all PIN-to-PIN messages to the BlackBerry Enterprise Server. A company can also install on the device third-party applications to report PIN-to-PIN messages.

Getting a BlackBerry PIN

When you try to call someone on the telephone, you can't get far without a telephone number. As you may expect, the same principle applies to PIN-to-PIN messaging: no PIN; no PIN-to-PIN messaging.

In practical terms, you need the PIN of any BlackBerry to which you want to send a PIN message. (You also need to find out your own PIN so that you can hand it out to folks who want to PIN-message you.)

The cautious side of you may wonder why on earth you'd give your PIN to someone. Here's the difference: Unlike a PIN for an ATM account, this PIN isn't your password. In fact, this PIN doesn't give anyone access to your BlackBerry or do anything to compromise security. It's simply an ID; think of it like a phone number.

Here are three quick paths to PIN enlightenment:

- **From the Help screen:** You can find the PIN for any device right there on its Help screen. Open the Help screen by pressing Alt+Num+H.

- **From the Message screen:** Send your PIN from the Message screen with the help of a keyword. When you type a preset word, your BlackBerry replaces what you type with a bit of information specific to your device.

  Sound wacky? It's easier than it sounds:

  a. **Compose a new message.**

     If you need a refresher on the whole e-mail message and messaging thing, visit Chapter 8.

  b. **In the subject or body of your message, type** mypin **and add a space.**

     See the left side of Figure 9-1. As soon as you type the space, `mypin` is miraculously transformed into your PIN in the format `pin:`*your-pin-number*, as shown on the right side of Figure 9-1. Isn't that neat? ***Note:*** Case doesn't matter here.

mypin isn't the only keyword that RIM predefines for you. mynumber and myver give you the phone number and OS version, respectively, of your BlackBerry Curve.

✔ **From the Status screen:** You can also find your PIN on the Status screen. Display the Status screen by choosing the following links in succession, starting from the Home screen: Settings, Options, and Status. Use the trackball or trackpad to highlight and click each link. Figure 9-2 shows a typical Status screen.

Figure 9-1: Type a keyword (left) and add a space, and the keyword gets translated (right).

```
To:
Cc:
Subject:
Mypin|
```

```
To:
Cc:
Subject:
pin:2100000a |
```

Figure 9-2: Find your PIN on the Status screen.

```
Status
Signal:                    -40 dBm
Battery:                     100 %
File Free:          69373017 Bytes
PIN:                      2100000A
IMEI:          123456.78.364813.8
WLAN MAC:       30:74:7C:CB:B8:AB
IP Address:                0.0.0.0
```

Assigning PINs to names

So you convince your BlackBerry-wielding buddies to go to the trouble of finding out their PINs and passing said PINs to you. Now the trick is finding a convenient place to store your PINs so that you can use them. Luckily for you, you have an obvious choice: BlackBerry Contacts. And RIM, in its infinite wisdom, makes storing such info a snap. To add a PIN to someone's contact info in Contacts, do the following:

1. **From the BlackBerry Home screen, select Contacts.**

   Contacts opens.

2. **Highlight a contact name, press the menu key, and then select Edit.**

   The Edit Contact screen for the contact name you selected makes an appearance.

3. **On the Edit Contact screen, scroll down to the PIN field (as shown in Figure 9-3).**

4. **Type the PIN.**

5. **Press the menu key and then select Save.**

   The edit you made for this contact is saved.

Edit Contact	123

Fax:
Other:
PIN: A111111**1**

Work Address
Address 1:
Address 2:
City:
State/Prov:
Zip/Postal Code:
Country:

Figure 9-3:
Add a contact's PIN info here.

It's that simple. Of course, it's even easier if you think ahead and enter the PIN information you have when you set up your initial contact info (by using the New Contact screen), but we understand that a PIN isn't the kind of information people carry around.

If all this talk about New Contact screens and Edit Contact screens doesn't sound familiar, check out Chapter 4, which covers the Contacts application in more detail.

Sending a PIN-to-PIN message

PIN-to-PIN just means *from one BlackBerry to another.*

Sending a PIN-to-PIN message is no different from sending an e-mail. Here's how:

1. **From the BlackBerry Home screen, select Contacts.**

2. **In Contacts, highlight a contact name and then press the menu key.**

   If a contact has a PIN, you see a menu item titled PIN *<contact name>*. Say, for example, you have a contact named Dante Sarigumba. When you highlight Dante Sarigumba in the list and then press the menu key, the menu item PIN Dante Sarigumba appears as an option, as shown in Figure 9-4.

3. **Select PIN *<contact name>* from the menu.**

   You see the ever-familiar New Message screen, with the PIN of your buddy already entered as an address.

4. **Enter the rest of the text fields — subject, message, and signature text — just as you would with an e-mail.**

Figure 9-4:
Send a PIN
message
via your
Contacts.

Alternatively, if you know the PIN, you can type it directly. Here's how:

1. **From the BlackBerry Home screen, select Messages.**

   The Messages application opens.

2. **Press the menu key and then select Compose PIN.**

   The New Message screen makes an appearance.

3. **In the To field, enter the PIN and then press the trackball or trackpad.**

   You just added a recipient in the To field.

4. **Add a subject line, the message, and then the signature text, just like you would in an e-mail.**

Unlike e-mails, when you send a PIN-to-PIN message, you can tell almost instantly whether the recipient got your message. Viewing the Message list, you see the letter *D* — which means *delivered* — on top of the check mark next to the PIN-to-PIN message you sent.

Because of the nature of PIN-to-PIN messaging (the conspicuous lack of a paper trail, as it were), companies can disable PIN-to-PIN messaging on your BlackBerry device. (No paper trail can mean legal problems down the road — can you say *Sarbanes-Oxley?*)

Receiving a PIN-to-PIN message

Receiving a PIN-to-PIN message is no different from receiving a standard e-mail. You get the same entry in your Messages list for the PIN-to-PIN message, and the same screen appears when you open the message.

By default, your BlackBerry vibrates to alert you, but you can change this in Profiles. (Check out Chapter 3 for more details on changing your profile.) When you reply to the message, the reply is a PIN-to-PIN message as well.

Keeping in Touch, the SMS/MMS Way

Short Messaging Service (also known as *SMS,* or *text messaging*) is so popular that you've probably seen TV shows asking for your feedback via SMS. Multimedia Messaging Service (MMS) is a much later evolution of SMS. Rather than sending a simple text message, you can also send someone an audio or a video clip.

How short is *short?* The maximum size per message is about 160 characters. If you send more than that, it gets broken down into multiple messages.

SMS is an established technology (not a new and unproven thing, in other words) that's been popular for years in Europe and Asia.

Text messaging does pose a challenge for beginners. It isn't tough; it's just cumbersome to type the letters on a small keyboard and keep up with the conversation. Also, you need to know the trends and options for text messaging. In-the-know folks use abbreviations that may be difficult for you to understand in the beginning, so don't dive in without your oxygen tank.

A quick preparation goes a long way toward avoiding being labeled uncool when it comes to your SMS syntax. The upcoming sections help smooth your path a bit by filling you in on the basics of SMS-speak.

Using shorthand for speedy replies

On a regular cellphone, three letters share a single key. Typing even a single paragraph can be a real pain.

Human ingenuity prevails. Abbreviations cut down on the amount of text you need to enter. *Texting* (short for *text messaging*) language is quite fashionable, especially among the 14–18-year-old set. Veteran text messagers (the hip ones, at least) can easily spot someone who's new to SMS technology by how that person doesn't use the right lingo — or uses such lingo incorrectly.

AWHFY?

In text messaging, the challenge lies in using abbreviations to craft a sentence with as few letters as possible. Because text messaging has been around for a number of years, plenty of folks have risen to this challenge by coming up with a considerable pool of useful abbreviations. Don't feel that you have to rush out and memorize the whole shorthand dictionary at once, though.

As with mastering a new language, start with the most commonly used words or sentences. When you become familiar with those, slowly gather in more and more terms. In time, the language will be second nature.

Table 9-1 gives you our take on the most common abbreviations, which are enough to get you started. With these under your belt, you can at least follow the most important parts of an SMS conversation. Feel free to check out the Web site associated with this book (www.blackberryfordummies.com) for a more comprehensive list of shorthand abbreviations.

Table 9-1	SMS Shorthand and Its Meanings		
Shorthand	*Meaning*	*Shorthand*	*Meaning*
2D4	To die for	CUL8R	See you later
2G4U	Too good for you	CUS	See you soon
2L8	Too late	F2F	Face to face
4E	Forever	FC	Fingers crossed
4YEO	For your eyes only	FCFS	First come, first served
A3	Anytime, anywhere, anyplace	FOAF	Friend of a friend

Shorthand	Meaning	Shorthand	Meaning
AFAIK	As far as I know	FWIW	For what it's worth
ASAP	As soon as possible	GAL	Get a life
ASL	Age, sex, location	GG	Good game
ATM	At the moment	GR8	Great
ATW	At the weekend	GSOH	Good sense of humor
AWHFY	Are we having fun yet?	H2CUS	Hope to see you soon
B4	Before	IC	I see
BBFN	Bye-bye for now	IDK	I don't know
BBL	Be back later	IMHO	In my honest opinion
BBS	Be back soon	IMO	In my opinion
BCNU	Be seeing you	IOU	I owe you
BG	Big grin	IOW	In other words
BION	Believe it or not	KISS	Keep it simple, stupid
BOL	Best of luck	LOL	Laughing out loud
BOT	Back on topic	OIC	Oh, I see
BRB	Be right back	RUOK	Are you okay?
BRT	Be right there	W4U	Waiting for you
BTW	By the way	W8	Wait
CMON	Come on	WTG	Way to go
CU	See you	TOM	Tomorrow

Showing some emotion

Written words can get folks into trouble every now and then; the very same words can mean different things to different people. A simple example is the phrase "You're clueless." When you speak such a phrase (with the appropriate facial and hand gestures), your friend knows (you hope) that you're teasing and that it's all a bit of fun. Write that same phrase in a text message, and, well, you may get a nasty reply in return — which you then have to respond to, which prompts another response, and soon enough, you've just ended a seven-year friendship.

SMS is akin to chatting, so *emoticons* show what you mean when you write "You're clueless." (I'm joking! I'm happy! I'm mad!) These cutesy codes help you telegraph your meaning in sledgehammer-to-the-forehead fashion.

We're talking smileys here — those combinations of keyboard characters that, when artfully combined, resemble a human face. The most popular example — one that you've probably encountered in e-mails from especially chirpy individuals — is the happy face, which (usually at the end of a statement) conveys good intentions or happy context, like this :). (Tilt your head to the left to see the face.)

Table 9-2 shows you the range of smiley choices. Just remember that smileys are supposed to be fun. They could be the one thing you need to make sure that your "gently teasing remark" isn't seen as a hateful comment. Smileys help, but if you aren't sure if what you're about to send can be misconstrued even with the help of the smileys, just don't send it.

Table 9-2		Smileys and Their Meanings	
Smiley	*Meaning*	*Smiley*	*Meaning*
:)	Happy, smiling	:(	Sad, frown
:-)	Happy, smiling, with nose	:-(	Sad, frown, with nose
:D	Laughing	:-<	Super sad
:-D	Laughing, with nose	:'-(	Crying
:'-)	Tears due to laughter	:-0	Yell, gasped
:-)8	Smiling with bow tie	:-@	Scream, what?
;)	Winking	:-(o)	Shouting
;-)	Winking, with nose	|-0	Yawn
0:-)	I'm an angel (male)	:----(	Liar, long nose
0*-)	I'm an angel (female)	%-(	Confused
8-)	Cool, with sunglasses	:-|	Determined
:-!	Foot in mouth	:-()	Talking
>-)	Evil grin	:-ozz	Bored
:-x	Kiss on the lips	@@	Eyes
(((H)))	Hugs	%-)	Cross-eyed
@>--;--	Rose	|@@|	Face

Smiley	Meaning	Smiley	Meaning
:b	Tongue out	#:-)	Hair is a mess
;b	Tongue out with a wink	&:-)	Hair is curly
:-&	Tongue tied	$-)	Yuppie
-!-	Sleepy	:-($)	Put your money where your mouth is
<3	Heart, or love	<(^(oo)^)>	Pig

Shorthand and smileys may not be appreciated in business. Use them appropriately.

Messaging etiquette and a few words of caution

Here are some commonsense messaging rules as well as a few words of caution. Even if you're new to messaging, being a neophyte doesn't give you license to act like a jerk. Play nice and take the following pointers to heart:

- **Use smileys to avoid misunderstandings.** Read more about emoticons and smileys earlier in this chapter.

- **Don't ever forward chain letters.** We mean it. Never.

- **If you need to forward a message, check the entire message content first.** Make sure nothing offends the recipient.

- **Some things in this world need to be said face to face, so don't even think of using messaging for it.** Ever try dumping your girlfriend or boyfriend over the phone? Guess what? Using messaging is far worse.

- **Keep your tone gender neutral.** Some messages that are forwarded through e-mails are inappropriate to the opposite sex.

- **Capital letters are as rude as shouting, so *DON'T USE THEM.***

- **Know your recipient.** A newbie might not easily grasp smileys and shorthand at first, so act accordingly. (Read more about shorthand earlier in this chapter.)

- **Don't reply to any message when you're angry.** You can't unsend a sent message. It's better to be prudent than sorry.

- **Don't gossip or be rude.** Beware! Your messages can end up in the wrong hands and haunt you in the future.

- **Easy does it.** No documented evidence reveals the deleterious effects (physical or psychological) of too much texting. However, don't text as if you want to enter the books as the first recorded case of Instantmessagingitis. As your great-grandma would tell you, too much of anything is bad for you. It's easy to lose track of time when IMing.

- **Drive safely.** Tuck away your BlackBerry whenever you're in the driver's seat.

Sending a text message

After you have the shorthand stuff and smileys under control, get your fingers pumped up and ready for action: It's message-sending time! Whether it's SMS or MMS, here's how to do it:

1. **From the BlackBerry Home screen, select Contacts.**

2. **In Contacts, highlight a contact who has a cellphone number, press the menu key, and select SMS (or MMS) <contact name> from the menu that appears.**

   SMS works only on mobile phones.

   The menu item for SMS or MMS is intelligent enough to display the name of the contact. For example, if you choose John Doe, the menu item reads SMS John Doe or MMS John Doe, as shown in Figure 9-5.

```
New Group           ▲
View
Edit
Delete
Activity Log
Email John Doe
Call John Doe
SMS John Doe
SIM Phone Book
Send As Attachment  ▼
```

Figure 9-5:
Start your
text mes-
sage here.

3. **If you choose MMS, browse your multimedia folders, and select the audio or video file you want to send.**

   When choosing MMS, this extra step allows you to choose the multimedia file, which is the only difference from composing an SMS message.

4. **Type your message.**

   Remember that shorthand business? You should start taking advantage of it the first chance you get. (Practice makes perfect.)

5. **Press the trackball or trackpad and then select Send from the menu that appears.**

   Your message is sent on its merry way.

Viewing a message you receive

If you have an incoming SMS or MMS message, you get a notification just like you do when you receive an e-mail. Also, as with e-mail, the e-mail icon at the top of the Home screen indicates a new message. Viewing an SMS or MMS message is the same as reading an e-mail. The basic run-through is as follows:

1. **Open Messages.**
2. **Scroll and highlight the unread message.**
3. **Press the trackball or trackpad.**

   Bob's your uncle: The message appears onscreen.

Customize how your BlackBerry notifies you when you receive an SMS message. Look for the "Using factory settings" and "Creating your own profile" sections in Chapter 3 for more details.

Always Online Using Instant Messaging

Real-time (as they happen) conversations with your friends over the Internet are easier with IM (instant messaging). IM enables two or more people to send and receive messages over the Internet. It all started with pure text messages and evolved into a rich medium involving voice and even video conversation in real time.

IM may not be available on your BlackBerry Curve. Service providers choose whether to include it. (Most providers, however, do support it for the BlackBerry Curve.) You can add IM to your BlackBerry even if it didn't come with it.

1. **Open your browser.**
2. **Go to** `http://mobile.blackberry.com`.
3. **Navigate to IM and Social Networking.**

   Here, you'll find download links for all the free applications for the popular IM networks and also a download link for BlackBerry Messenger. (Chapter 10 covers BlackBerry Messenger.)

Chatting using IM rules

When you're IMing — that's right; it's a verb — you can tell lots of things:

- ✔ When someone's typing a message to you
- ✔ Whether your buddies are online
- ✔ When your buddies are away from their computers
- ✔ When your buddies are simply too busy to be interrupted at the moment

IM adds a totally different slant on long-distance communication, opening a wide array of possibilities — possibilities that can be used for good (team collaboration) or ill (mindless gossip), depending on the situation.

As you may expect, IM is great for both personal and business applications. Whether you're maintaining friendships or working to create new ones, IM is definitely one powerful tool to consider adding to your social-skills toolbox.

Instant messaging on your BlackBerry

Most network providers dish out the three most popular IM services to their BlackBerry customers:

- ✔ Google Talk
- ✔ Yahoo! (Y!) Messenger
- ✔ Windows Live Messenger

Those three IM programs aren't the only popular ones. Here are a few more:

- ✔ AOL Instant Messenger (AIM)
- ✔ ICQ Instant Messenger
- ✔ iChat AV (on the Macintosh)
- ✔ Jabber (open source)

If you're using an IM network that isn't preloaded, you can always check the RIM Web site to download the applications: mobile.blackberry.com. On this page, go to IM and Social Networking. The list of IM applications should be listed on the next page with a link for download.

IM basics: What you need

Assuming that you have the IM application available on your BlackBerry, you need just two things to start using the standard five IM programs:

- ✔ User ID
- ✔ Password

Getting a user ID/password combo is a breeze. Just go to the appropriate registration Web page (from the following list) for the IM application(s) you want to use. Note that it's easier and faster to use your desktop or laptop to sign up.

- ✔ **Google Talk**
  www.google.com/accounts/NewAccount?service=talk
- ✔ **AOL Instant Messenger (AIM)**
  https://reg.my.screenname.aol.com/_cqr/registration/initRegistration.psp
- ✔ **ICQ Instant Messenger**
  www.icq.com/register
- ✔ **Windows Live Messenger**
  http://messenger.msn.com/download/getstarted.aspx
- ✔ **Yahoo! Messenger**
  http://edit.yahoo.com/config/eval_register?.src=pg&.done=http:// messenger.yahoo.com

Given the many IM network choices available, your friends are probably signed up on a bunch of different networks. You might end up having to sign up for multiple networks if you want to reach them all via IM.

Going online with IM

After you obtain the user ID/password combo for one (or more) of the IM services, you can use your BlackBerry to start chatting with your buddies by following these steps:

1. **From the BlackBerry Home screen, select the IM application of your choice.**

   To illustrate how to do this, we use Google Talk. An application-specific logon screen shows up for you to sign on, similar to the one shown in Figure 9-6. It's straightforward, with the standard screen name (also called a username or ID) line and password line.

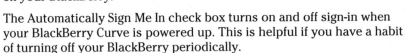

Figure 9-6:
Logon
screen for
Google Talk.

2. **Enter your screen name/ID and password.**

3. **(Optional) If you want, select the Remember Password check box.
   Also if you want, select the Automatically Sign Me In check box.**

   When the Remember Password check box is enabled, the ID/password
   information is pre-entered the next time you come back to this screen.
   (Um, that is, you don't have to type this stuff every time you want to IM.)

   We recommend that you select this check box to save time but also set
   your handheld password to Enabled so that security isn't compromised.
   Refer to Chapter 3 if you need a refresher on how to enable passwords
   on your BlackBerry.

   The Automatically Sign Me In check box turns on and off sign-in when
   your BlackBerry Curve is powered up. This is helpful if you have a habit
   of turning off your BlackBerry periodically.

4. **Press the trackball or trackpad and then select Sign In.**

   At this point, IM tries to log you on. This can take a few seconds, during
   which time the screen reads `Sending request to AOL` or something
   similar while it's in this phase. After you're logged on, a simple listing of
   your contacts, or buddies, appears onscreen.

5. **Select the person you'd like to chat with.**

   A menu appears, listing various things you can do. Features could differ
   a little bit for each IM application, but for Google Talk, here's a sample of
   what you can do: Start Chat, Send File, Add a Friend, Rename, Remove,
   and Block.

6. **Select the action you'd like.**

Adding a contact/buddy

Before you can start chatting with your buddies, you need to know their user IDs (see Table 9-3).

Table 9-3	How to Obtain Your Friend's Credentials
Provider	*Where You Get Someone's User ID*
AOL Instant Messenger	Your friend or by searching AOL's directory
Google Talk	The text before the @ sign in his or her Google e-mail address
ICQ Instant Messenger	Your friend's e-mail or the ICQ Global Directory
MSN Live Messenger	MSN passport ID or Hotmail ID
Yahoo! Messenger	The text before the @ sign in his or her Yahoo! e-mail address

Luckily for you, you don't need to search around for IDs every time you want to IM someone. You can store IDs as part of a contacts list. Follow these steps:

1. **Starting within the IM service of your choice, press the menu key.**

2. **Select Add a Friend, as shown in Figure 9-7.**

   The Add a Friend screen appears.

Help
Collapse All
Add a Friend
My Status (Available)
My Details
Settings
Sign Out
Switch Application
Close

Figure 9-7: Adding a friend.

3. **Enter the user ID of your contact on the Add a Friend screen.**

4. **Press the trackball or trackpad.**

   IM is smart enough to figure out whether this contact has a valid user ID. If the ID is valid, the application adds the ID to your list of contacts. The buddy goes either to the Online or Offline section of your list, depending on whether he or she is logged on. You'll be warned if the ID you entered isn't valid.

Doing the chat thing

Suppose you want to start a conversation with one of your contacts (a safe assumption, we think). When you send a message within the IM application, you're initiating a conversation. Here's how:

1. **Log on to the IM application of your choice.**

2. **Select the person you want to contact.**

   A typical online chat screen shows up. The top portion lists old messages sent to and received from this contact. You type your message in the bottom part of the screen.

3. **Type your message.**

4. **Press the enter key.**

   Your user ID and the message you just sent show up in the topmost (history) section of the chat screen. When you get a message, it's added to the history section so that both sides of your conversation stay in view.

Sending your smile

You can quickly add emoticons to your message (without having to remember all the character equivalents in Table 9-1). Follow these steps:

1. **While you're typing your message, press the menu key.**

2. **From the menu that appears, select Show Symbols.**

   All the icons appear, as shown in Figure 9-8.

3. **Select the emoticon you want.**

   The emoticon is added to your message.

Taking control of your IM app

If you use IM frequently — and you tend to chat with many contacts at the same time — your BlackBerry's physical limitations may cramp your IM style. No matter whether you use AIM, Y! Messenger, ICQ Instant Messenger, MSN

Live Messenger, or BlackBerry Messenger (see Chapter 10), it's still slower to type words on the tiny keypad than it is to type on your PC.

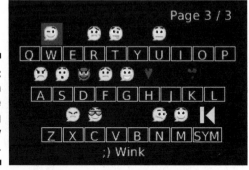

Figure 9-8: You can choose among many smileys.

Do you just give up on the dream of IMing on the go? Not necessarily. The following sections show how you can power up your BlackBerry IM technique.

Less is more

If you can't keep up with all your buddies, your best bet is to limit your exposure. Take a whack at your contacts list so that only your true buddies remain as contacts whom you want to IM from your BlackBerry. Trimming your list is easy. To delete a contact from your IM application, highlight the contact from the main screen of the IM application, press the menu key, and select Delete.

Deleting a contact or buddy from an IM application on your BlackBerry also deletes it from the desktop or laptop computer version of the app. That's because the list of contacts is maintained at a central location — an IM server, to be precise — and not on your BlackBerry.

Set up two accounts of your favorite IM application: one for your BlackBerry and one for your desktop PC. By using these accounts separately, you can limit the number of contacts you have on your BlackBerry and still maintain a full-blown list of contacts on your desktop.

Less typing — use shorthand

Cut down your typing time. Don't forget the shorthand described earlier in this chapter. It's widely used in IM as well as texting, so refer to Table 9-1 whenever you can so that you can respond quickly. Before you know it, you will have the abbreviations memorized and will be using them with ease. Emoticons also make your conversation interesting, so make sure you take them out of your toolbox. Refer to Table 9-2 earlier in this chapter for a list of the most common ones.

SMS versus connecting via the Web

SMS messages are short messages designed for cellphones. IM is a step up, evolving from the Internet, where bandwidth is no longer a concern. It provides a better real-time conversation experience across distances. These two technologies evolved in parallel. As more people use IM, it becomes apparent that this technology has a place in handheld devices, where mobility is an advantage. Some of the IM programs developed and used in the BlackBerry in the past use SMS behind the scenes. And because your BlackBerry can connect to the Internet, other programs use the Internet directly. These differences can affect your monthly bill as well as your messaging experience. Read on.

If you don't have unlimited SMS but have an unlimited data plan, be careful with any third-party IM software. Make sure that it uses the Internet instead of SMS. If it uses SMS, you'll incur charges for every message sent and received, and most network providers charge 20 cents for every SMS message, which can add up quickly and lead to a nasty surprise on your monthly bill.

Jive on

If you want to make sure that you won't have text-messaging fees for using an IM client, check out these IM programs:

✔ **BeejiveIM (`www.beejive.com/download/blackberry.htm`):** This one-time-fee program connects directly to the Web instead of using SMS. It works with multiple IM networks and multiple accounts per network: AIM, Windows Live Messenger, Yahoo! Messenger, Google Talk, ICQ Instant Messenger, Jabber, and MySpace IM. This is one of the best options. On their Web site, they have versions to support old BlackBerry devices, BlackBerry Storm, and high-resolution screens. Download the version for high-resolution screens.

✔ **Nimbuzz (`www.nimbuzz.com`):** Nimbuzz supports many of the popular IM networks. It even supports calls using the Skype network. And the best thing is that it's free and doesn't use SMS.

✔ **IM+ (`www.shapeservices.com/eng/im/blackberry`):** If you don't want to pay annually, consider this service. IM+ asks for a one-time fee and also supports Yahoo!, MSN, AOL, ICQ, Google Talk, and Jabber networks. The best thing about IM+ is that it sends messages by using the Internet rather than SMS, so it's best suited for people who have the unlimited data plan. You have to choose a version: The Regular version connects to BlackBerry Enterprise Server, which is used by companies as a way of connecting the BlackBerry platform to a corporate network and e-mail server. The WAP version allows a personal BlackBerry to use the network provider's WAP gateway to connect to the Internet. The Shape Services Web site has a comprehensive FAQ list for details about the software.

Check out the Web site associated with this book (`www.blackberryfordummies.com`) for updates regarding these (and other) recommendations.

Chapter 10

Instant Messaging on BlackBerry Messenger

*I*n Chapter 9, you find a slew of ways to send messages on your BlackBerry Curve. In this chapter, you get the scoop on another way to send messages, using a special application known and loved by BlackBerry.

RIM has entered the IM (instant messaging) horse race in the form of a spirited filly named (you guessed it) BlackBerry Messenger. This application is based on the PIN-to-PIN messaging technology (refer to Chapter 9), which means that it is mucho fast and quite reliable.

However, with BlackBerry Messenger, you can chat with only those buddies who have a BlackBerry and also have PIN-to-PIN messaging enabled. The application supports IM features common to many other applications, such as group chatting and the capability to monitor the availability of other IM buddies.

Using BlackBerry Messenger

You can access BlackBerry Messenger in the Applications folder from the Home screen, as shown in Figure 10-1. The first time you run BlackBerry Messenger, a welcome screen asks you to enter your display name. This display name is the one you want other people to see on their BlackBerry Messenger when you send them a message.

Figure 10-1:
Launch
BlackBerry
Messenger
here.

You see a contacts list the next time you open the application, as shown on the left in Figure 10-2. (Okay, the picture here displays some contacts, but your list should be empty; we'll show you how to populate the list in a minute.)

Figure 10-2:
The
contacts list
(left) and
menu (right).

Pressing the menu key lets you do the following, as shown on the right side of Figure 10-2:

- ✔ **Broadcast Message:** Send a message to multiple contacts in your BlackBerry Messenger. The messages appear as conversations in the recipients' BlackBerry Messenger.

- ✔ **Open Chat:** Initiate a conversation with the currently highlighted contact.

- ✔ **Start Group Chat:** Initiate a group conversation. See the later section "Starting a group conversation" for details.

- ✔ **Add Contact:** Add a new contact to BlackBerry Messenger (see the next section).

- ✔ **Add Group:** Create custom groupings for your contacts.

This option is helpful if you have a lot of contacts in BlackBerry Messenger. Simply select this menu item, and an Add Group screen appears so you can enter a group name.

✔ **Contact Info:** When selected, display a screen showing the information of the currently highlighted contact.

✔ **Delete Contact:** Allows you to delete the currently highlighted contact.

The menu has more items. Although these items are not shown on the right side of Figure 10-2, scroll down the menu screen to see the following:

✔ **Edit My Info:** Customize your personal information and control how you want others to see you from their BlackBerry Messenger Contacts list. You can do the following (see Figure 10-3):

• Change your picture

• Change your display name

• Allow others to see the title of the song you're currently listening to

• Allow others to see that you're currently using the phone

• Enter a personal message that others could see

• Set your time zone

• Allow others to see your country and time zone information

✔ **Back Up Contacts List:** Save your list of BlackBerry Messenger contacts to the file system. The location defaults to the media card, but the screen that follows after you select this option allows you to select a different folder and enter a different name for the backup file.

✔ **Restore Contacts List:** Restore your list of BlackBerry Messenger contacts from the file you created from the Back Up Contacts List option.

✔ **Delete Backup Files:** Delete a backup file. If you have multiple backups, this option allows you to choose which file to delete.

✔ **Options:** Customize the behavior of your BlackBerry Messenger.

Figure 10-3:
Set your personal information (left) and the rest of the Edit My Info screen (right) .

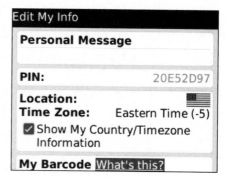

Adding a contact

With no one in your contacts list, BlackBerry Messenger is a pretty useless item. Your first order of business is to add a contact to your list — someone you know who

- ✔ Has a BlackBerry
- ✔ Is entered in your Contacts
- ✔ Has PIN-to-PIN messaging enabled
- ✔ Has a copy of BlackBerry Messenger installed on his or her device

If you know someone who fits these criteria, you can add that person to your list by doing the following:

1. **In BlackBerry Messenger, press the menu key.**

2. **Select Add a Contact.**

   The Add Contact screen appears, listing actions related to adding a contact, as shown on the left side of Figure 10-4. The top two options in the list are ways to add a contact in BlackBerry Messenger.

Figure 10-4: Add a contact (left) and an invitation barcode (right).

3. **If you want to *scan* your friend's BlackBerry barcode:**

   a. **On the same screen (Figure 10-4, left), but using your friend's BlackBerry, select the third option, which says Show Your Invitation Barcode to Another BlackBerry.**

      A barcode image similar to Figure 10-4, right, appears on your friend's BlackBerry.

b. **On your BlackBerry Curve, select the second option, Scan Invitation Barcode from Another BlackBerry.**

A Camera application appears to allow you to capture the barcode. Once captured, the contact information is immediately added to your BlackBerry Messenger contacts list.

That's it. You're finished. The following steps show how to enter your contact directly from the Add Contact screen.

4. **If instead you want to enter your contact directly:**

a. **On the Add Contact screen, select the first option, Add a Contact by Entering Their Email Address or PIN.**

b. **Start typing the name of the contact, and when a list of possible contacts appears, select the name you want to add.**

c. **Type your message.**

A default message is provided, as you can see in Figure 10-5, but you can edit this message. This is the message that the contact will receive after you're finished with Step d.

d. **Select OK and then select OK again in the screen that follows.**

The application sends your request. As long as the person hasn't responded to your request, his or her name appears as part of the Pending group, as shown in Figure 10-6. When your contact responds positively to your request, that name goes to the official contacts list.

Figure 10-5:
Potential
contacts
are asked
before being
added.

Add Contact

To: testing@test.us

Dante ▒ would like to add you to his or her BlackBerry Messenger Contact List.

Email:
                    @tmo.blackberry.net

Security Question: None

Privacy Setting for Contact

Figure 10-6:
To-be-
approved
contacts
are in the
Pending
Contacts
group.

Starting a conversation

You can easily start a conversation with any of your contacts. Follow these steps:

1. **On the BlackBerry Messenger main menu, select the name in your contacts list.**

   A traditional chat interface opens, with a list of old messages at the top and a text box for typing messages at the bottom.

2. **Type your message.**

3. **Press the enter key.**

   Any messages you send (as well as any responses you get) are appended to the history list at the top.

Starting a group conversation

You can easily invite others to your BlackBerry Messenger conversation. Follow these steps:

1. **During a conversation, press the menu key.**

   The BlackBerry Messenger main menu appears. This time, an Invite option has been added.

2. **Select Invite to Group Chat.**

   The Select Contacts screen opens, listing your BlackBerry Messenger contacts who are currently available (see Figure 10-7). For each contact, you can select the check box to indicate that you want to invite that person to the chat.

3. **Select people by selecting the corresponding check boxes.**

   You can choose any number of people.

4. **Select OK.**

   You're back to the preceding conversation screen, but this time, the history list shows the contacts you added to the conversation. The newly selected contact(s) can now join the conversation.

Figure 10-7:
See your available contacts here.

You can set a subject for your message. This is especially useful for group conversations. To add a subject to a conversation, follow these simple steps:

1. **Press the menu key while you're on the conversation screen and then select Set Subject.**

   On the screen that follows, the cursor is in the subject line, waiting for you to enter a subject (see Figure 10-8).

2. **On the screen that follows, enter the subject and then select OK.**

   The conversation screen is updated with the subject.

You can make your name appear snazzy by adding symbols, such as Dante☺ and Yosma☞ (see Figure 10-9):

1. **On the BlackBerry Messenger screen, press the menu key.**

2. **Select Edit My Info.**

3. **Press the menu key, and select Add Smiley to choose the symbol you want.**

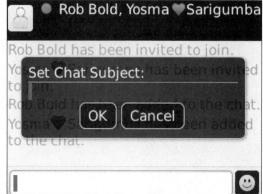

Figure 10-8:
Add a subject to your conversation here.

Figure 10-9:
Add symbols to your name here.

Sending a file

BlackBerry Messenger, like any other IM application, can send files. While on a conversation, just press the menu key, and you'll see several menu items allowing you to share a file:

- ✓ **Send Picture:** Selecting this option shows a screen similar to the left side of Figure 10-10, where you can either launch the Camera application to take a picture to send or select the picture file you want to send (you can navigate to a specific folder if necessary). The default location for picture files is the Media Card pictures folder. Just select Camera to launch the Camera application.

- ✓ **Send Voice Note:** Selecting this option gives you the Voice Note screen (refer to Figure 10-10, right), where you can record the voice message you want to send. When you're ready to record, follow these steps:

a. **Select Start.**

Curve is ready to record your voice message. A screen indicating recording appears with a Stop button, as shown on the left side of Figure 10-11.

b. **When you have finished speaking your message, select Stop.**

A screen similar to the right side of Figure 10-11 appears. You can play the message to review what you said, send the message if you're satisfied, or cancel sending a voice note.

c. **Select Send.**

A prompt asks you to add a description of your voice message. Selecting No sends the message right away.

d. **Select Yes.**

e. **Enter a description and then select OK.**

A request to transfer the file is sent, and your friend needs to accept it in his or her BlackBerry Messenger for the transmission to begin.

✔ **Send File:** Displays a screen that lists which file types you can send. Aside from giving you a different way of sending picture and voice message, the screen lists the following options:

- **File:** Sends any type of file. When selected, it shows an Explorer-type screen so you can navigate to the file you want to send. The default folders shown are Media Card and Device Memory.

- **BlackBerry Contact:** Sends a vCard (see Chapter 4 for details on the vCard). When selected, it displays Contacts, allowing you to select the contact you want to send.

- **Messenger Contact:** Lets you choose a contact from your list of BlackBerry Messenger contacts and send the info as a file.

Figure 10-10:
Send a picture (left) or start recording a voice message (right).

Saving the conversation history

While you are on the conversation screen, you can save your chat history in two ways. Both methods are accessible by a simple press of the menu key:

- **Copy History:** Copies the existing chat history to the Clipboard. Then you paste it into the application where you want it saved, such as Calendar or MemoPad.
- **Email History:** Displays the Compose Message dialog screen, shown in Figure 10-12, with the Subject field prepopulated with `Chat with <Contact> on <Date>` and the body of the message prepopulated with the chat history.

Send Using: [Default]

To:

Cc:

Subject: Chat with Rob Bold on 8/16/2009

Participants:

Dante *US* , Rob Bold

Messages:

Broadcasting a Message

Do you feel the need to start a conversation on the same subject with several people? You can start with a group chat, but what if you want to get a personal opinion from each individual, something that each person isn't comfortable saying in front of the crowd? The best way to do this is to broadcast a message to multiple recipients:

1. **On the BlackBerry Messenger screen, press the menu key.**

2. **Select Broadcast Message.**

   The Broadcast Message screen appears, as shown in Figure 10-13, allowing you to enter your message and select the recipients.

3. **Enter your message.**

4. **Select the recipients.**

5. **Select Send.**

Figure 10-13:
Broadcast a message here.

Chapter 11

Surfing the Internet Wave

. . . .

In This Chapter

▶ Using BlackBerry's Browser to surf the Web

▶ Creating and organizing bookmarks

▶ Customizing and optimizing Browser

▶ Downloading and installing applications from the Web

▶ Using browsers in business

. . . .

*I*t's hard to believe that about 15 years ago, more folks didn't have access to the Internet than did. Today, you can surf the Web anytime and any-where from a desktop computer, a netbook, or even a tiny mobile device such as a PDA or a smartphone. Having said that, it should be no surprise that your BlackBerry Curve has a Web browser of its own.

In this chapter, we show you how to use BlackBerry Browser. We give you shortcuts and timesaving tips, including the coolest ways to make pages load faster, as well as a complete neat-freak's guide to managing your bookmarks.

And because your network service provider may also have its own custom browser for you to use, we compare these proprietary browsers with the default BlackBerry Browser so you can decide which best suits your needs.

Kicking Up Browser

BlackBerry Browser comes loaded on your smartphone and accesses the Web with a cellphone connection. Browser can be named differently, depending on how the service provider customizes it. Sometimes it's named *BlackBerry Browser; Internet Browser; Hotspot Browser;* or, most likely, just *Browser.* We just use *Browser* to make things easier.

Browser has multiple personalities:

- **One that's connected to your company's BlackBerry Enterprise Server**

  BlackBerry Enterprise Server is a software application from RIM (Research In Motion) that companies can use to control and manage BlackBerry devices. The software also allows your device to see your company's network and connect to your company's databases.

  If you're a corporate BlackBerry user, your company administrator may turn off or not install all browsers except for the one that connects through the company's BlackBerry Enterprise Server.

- **One that goes directly to your service provider's network**

  This might be called by the network service provider's brand name.

- **A browser that uses a Wi-Fi connection**

- **A WAP browser**

  Wireless application protocol, or WAP, was popular in the 1990s, when mobile device displays were limited and could display only five or six rows of text. WAP lost its appeal with the advent of high-resolution screens.

The following sections get you started using Browser. After you get your feet wet, we promise that you'll be champing at the bit to find out more!

Getting to Browser

Browser is one of the main applications of your device, with its Globe icon visible right on the Home screen, as shown in Figure 11-1. In most cases, you open Browser by scrolling to this icon and then pressing the trackball or trackpad.

Figure 11-1: You can open Browser from the Home screen.

Opening Browser by clicking its icon on the Home screen gives you a list of bookmarks.

If you haven't yet added bookmarks, the opening Browser screen looks like Figure 11-2. You find out more about adding bookmarks later in this chapter.

Figure 11-2: Browser with the default empty Bookmarks screen.

 If Browser is your default browser, you can access it from any application that distinguishes a Web address. For example, from Contacts, you can open Browser by opening the link on the Web Page field. If you get an e-mail that contains a Web address, just scroll to that link. The link is highlighted, and you can open the page by pressing the trackball or trackpad.

 When you access Browser from another application, you don't have to close that application to jump to Browser. Just press the Alt key (to the left of the Z key) and the escape key at the same time to open a pop-up screen with application icons. Use your trackball or trackpad to highlight the Browser icon; then press the trackball or trackpad to launch Browser.

By default, accessing Browser by clicking a Web address or a Web link within another application opens the Web page associated with that address. (In Figure 11-3, we're opening Browser from the Messages application.)

Hitting the (air)waves

After you locate Browser, you're ready to surf the Web. Here's how:

1. **Open Browser.**
2. **Press the menu key and then select Go To.**
3. **Type a Web address, as shown in Figure 11-4.**

4. Select OK.

While the page is loading, progress is indicated at the bottom of the screen.

Unless you change its configuration (see Start Page in the "Configuring Browser" section, later in this chapter), BlackBerry displays your bookmarks when you open Browser. And if you already have bookmarks, just select the bookmark. For the lowdown on adding bookmarks, see the upcoming section "Bookmarking Your Favorite Sites."

When you see a phone number or an e-mail address on a Web page, you can scroll to that information to highlight it. Then press the trackball or trackpad to initiate a phone call or open a new e-mail message (depending on which type of link you highlighted).

Figure 11-3: Open Browser from Messages.

Figure 11-4: Opening a Web page is simple.

Navigating Web pages

Using Browser to navigate to a Web page is easy. Note that hyperlinks are highlighted onscreen. To jump to a particular hyperlink, scroll to the highlighted link and press the trackball or trackpad.

Here are a few shortcuts you can use while navigating a Web page:

- ✓ **Move up and down one full display page at a time.** Press 9 (down arrow) or 3 (up arrow).

- ✓ **Switch between full-screen mode and normal mode.** Press the exclamation-point (!) key. In full-screen mode, the BlackBerry doesn't show anything extra (for example, the signal level) on the top portion of the display screen. Normal mode is the default.

- ✓ **Stop loading a page.** Press the escape key.

- ✓ **Go back to the previous page (if there is one).** Press the escape key.

And don't forget the Browser menu (press the menu key). It has some useful shortcuts, as shown in Figure 11-5.

Here are the Browser menu options:

- ✓ **Help:** Like the rest of BlackBerry applications, Help is always available in the menu screen to display a quick guide.

- ✓ **Column View:** The default view; it appears only if you are in Page view. With this view, the Web page is displayed vertically, meaning that a wide Web page wraps down, and you can use the trackball or trackpad to scroll up and down the page.

Figure 11-5:
The Browser menu has lots of good stuff.

Help
Column View
Zoom In
Zoom Out
Find
Home
Go To...
Recent Pages
History
Refresh

Refresh
Set Encoding
Add Bookmark
Bookmarks
Page Address
Send Address
Options
Save Page
Switch Application
Close

- **Page View:** Appears only if you are in Column view. (See the preceding bullet.) With this view, you see the page as you typically would in a PC's Internet browser. The compressed version of the Web page takes up the entire screen first.

- **Zoom In/Out:** Zooms in and out.

- **Find:** Locates and highlights text within the current page. Like any other basic Find tool, this option displays a prompt to enter the text you want to find. After the initial search, a Find Next menu appears for finding the next matching text.

- **Select:** Appears only if the trackball or trackpad pointer is placed on text. Use this feature to highlight text onscreen for copying.

- **Stop:** Appears only if you're in the middle of requesting a page. Use Stop to cancel such a request. This is the same as pressing the escape key.

- **Copy:** Appears if you have highlighted text. Selecting Copy copies the highlighted text into memory so that you can use it later for pasting somewhere else, such as in MemoPad.

- **Full Image:** Appears only if you highlight an image and only a portion of the image is displayed onscreen.

- **Save Image:** Appears only if you highlight an image, allowing you to save the image in the Curve's built-in memory or to an SD card.

- **Home:** The shortcut to your Home page. The default Home page can vary from carrier to carrier, but to change it, open the Browser menu, choose Options⇨Browser Configuration, and change the Home Page Address field.

- **Get Link:** Appears only if you have a highlighted link. Choosing this menu item opens that page of the link.

  The faster way to open a link is to press Enter.

- **Go To:** Opens a Web page when you enter a Web address and press the trackball or trackpad. As you enter more addresses, they are listed in the History portion of the screen so you don't have to retype them. To find out how to clear this list, see the "Cache operations" section, later in this chapter.

- **Back:** This menu item appears only if you have navigated to more than one Web page. The Back option goes back to the preceding page you viewed.

  You can achieve the same function by pressing the escape key.

- **Forward:** This menu item appears only if you have gone back at least one Web page. The Forward option progresses one page at a time.

- **Recent Pages:** Jumps to any of those Web pages when you highlight the history page and press the enter key twice. Browser can track up to 20 pages of Web addresses you've visited, which you can view on the History screen.

- **History:** Displays a list of the Web pages you've visited and allows you to jump back quickly to those pages. The list is grouped by date.

✔ **Refresh:** Updates the current page. This is helpful when you're viewing a page with data that changes frequently (such as stock quotes).

✔ **Set Encoding:** Specifies the encoding used in viewing a Web page. This is useful when viewing foreign languages that use different characters. Most BlackBerry users don't have to deal with this and probably don't know what type of encoding a particular language could display.

When you try to open a Web page, indicators that show the progress of your request appear at the bottom of the screen. Figure 11-6 (left) shows Browser requesting a page. Figure 11-6 (right) shows that you've reached the page and the page is still loading.

Figure 11-6:
Requesting
a page (left)
and then
loading
it (right).

The icons in the top-right corner of both screens in Figure 11-6 are (from right to left)

✔ Your **connection type** appears in the rightmost portion. In Figure 11-6, WiFi means that the connection is using a Wi-Fi network.

If you're not connected to Wi-Fi, an icon with vertical bars and an antenna appears to the right of the connection type, showing the strength of the network signals (the same signal indicators for phone and e-mail).

✔ The **lock icon** indicates whether you're at a secure Web page. Figure 11-6 shows a nonsecure page. Whether a page is secure depends on the Web site you're visiting. If you're accessing your bank, you most likely see the secured icon (a closed lock). On the other hand, most pages don't need to be secure, so you see the unsecured icon (an open lock).

✔ The **connection information icon** to the left of the lock is a way for you to know the amount of Web page data transferred between your BlackBerry Curve and the network provider. In Browser, you should see a trackball or trackpad pointer in the screen, which is similar to a PC mouse pointer. Scroll the trackball or trackpad until the pointer hovers in the connection information icon; then press the trackball or trackpad. The next screen displays the connection information.

If you lose patience waiting for a page to load and want to browse somewhere else, press the escape key to stop the page from loading.

Saving a Web page address

Entering a Web address to view a page can get tedious. Fortunately, you can return to a page without typing the same address. While you're viewing a Web page, simply use the Browser menu (shown in Figure 11-7) to save that page's address.

Figure 11-7:
Use the
Browser
menu to
save a
Web page
address.

You can save a Web page address in several ways:

- ✔ **Page Address:** This option allows you to view the Web address of the current page through a pop-up screen, which presents you with two options:

  - • Copy Address saves the page's address to your BlackBerry Clipboard and allows you to paste it somewhere else.

  - • Send Address is the same Send Address you see in the Browser menu (as described in the next item).

- ✔ **Send Address:** Presents another screen so that you can choose whether to send the address by e-mail (Chapter 8), MMS (Chapter 9), PIN (Chapter 9), SMS (Chapter 9), or Messenger Contact (Chapter 10).

- ✔ **Save Page:** Use this option to save the Web address of the current page to Messages. A message appears with the Browser globe icon to indicate that it's a Web link, as shown in Figure 11-8. Highlighting that entry and pressing the trackball or trackpad launches Browser and opens the page for your viewing pleasure.

Saving a page to your message list has a different purpose from book-marking a page. The saved page initially shows as unread in Messages, to remind you to check back later.

Figure 11-8:
Save a Web
page link in
Messages.

Note: When you don't have network coverage, and you try to access a Web page, you're prompted to save your request. When you do, your request is automatically saved in the message list. When you do have coverage later, you can open the same Web page from the message list, with the content loaded already!

If you press a letter key while a menu is displayed, you select the first menu item that starts with that letter. Pressing the same letter again selects the next menu item that starts with that letter.

Sending an address by e-mail

You can send a Web address to any recipient via e-mail by using the Page Address option in the Browser menu. For a more direct way, simply select Send Address from the Browser menu while the Web page is displayed. If you know right away that you'll need to send an address to someone, save a few clicks and use the more direct method.

Saving Web images

You can save images in JPEG, PNG, GIF, and BMP formats from a Web page. Any saved image is kept in the Pictures application, which enables you to view it later. To save an image, just click the image and then select Save Image from the menu that appears.

No place like Home

Changing your Home screen background is a neat trick. You can use an image you have saved in your Pictures list as the background on your Home screen. Here's how:

1. **From the Home screen, select the Media icon and then select Pictures.**

   The Pictures application opens.

2. **Scroll to and select the image you want to set as your background.**

3. **Press the menu key and then select Set as Home Screen Image.**

Bookmarking Your Favorite Sites

You don't have to memorize all the addresses of your favorite sites. Instead, use BlackBerry Browser to keep a list of sites you want to revisit. In other words, make a *bookmark* so that you can come back to a site quickly.

Adding and visiting a bookmark

Add a new bookmark this way:

1. **Open Browser, and go to the Web page you want to bookmark.**

2. **Select Add Bookmark from the Browser menu.**

   The menu is always accessible by pressing the menu key.

3. **(Optional) In the Add Bookmark dialog box, change the bookmark name.**

   The name of the bookmark defaults to the Web site title and, in most cases, is appropriate to use as the name. You always have the option to change this name; refer to the next section, "Modifying a bookmark."

4. **In the Add Bookmark dialog box, navigate to the folder where you want to save the bookmark.**

   The dialog box is shown in Figure 11-9. The default bookmark save folder is BlackBerry Bookmarks, but you can save the bookmark in any folder you create. To see how to create a bookmark folder, skip to the section "Adding a bookmark subfolder."

5. **Scroll to the bottom of the dialog box, and Select Add.**

Available offline

In the Add Bookmark dialog box is the Available Offline check box. When that check box is selected, you not only save a page as a bookmark, but also *cache* it so you can see it even when you're out of range (such as when you're stuck deep in a mountain cave). The next time you click the bookmark, that page comes up very fast. We recommend making bookmarks available offline for pages that don't change from day to day, such as search engines (for example, Google).

Figure 11-9:
Name the
bookmark,
and specify
where to
store it.

Add Bookmark

Name: SmrtGuard :: Your
Smartphone Guardian™

Folder: BlackBerry Bookmarks

☐ Available Offline
Auto Synchronize: Never
Browser: Internet Browser
Browser Identification: Auto

Here's how to go to a bookmarked page:

1. **In Browser, select Bookmarks from the Browser menu.**

   You're taken to the Bookmarks screen. From here, you can find all the pages you've bookmarked.

2. **Select the bookmark for the page you want to visit.**

Modifying a bookmark

You have the option of changing the attributes of existing bookmarks. Why change them? Say you bookmarked a few pages from the same Web site, but the author of the Web pages didn't bother to have a unique title for each page. While happily bookmarking pages, you didn't bother to change the names of the bookmarks that default to the Web page title. Now you end up with several bookmarks with the same name. But changing a bookmark is a snap. Follow these steps:

1. **Select Bookmarks from the Browser menu.**

2. **From the Bookmarks screen, highlight the name of the bookmark you want to modify, press the menu key, and then select Edit Bookmark.**

3. **On the screen that follows, edit the existing name, the address the bookmark is pointing to, or both.**

4. **Select Accept to save your changes.**

Organizing your bookmarks

Over time, the number of your bookmarks will grow. And trying to find a certain site on a tiny screen can be tough. A handy work-around is to organize your bookmarks with folders. For example, you can group related sites in a folder, and each folder can have one or more other folders inside it (subfolders). Having a folder hierarchy narrows your search and allows you to easily find a site.

For example, your sites might fall into these categories:

- Reference

    NY Times

    Yahoo!

- Fun

    Flickr

    The Onion

- Shopping

    Etsy

    Gaiam

Adding a bookmark subfolder

You can add subfolders only to folders that are already listed on the Bookmarks page. That is, you can't create your own root folder. Your choices for adding your first subfolder are under WAP Bookmarks or BlackBerry Bookmarks.

Suppose you want to add a Reference subfolder within your BlackBerry Bookmarks folder. Here are the quick and easy steps:

1. **On the Bookmarks screen, highlight BlackBerry Bookmarks.**

    The BlackBerry Bookmarks folder is the *parent* of the new subfolder. In this case, the BlackBerry Bookmarks folder will contain the Reference subfolder.

2. Press the menu key and then select Add Subfolder, as shown in Figure 11-10.

You see a dialog box where you can enter the name of the folder. (We're using Reference.)

Figure 11-10:
Add a folder here.

Help
Collapse
Go To...
History
Add Bookmark
Add Subfolder
Options
Switch Application
Close

3. Type the folder name, and select OK.

The Reference folder now appears on the Bookmarks screen (as shown in Figure 11-11), bearing a folder icon.

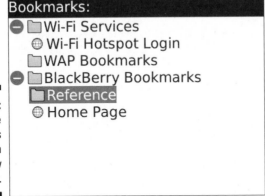

Figure 11-11:
The Bookmarks screen with a new subfolder.

Bookmarks:
⊖ Wi-Fi Services
　⊕ Wi-Fi Hotspot Login
　WAP Bookmarks
⊖ BlackBerry Bookmarks
　Reference
　⊕ Home Page

Renaming a bookmark folder

Although you can't rename the root bookmark folders, such as BlackBerry Bookmarks and WAP Bookmarks, the folders you create under them are fair game. Renaming a bookmark folder that you created is as easy as editing a bookmark. Follow these steps:

1. On the Bookmarks screen, highlight the name of the folder you want to change.

2. **Press the menu key and then select Rename Folder.**

3. **Type the name of the folder.**

4. **Select OK to save your changes.**

Moving a bookmark

If you keep going astray looking for a bookmark that you think exists in a particular folder but is instead in another, move that bookmark where it belongs.
Follow these steps:

1. **Highlight the bookmark, press the menu key, and then select Move
   Bookmark.**

2. **Use the trackball or trackpad to move the bookmark to the location in
   the list where you want it to appear.**

3. **After you find the right location, press the trackball or trackpad.**

   Your bookmark is in its new home.

Cleaning up your bookmarks

Maybe you really like a site but eventually stop visiting it. Or maybe a site
disappears, and every time you click the bookmark, you get a 404 Not Found
error. Time for a little spring cleaning. From the Bookmarks screen, highlight
the name of the bookmark you want to delete. Press the menu key and then
select Delete Bookmark. It's just that easy.

You can — repeat, *can* — clean up bookmarks wholesale by deleting a folder.
A word to the wise, though: All contents of that folder will be deleted, so purge
with caution.

Exercising Options and Optimization Techniques

Sure, Browser works out of the box, but folks have their own tastes, right?
Look to Browser Options for attributes and features you can customize.

Press the menu key and then select Options. The Browser Options screen
that opens offers three main categories to choose among, as shown in
Figure 11-12:

  ✔ **Browser Configuration:** A place to toggle Browser features

  ✔ **General Properties:** Settings for the general look and feel of Browser

  ✔ **Cache Operations:** Options for clearing file caches used by Browser

If you feel speed-greedy after adjusting the options, see the sidebar "Speeding up browsing," later in this chapter.

> Browser Options
> **Browser Configuration**
> General Properties
> Cache Operations

Configuring Browser

You can define browser-specific settings from the Browser Configuration screen, which you access from the Browser Options screen. The customization items you can amend (shown in Figure 11-13) are as follows:

   ✓ **Support JavaScript:** JavaScript is a scripting language used heavily to make dynamic Web pages. A Web page might not behave normally when this option is turned off. This option is off by default.

> Browser Configuration
> Browser: Browser
> ☐ Support JavaScript
> ☑ Prompt to enable JavaScript
> ☑ Show Images
> ☑ Use Background Images
> ☑ Support Embedded Media
> Browser Identification: BlackBerry
> Start Page: Start Page
>
> Home Page Address: http://
> mobile.blackberry.com/

✔ **Allow JavaScript Popups:** Most ad pages are launched as JavaScript pop-ups, so having this check box selected minimizes these ads. Be aware, though, that some important pages are also displayed as JavaScript pop-ups.

Note: This option appears only if you select the Support JavaScript check box.

✔ **Prompt to Enable JavaScript:** This option appears and comes into play only if you haven't selected Support JavaScript. The default value for this option is selected (if you browse a page that has JavaScript, Browser will prompt you to either enable JavaScript or not).

✔ **Terminate Slow Running Scripts:** Sometimes you find Web pages with scripts that aren't written well. Leave this option selected to keep Browser from hanging. This option appears only if you select the Support JavaScript check box.

✔ **Show Images:** This option controls the display of images depending on the content mode of WML, HTML, or both. Think of WML pages as Web pages made just for mobile devices, such as the BlackBerry. We recommend leaving this option selected for both WML and HTML.

Turn on and off the display of image placeholders if you opt to not display images.

✔ **Use Background Images:** A Web page background image can make the page look pleasing, but if the image is big, it could take time to download it.

✔ **Support Embedded Media:** Select this option to support media such as SVG (scalable vector graphics). Think of SVG as Adobe Flash for mobile devices such as the BlackBerry Curve. SVG can be a still image or an animated one.

✔ **Browser Identification:** This option specifies which browser type your browser emulates. The default is BlackBerry, but Browser can also emulate Microsoft Internet Explorer and Mozilla Firefox.

Keep the default BlackBerry mode. We don't see much difference in any of them.

✔ **Start Page:** Use this to specify a starting page to load when you open Browser.

✔ **Home Page Address:** Use this to set your home page. Note that the Home page is always available from the Browser menu.

General Browser properties

The General Properties screen is similar to the Browser Configuration screen (see the preceding section) in that you can customize some Browser behaviors. General Properties, however, is geared more toward the features of the

Browser content. As shown in Figure 11-14, you can configure features and also turn features off or on.

```
General Properties
Default Browser:              Browser
Default Font Family:     BBAlpha Sans
Default Font Size:                    8
Minimum Font Size:                   6
Minimum Font Style:              Plain
Default View:                     Page
Image Quality:                  Medium
Repeat Animations:          100 times
■Enable JavaScript Location
  support
```

Figure 11-14:
The General
Properties
screen.

From this screen, use the Space key to change the value of a field. You can configure the following features:

- ✔ **Default Browser:** If you have multiple browsers available, use this to specify which one you want to use when opening a Web link.

- ✔ **Default Font Family:** When a Web page doesn't specify the text font, Browser will use the one you selected here.

- ✔ **Default Font Size:** When a Web page doesn't specify the text font size, Browser uses the one you selected here. The smaller the size, the more text can fit onscreen.

- ✔ **Minimum Font Size:** A Web page might specify a font size too small to be legible. Specifying a legible font size will override the Web page.

- ✔ **Minimum Font Style:** When Browser is using the minimum font size, you can choose what font to use. Some fonts are more legible, even in a small size, than others. If you aren't sure which one to use, leave this set to the default.

- ✔ **Default View:** You can toggle the default view:

  - • Column: Wraps all Web page elements vertically, so you just scroll up and down by panning the page.

  - • Page: Displays the page as you normally see it in your PC's Internet browser. Pan the page to scroll left, right, up, and down.

- ✔ **Image Quality:** The higher the quality, the slower the page loads. You have three options: low, medium (the default), and high.

- ✔ **Repeat Animations:** Sets the number of times an animation repeats. This pertains to animated images that most banner ads use. Your choices are Never, Once, 10 Times, 100 Times (the default), and As Many as the Image Specifies.

✔ **Enable JavaScript Location Support:** Web pages that have scripts that take advantage of your BlackBerry's location through GPS will work if you have this selected.

✔ **Prompt Before:** You can have BlackBerry Browser give you a second chance before you do the following:

- Closing Browser on Escape: You're notified right before you exit BlackBerry Browser.

- Closing Modified Pages: You're notified right before you exit a modified Web page (for example, some type of online form you fill out).

- Running WML Scripts: WML is a script that tells a wireless device how to display a page. It was popular years ago, when resolutions of device screens were low, but very few Web sites are using it now. We recommend leaving this field deselected.

Cache operations

At any given time, your BlackBerry uses a few cache mechanisms. A *cache* (pronounced *cash*) temporarily stores information used by Browser so that the next time the info is needed, Browser doesn't have to go back to the source Web site. The cache can speed up displays when you want to view the Web page again and is also useful when you're suddenly out of network coverage. When you visit a site that uses cookies, Browser caches that cookie. (Think of a *cookie* as a piece of text that a Web site creates and places in your BlackBerry's memory to remember something about you, such as your username.)

Some Web sites *push* (send) Web pages to BlackBerry devices. An icon will appear on the Home screen, allowing you to quickly view the page. After the Web page is delivered to your BlackBerry, it becomes available even if you go out of the coverage area. If you subscribe to this service, your device will store Web pages in the cache. Also, the addresses of the pages that you visited (or your latest 20 in your history list) comprise a cache.

The Cache Operations screen, shown in Figure 11-15, allows you to manually clear your cache. To view the Cache Operations screen, follow these steps:

1. **From the Browser screen, press the menu key.**

2. **Select Options.**

3. **Select Cache Operations.**

Speeding up browsing

On a wireless network, many factors can affect the speed with which Web pages display. If you find that browsing the Web is extremely slow, you can make your pages load faster in exchange for not using a few features. Here are some of the speed-enhancing work-arounds you can use:

✔ **Don't display images.** You can achieve a big performance improvement by turning off image display. From the Browser menu, select Browser Options⇨Browser Configuration, scroll to Show Images, and change the value to No.

✔ **Check your BlackBerry memory.** When your BlackBerry's memory is depleted, its performance degrades. The BlackBerry low-memory manager calls each application every now and then, telling each one to free resources.

Hint #1: Don't leave many e-mail messages unread. When the low-memory manager kicks in, Messages tries to delete old messages, but it can't delete unread messages.

Hint #2: Purge the BlackBerry event log to free needed space. Enter the letters **LGLG** while pressing down the Shift key. This opens an event log. The event log entries may not make sense to you because they're mostly cryptic and in codes. These are usually helpful for technical folks to figure out what's going on in your BlackBerry but are something you don't really need. You can clear the event log to free memory.

✔ **Turn off other features.** If you're mostly interested in viewing content, consider turning off features that pertain to how the content is processed, such as Support HTML Tables, Use Background Images, Support JavaScript, Allow JavaScript Popups, and Support Style Sheets. To turn off other Browser features, navigate to Browser Options⇨General Properties.

Warning: We don't advise turning off features while performing an important task such as online banking. If you do, you may not be able to perform some of the actions on the page. For example, the Submit button might not work. Not good.

Figure 11-15: The Cache Operations screen.

The size for each type of cache is displayed on this screen. If the cache has content, you also see the Clear button, which you can use to clear the specified cache type. This is true for all types of cache except for history, which has its own Clear History button. You find four types of cache:

- **Content Cache:** Any offline content. You may want to clear this whenever you're running out of space on your BlackBerry and need to free some memory. Or maybe you're tired of viewing old content or tired of pressing the Refresh option.

- **Pushed Content:** Any content that was pushed to your BlackBerry from Push Services subscriptions. You may want to clear this to free memory on your BlackBerry.

- **Cookie Cache:** Any cookies stored on your BlackBerry. You may want to clear this for security's sake. Sometimes you don't want a Web site to remember you.

- **History:** The list of sites you've visited by using the Go To function. You may want to clear this for the sake of security if you don't want other people knowing which Web sites you're visiting on your BlackBerry.

You can easily check how much memory your device has in the Help Me! screen. To go to the Help Me! screen, press and hold Alt+Shift+H while in the Home screen. Shift is the ↑ bottom-left key to the left of the 0 key.

Installing and Uninstalling Applications from the Web

You can download and install applications on your BlackBerry via Browser — that is, if the application has a link that lets you download and install the files (see Chapter 19 for other installation options). The downloading and installing parts are easy. Follow these steps:

1. **From Browser, click the application's link.**

   You see a simple prompt that looks like the screen shown in Figure 11-16.

2. **Select the Download button.**

   The download starts, and you'll see a progress screen.

As long as you stay within network coverage while the download is progressing, your BlackBerry can finish the download *and* install the application for you. If it finishes without any problems, you see the screen shown in Figure 11-17.

Figure 11-16:
A typical page that lets you download an application on your BlackBerry.

Figure 11-17:
The download and installation were completed.

As with a desktop computer, the download might or might not work for a variety of reasons. Sometimes the application

 ✔ Requires you to install libraries

 ✔ Works only on a certain version of the BlackBerry OS

These issues can be prevented, depending on the sophistication of the site where the link is published. With most reputable sources, these issues have been resolved, and successful downloading and installation are a snap.

Installing applications from a source that is not reputable can cause your BlackBerry to become unstable. Before you download an application from the Web, be sure to read reviews about that particular application. Most of the time, other people who tried the software provide reviews or feedback. Don't be the first to write the bad review!

Your BlackBerry Enterprise Server administrator can disable the feature in your BlackBerry to download and install an application. This is mostly the case for a company-issued device. If you have problems downloading and installing an application, check your company policy or contact the BlackBerry support person in your company.

If you download an application that turns out to be a dud, you need to uninstall it. See Chapter 19 for more on uninstalling an application from your BlackBerry.

Browser's Behavior in Business

Getting a device from your employer has both a good and an ugly side:

- ✔ **Good:** Your company foots the bill.
- ✔ **Ugly:** Your company foots the bill.

Because your company pays, the company dictates what you can and cannot do with your BlackBerry Curve. This is especially true with respect to browsing the Web.

Two scenarios come into play when it comes to your browser:

- ✔ Your browser might be running under your company's BlackBerry Enterprise Server. With this setup, your BlackBerry Browser is connecting to the Internet by using your company's Internet connection. It's like using your desktop machine at work.
- ✔ Your browser is connected through a network service provider. Most of the time, this kind of browser is called by the company's name.

In most cases, your device fits in only one scenario, which is the case where your browser is connected through your company's BlackBerry Enterprise Server server. Some lucky folks may have both. Whatever scenario you're in, the following sections describe the major differences between the two and indicate what you can expect.

Using Browser on your company's BlackBerry Enterprise Server

In an enterprise setup, your BlackBerry Browser is connected through your company's BlackBerry Enterprise Server server. With this setup, the browser is actually named *BlackBerry Browser.* BlackBerry Enterprise Server is located inside your company's intranet. This setup allows the company to better manage the privileges and the functions you can use on your device.

For the BlackBerry Browser application, this setup allows the company to use the existing Internet infrastructure, including the company's firewall.

Because you are within the company's network, the boundaries that your network administrator set up on your account apply to your BlackBerry as well. For example, when browsing the Web, your BlackBerry won't display any Web sites that are blocked by your company's server.

The good thing, though, is that you can browse the company's intranet: That is, all the Web pages you have access to inside your company through your company's PC are available also in your BlackBerry.

Know (and respect) your company's Web-browsing policy. Most companies keep logs of sites you view on your browser and might even have software to monitor usage. Also, your company might not allow downloading from the Web.

Using your network provider's browser

Any new device coming from a network service provider can come with its own branded Web browser. It's the same BlackBerry Browser, but the behavior might differ in the following ways:

- ✓ **The name is different.**
- ✓ **The default home page usually points to the provider's Web site.** This isn't necessarily a bad thing. Most of the time, the network provider's Web site is full of links that you may not find on BlackBerry Browser.
- ✓ **You can browse more sites.** You aren't limited by your company's policy.

Setting the default browser

If you have two Web browsers on your Curve, you have the option to set the *default* browser. This comes into play when you view a Web address by using a link outside the Browser application. For example, when you view an e-mail with a Web link, selecting that link launches the default browser.

To set up the default browser, follow these steps:

1. **Go to the Home screen.**
2. **Choose Settings⇨Options⇨Advanced Options⇨Browser.**
3. **Use the Space key to change the value of the default browser configuration, as shown in Figure 11-18.**

Browser
Default browser configuration:
Browser
Default MDS browser configuration:
Browser

Part IV

Music, Pictures, and Movies on Your Curve

"You can do a lot with a BlackBerry Curve, and I guess dressing one up in G.I. Joe clothes and calling it your little desk commander is okay, too."

In this part . . .

Use your BlackBerry Curve as a still and video camera (Chapter 13). Get entertained and have fun with Curve's multimedia capabilities (Chapter 14). And finally, manage your media files (Chapter 15).

Chapter 12

Getting Around with Your BlackBerry GPS

A few years back, when some of the North American network carriers introduced GPS on their versions of the BlackBerry, we were quite impressed . . . until we tried it. The response time was slow, and it wasn't accurate. On top of that, the network carriers charged users an arm and a leg for this inferior service. As it turns out, those GPS functions were implemented by using the network — that is, GPS wasn't embedded in the BlackBerry. How low-tech!

Today, your BlackBerry Curve can come with built-in GPS, which makes finding yourself easy. In this chapter, we show you how to use your BlackBerry's built-in GPS and show you the best GPS applications you can use on your BlackBerry, two of which are free!

The BlackBerry Curve 8900 model has built-in GPS, but some BlackBerry Curve 8500 models do not. If you have a BlackBerry Curve 8500, please check with your network carrier for the status of your Curve.

Putting Safety First

Some GPS features are useful while you're driving a car. However, even when tempted to use your BlackBerry GPS while driving, we *strongly* suggest that you *do not* adjust it while you're driving.

Before you start using BlackBerry GPS in your car, you need a BlackBerry car holder — preferably a car kit with a car charger. You can buy a car kit on the Internet; just search for *BlackBerry car kit*. Or go to one of the following Web sites:

    ✔ www.shopblackberry.com

    ✔ http://shop.crackberry.com

Now that you have all you need to keep you safe, keep on reading.

What You Need

For GPS to work on your BlackBerry, it needs navigation maps, which are usually downloaded in little pieces as required. And because these maps are downloaded, you must be subscribed to a data plan and have a radio signal to obtain them.

If you didn't subscribe to an unlimited data plan from your network carrier, be aware that the more you use your GPS as you move about, the more data (map pieces) you'll download, which means the more charges you'll incur.

In summary, for your BlackBerry GPS to work, you need

    ✔ **A data plan from your network carrier.** We recommend an unlimited data plan.

    ✔ **To be in an area where you have a radio signal.** That way, you can download the maps.

Your GPS Application Choices

The four GPS applications that you can use on your BlackBerry are

    ✔ **BlackBerry Maps** (comes with your BlackBerry): Free

    ✔ **Google Maps** (m.google.com/maps): Free

    ✔ **Garmin Mobile** (garmin.com/mobile/mobilext): $99 one-time fee

    ✔ **TeleNav GPS Navigator** (telenav.com/products/tn/): $9.99 per month

The icons for all are pictured in Figure 12-1.

BlackBerry Maps

As we mention earlier, your BlackBerry comes with the BlackBerry Maps application loaded (refer to Figure 12-1).

Figure 12-1:
BlackBerry
GPS
applications.

BlackBerry Maps | TeleNav GPS Navigator

Google Maps | Garmin Mobile

If you have a BlackBerry with AT&T as your network carrier, you might not have BlackBerry Maps installed out of the box. No worries; you can download it via `mobile.blackberry.com`. (Keep reading, too, for alternatives to BlackBerry Maps that still take advantage of your BlackBerry GPS.)

With or without GPS (built-in or external), you can use BlackBerry Maps to do the following (see Figure 12-2):

✔ Find a location by typing an address or by using Contacts

✔ Get point-to-point directions

✔ E-mail or SMS a location to colleagues and friends

✔ Turn GPS on or off

✔ Zoom in and out of the map

Of course, with GPS turned on, you can track where you are and follow point-to-point directions.

Google Maps

Google Maps is the mobile version of `http://maps.google.com`. It has most of the features of the online version, including satellite imaging and traffic information. Best of all, it's free.

Like BlackBerry Maps, you can use Google Maps even without a GPS. With Google Maps, you can search for businesses and landmarks; it's like having the ultimate 411 (with a map) at the tip of your fingers.

Figure 12-2:
BlackBerry
Maps on the
BlackBerry
Curve.

Because Google Maps doesn't come with your BlackBerry, you need to download it. To do so, go to www.google.com/gmm. After the program downloads, its icon appears on your Home screen (refer to Figure 12-1).

After Google Maps is loaded, press the menu key to display the menu shown in Figure 12-3.

Figure 12-3:
Google
Maps menu.

From the menu, you can do the following:

✔ Find businesses and landmarks, including phone numbers, address information, and Web addresses

✔ Find and map exact addresses

✔ Get step-by-step directions from point A to point B

✔ View a satellite image of the current map (see Figure 12-4)

✔ Get traffic information for major highways

Figure 12-4:
Google
Maps
showing
a satellite
photo.

With GPS or Google's MyLocation on, you can see your current location as a blue blinking dot.

Here are some keyboard shortcuts for Google Maps:

✔ **Zoom in:** I key

✔ **Zoom out:** O key

✔ **Go to the current location:** 0 (zero) key

You need to have a radio signal to download maps to your BlackBerry. In addition, we recommend that you have an unlimited data plan if you are a frequent user of the GPS feature on your BlackBerry.

TeleNav GPS Navigator

TeleNav GPS Navigator is a full-featured GPS solution. It's intended as a GPS device replacement, which means the folks at TeleNav want you to use your BlackBerry in the car. TeleNav's feature list is extensive. From 3D maps to a real-time compass to finding Wi-Fi hotspots, the list goes on and on. It even lets you input the address by speaking aloud instead of typing, and responds by speaking the directions aloud to you. Figure 12-5 shows the main menu for TeleNav. (Note that there are network-branded versions of TeleNav; for example, Figure 12-5 shows an AT&T version. The functionalities from TeleNav are the same, regardless of network branding.)

The extensive features come at a price. Depending on your network carrier, TeleNav costs about $10 per month. TeleNav does offer a 30-day free trial. Visit www.telenav.com/products/tn for more information. After the product is downloaded, its icon appears on your screen (refer to Figure 12-1).

Figure 12-5:
AT&T-branded version of TeleNav main menu.

Garmin Mobile

Like TeleNav, Garmin offers a full-featured GPS solution. They charge a one-time fee of $99, which is good for the life of the device. The features of Garmin Mobile are very similar to its GPS counterpart. If you have ever owned a Garmin GPS, the user interface is similar and friendly. Figure 12-6 shows the main menu for Garmin Mobile.

Figure 12-6:
Garmin Mobile's main menu.

We like the simplicity of Garmin's user interface and its one-time cost.

To find out more, visit www.garmin.com/mobile/mobilext.

Chapter 13

Taking Great Pictures and Capturing Videos

*O*h, shoot, you forgot your camera. Don't worry! Your BlackBerry is there when you need to capture the unbelievable: Grandma doing a handstand, Grandpa doing a cartwheel, or your roommate doing her laundry. And if pictures aren't enough, you can record your unbelievable scene in full motion.

Before you try taking pictures, read this chapter so you know what to expect and how to get the best shot. We walk you through the easy steps for capturing that funny pose and tell you how to store those photos and videos. And don't miss reading how to share the joy with your buddies.

Saying "Cheese"

Snapping shots with your BlackBerry Curve couldn't be easier. Just turn on the Camera app, line up your shot, and snap away. Here's the bird's-eye view:

1. **Press the right convenience key (bottom key on the right side of your BlackBerry) to bring up the Camera application.**

Figure 13-1 shows the 8900, and Figure 13-2, the 8500. Most network carriers set the right convenience key on the Curve to bring up the Camera application. However, network carriers may change this setting. So if you don't see the Camera app when pressing the right-side key, the alternative to launching the Camera application is selecting the Camera icon from the Home screen.

Make sure that your finger isn't blocking the lens on the back side of your device.

The camera button on the right side of your Curve is really a convenience key, which you can program to open your favorite application. By default, it's set to launch Camera. Chapter 3 shows how to change this setting.

2. **When you see the image onscreen, press the Camera key to take the picture.**

You should hear a funky shutterlike sound. Neat and easy, isn't it?

That's the quick version. Keep reading to discover more about Camera's features.

Figure 13-1:
The camera screen ready to take pictures on the 8900.

Number of pictures you can capture   Zoom   Low-light indicator

Flash

Figure 13-2:
The camera
screen
ready
to take
pictures on
the 8500.

Zoom

Low-light indicator

Number of pictures you can capture

Reading the screen indicators

When you open the Camera application, the first thing you see is the screen shown in Figure 13-1 (8900) or Figure 13-2 (8500). The top portion of this screen shows you the image you're about to capture. Immediately below the preview are icons that indicate (starting from the left)

✔ Number of pictures you can capture

✔ Zoom

✔ Flash for 8900

✔ Low-light indicator

Choosing the picture quality

Your Curve can capture images with as much resolution as 2.0 megapixels (MP) for the 8500 and 3.2 MP for the 8900. Saving images at this resolution requires considerable space, though. Just be mindful when shooting, and consider saving images at a lower quality to save some space on your BlackBerry.

Get a big microSD card. Nowadays, even a 32GB microSD card is inexpensive, and it holds thousands of pictures.

Here are the three resolutions you can choose:

- ✔ **Normal:** The default setting. This is the lowest quality but lets you save the most pictures. The trade-off is that Normal picture quality won't be as smooth or as fine as the other resolution choices.

  If you're just taking pictures of your friends' faces so you can attach them as Caller IDs, Normal is appropriate.

- ✔ **Fine:** A middle setting between Normal and SuperFine. This is a compromise if you're concerned about space and want to capture more pictures. The best use is for any electronic viewer; this option isn't good for printing.

- ✔ **SuperFine:** The best quality that your Camera can capture. Choose this if you plan on printing the images.

Changing picture quality is a snap. Follow these steps:

1. **Open the Camera application.**

2. **Press the menu key and then select the Options icon.**

3. **Highlight Picture Quality and then press the Space key until the setting you want is highlighted.**

   Pressing the Space key toggles the picture quality value among Normal, Fine, and SuperFine.

4. **Press the menu key and then select Save.**

   The picture quality you chose is active.

Zooming and focusing

You need to be steady to get a good focus while taking your shots. Although it's convenient to use one hand while taking pictures, most of the time, you'll get a blurry image if you try that.

When taking pictures, hold your Curve with both hands, one holding the smartphone steady and the other pressing the trackball or trackpad. If the right convenience key is set to Camera, you can press that instead of the trackball or trackpad.

Holding the smartphone with both hands is even more important if you're zooming in. Yes, your camera is capable of up to 3.0x digital zoom. Here's what you need to do to focus and zoom:

- ✔ **To focus:** Your camera has autofocus. Just hold it steady.
- ✔ **To zoom in:** Slide up with the trackball or trackpad.
- ✔ **To zoom out:** Slide down with the trackball or trackpad.

While zooming, the value in the indicator changes from 1.0x to 2.0x to 3.0x and vice versa, depending on the direction you scroll.

When zooming, your thumb is already on the trackball or trackpad. What a convenient way to take the picture — just press.

We don't recommend using the zoom. Digital zoom (which is what your camera has) gives poor results because it's done through software and degrades the quality of the picture. The higher the zoom factor, the more pixelated the picture becomes. To get a clearer picture, get closer to the object.

Setting the flash

If you have the BlackBerry Curve 8900, your smartphone comes with a flash. The rightmost indicator on the Camera screen is the flash. The default is Automatic, which shows a lightning bolt with the letter *A*. Automatic means that the camera detects the amount of light you have at the moment you capture the image. Where it's dark, the flash fires; otherwise, it doesn't.

You can turn the flash on, off, or to automatic. The default setting is Automatic. When set to Off, the lightning bolt is encircled with a diagonal line, just like you see on No Smoking signs. You can toggle the settings on the camera's Options screen, which is accessible by pressing the menu key and selecting Options.

The 8500 has no flash.

Setting the white balance

In photography, filters are used to compensate for the dominant light. For instance, a fluorescent versus an incandescent light could affect how warm the picture appears. Instead of using filters, most digital cameras, including the Curve, have a feature called *white balance* that corrects or compensates for many types of light settings.

You can choose Sunny, Cloudy, Night, Incandescent, Fluorescent, or Automatic (the default). *Automatic* means your camera determines what it thinks are the best settings to apply. You can change the white balance through the camera's Options screen, which is accessible by pressing the menu key and then selecting Options.

Setting the picture size

Aside from picture quality, you can adjust the size of the photo:

- ✔ **Large:** 1600 x 1200. This is the default setting.

  Large uses more memory.
- ✔ **Medium:** 1024 x 768
- ✔ **Small:** 640 x 480

Again, camera settings are accessible through the camera's Options screen — press the menu key and then select Options from the menu that appears.

Geotagging

Because your Curve has GPS capability, your location based on longitude and latitude can be determined easily. This information can be added to your media files, including pictures taken from your camera. Now you don't have to wonder where you took that crazy pose. Adding geographic information is known as *geotagging*.

Geotagging is disabled by default. Enable it from the camera's Options screen: Press the menu key and then select Options to get to the Options screen.

If you have longitude and latitude information from one of your photos, you can use one of the free sites on the Web to locate where you were when you took the photo. One such site is www.travelgis.com/geocode/default.aspx.

Working with Pictures

You've taken a bunch of pictures, and you want to see them. And maybe delete the unflattering ones. Or perhaps organize them. No problem.

Viewing pictures

If you take a picture, you want to see it, right? You can see an image you just captured right then and there, as shown in Figure 13-3.

Figure 13-3:
The Camera
screen after
taking a
picture.

All the pictures you took on your Camera are filed directly to a folder in your system. The possible default folder location of pictures is based on whether you opted to save it in

- **Device Memory:** /Device Memory/home/user/pictures
- **Media Card:** /Media Card/BlackBerry/pictures

Let your device file the pictures in the media card (microSD). The first time you use Camera, it prompts you whether to save pictures to the media card. If you aren't sure what the current setting is, simply close the Camera application and then take out the microSD card and put it back in. The next time you open Camera, it displays the same prompt about letting you save pictures to the media card.

The format of the filename is based on the current date and time and named as IMG<counter>-<yyyymmdd>-<hhmm>.jpg. So if you took the 21st picture at 9:30 a.m. on December 20, 2009, you end up with IMG00021-20091220-0930.jpg.

If you're browsing through your picture folders, view a picture by highlighting it and pressing the trackball or trackpad.

Creating a slide show

To see your pictures in a slide show, follow these steps:

1. **From the Camera screen, press the menu key, and then select View Pictures from the menu that appears.**

2. **Press the menu key.**

3. **Select Slide Show.**

   Voilà! Your BlackBerry displays your pictures one at a time at a regular time interval. The default interval between each picture is two seconds; if you aren't happy with this interval, change it in the Options screen. (Press the menu key and then select Options to get to the Options screen.)

Trashing pictures

If you don't like an image you captured, you can delete it. Follow these steps:

1. **Highlight the picture you want to trash.**

2. **Press the menu key and then select Delete from the menu that appears; alternatively, press the Del key.**

   A confirmation screen appears.

3. **Select Delete.**

You can also delete an image right after taking the picture; just select the trash-can icon when viewing the photo (refer to Figure 13-3).

Listing filenames versus thumbnails

When you open a folder packed with pictures, your BlackBerry automatically shows *thumbnails,* which are small previews of your pictures.

A preview is nice, but suppose you want to search for a picture by filename. Here's how:

1. **Go to a picture folder.**

2. **Press the menu key.**

3. **Select View List.**

   That's exactly what you get: a list of all the pictures in the folder. What's neat is that the option also displays the file size, which can give you a clue about what settings you used to take the picture. For example, a photo taken at a SuperFine quality produces a much bigger file size compared with one taken at Normal.

Checking picture properties

Curious about the amount of memory your picture is using? Want to know the time you took the photo?

1. **Highlight the picture from a list.**

   On the Camera screen, view the list of your pictures by pressing the menu key and then selecting View Pictures.

2. **Press the menu key.**

3. **Select Properties.**

   You see a screen similar to Figure 13-4, which displays the file's location in your BlackBerry, size, and last modification. The arrow with Removable text indicates that it's filed in the media card. The Hidden check box allows you to hide the file when navigating through your picture list. Once hidden, the file disappears from the list, and the only way to see the file in your Curve again is to use Explore. Check Chapter 14 for details about Explore.

Figure 13-4:
Your
picture's
properties.

/Device Memory/home/user/
pictures/IMG00001-
20090816-1943.jpg
Size: 247.1KB
Picture Size: 1200 x 1600
Image File
Last Modified:
              16 Aug 2009 19:43
☐Hidden

Organizing your pictures

Organization is all about time and the best use of it. After all, you want to spend your time enjoying looking *at* your pictures — not looking *for* them. Your BlackBerry Curve enables you to rename and move pictures to different folders. You can create folders, too. With those capabilities, you should be on your way to organization nirvana.

Renaming a picture file

BlackBerry autonames a file when you capture a picture. However, the name of the picture is generic, something like IMG*xxxx-currentdate-time,* where *x* is a number. Not very helpful.

Make it a habit to rename a photo as soon as you capture it. Using a name like *Dean blows birthday candles* is much more helpful than *IMG0029-20081013-0029.*

Renaming a photo file is a snap. Here's how:

1. **Display the picture screen or highlight the photo file in the list.**

   The list is displayed from Camera when you press the menu key and select View Pictures.

2. **Press the menu key and select Rename.**

   A Rename screen appears, as shown in Figure 13-5.

3. **Enter the name you want for this picture and then select Save.**

   Your picture is renamed.

Figure 13-5:
Rename
your picture
here.

Creating a folder

Being the organized person you are, you must be wondering about folders. Don't fret; it's simple to create one. Here's how:

1. **From the Camera screen, press the menu key and then select View Pictures.**

   The screen displays the list of pictures in the folder where Camera saves the pictures.

   - If the current folder is still the default pictures-folder location, this folder will be the root of where you can create your subfolder. You can proceed to Step 3.

   - Otherwise, follow Step 2 to select the Up icon to navigate up to the folder above this folder.

2. **Select the Up icon to navigate to the main folder where you want your new folder to be created.**

   You should be *within* the folder where you want your new folder to be created. If you are not, repeat this step to navigate to that folder.

3. **Press the menu key and then select New Folder.**

4. **Type the name of the folder and then select OK.**

   Your folder is created.

Moving pictures

Here's how to move pictures to a different folder:

1. **From the Camera screen, press the menu key and then select View Pictures.**

   The screen displays the list of pictures in the current folder. If the picture you want to move isn't in this folder, click the Up icon to navigate up to other folders.

2. **Highlight the picture you want to move, press the menu key, and then select Move.**

   In the screen that opens, navigate to the folder where you want to move this picture.

3. **Click the Up icon, and use the trackball or trackpad to navigate to the folder where you want to move this picture.**

4. **Press the menu key and then select Move Here.**

   Your picture is moved.

You can easily transfer your pictures to your PC or copy pictures from your PC to your Curve. See Chapter 15 for details.

Sharing your pictures

Where's the joy in taking great pictures if you're the only one seeing them? Your BlackBerry has several options for sharing your bundle of joy:

1. **From the Camera screen, press the menu key and then select View Pictures.**

2. **Highlight a picture you want to share.**

3. **Press the menu key.**

4. **Select one of the choices listed here:**

   • Send as E-mail: This goes directly to the Message screen for composing an e-mail, with the selected picture as an attachment.

   • Send as MMS: Similar to Send as Email, this opens a Compose MMS screen with the selected picture as an attachment. MMS first displays Contacts, though, letting you select the person's phone number to receive the MMS before going to the Compose screen. Another difference is that in MMS, the Curve sends a tiny version of the picture.

   • Send to Messenger Contact: This option is available if you have BlackBerry Messenger installed. This function is similar to Send as MMS but displays only those contacts you have in BlackBerry Messenger. It uses BlackBerry Messenger to send a tiny version of the picture file.

   • Send Using Bluetooth: Send the picture to any Bluetooth-capable device.

You might see other ways to send a picture file if you have other instant messaging (IM) clients installed. For example, if you have Google Talk installed, you will see the Send as Google Talk option.

Setting a picture as Caller ID

Wouldn't it be nice when your girlfriend calls if you also could see her beautiful face? You can. Start with a photo of her saved on your BlackBerry Curve. Then follow these steps:

1. **Select the Media icon from the Home screen and then select Pictures.**

2. **Navigate to the location of the photo.**

3. **Highlight the photo you want to appear when the person calls.**

4. **Press the menu key and then select Set as Caller ID.**

   The photo is displayed onscreen, with a superimposed, portrait-size cropping rectangle. Inside the rectangle is a clear view of the photo; outside the rectangle, the photo is blurry. The clear view represents the portion of the photo that you want to show up as Caller ID. You can move the trackball or trackpad to move the rectangle to make sure that you crop to capture the face.

5. **Crop the photo by pressing the trackball or trackpad and selecting Crop and Save.**

   Contacts appears.

6. **Select the contact you want this picture to appear for.**

   A message indicating a picture is set for that contact appears. You're set.

Adding a photo to your contacts can also be done through the Contacts application (refer to Chapter 4).

Setting a Home screen image

Suppose you have a stunning picture that you want to use as the background image for your BlackBerry. Follow these steps to set the image:

1. **Select the Media icon from the Home screen and then select Pictures.**

2. **Navigate to the location of the picture you want to use.**

3. **Highlight the picture.**

4. **Press the menu key and then select Set as Wallpaper.**

   You can always reset the screen image or go back to the default Home screen image by following the preceding steps but selecting Reset Wallpaper from the Menu screen in Step 4.

Say Action: Capturing Video

Your BlackBerry Curve camera application can do more than take still photos. You can also use it to take videos.

Here are the quick and easy steps to use Video Camera mode:

1. **Open the Camera application.**

2. **Press the menu key and then select Video Camera.**

The screen displays like a viewfinder on a typical digital video camera, as shown in Figure 13-6. Press the trackball or trackpad to start recording.

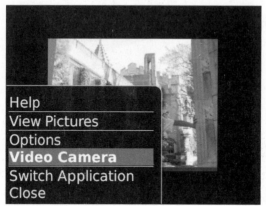

Figure 13-6: Toggle to Video Camera mode here.

The onscreen controls are all context related. When you first launch the video camera, all you see is the Record button with the big white dot at the bottom of the screen (shown in Figure 13-7). When you use the trackball or trackpad to select the Record button, the video camera starts taking video, and the only available control is a Pause button.

Figure 13-7: BlackBerry as a digital video camera on the 8900 (left) and 8500 (right).

Available memory   Video light   Available memory   Recorded time

Record   Recorded time   Record

The indicators on your screen, as shown in Figure 13-7, are as follows:

✔ **Available Memory:** The more squares you see, the more free space you have for saving videos to the device memory or the media card.

✔ **Video Light:** Shows up only if you have the 8900. A circle around the lightning icon, like you see on the left side of Figure 13-7, indicates that Video light is off, which is the default setting.

The following section shows how to enable Video light.

✔ **Zoom:** Like your still camera, it's capable of giving you 3.0x digital zoom.

✔ **Recorded Time:** Tells you how long, in seconds, you've been recording.

You can use the escape key to stop recording and save the captured video or press the trackball or trackpad to pause recording. When you pause the recording, the screen updates to show the rest of the controls, as you see in Figure 13-8.

Figure 13-8:
The video camera controls.

Record Stop Play Rename Delete Send

The controls are the familiar buttons you see on a typical video recorder/player. From left to right, they are as follows:

✔ **Record:** Continue recording.

✔ **Stop:** End the current recording.

✔ **Play:** Play the current video you just recorded.

✔ **Rename:** Rename the video file.

✔ **Delete:** Get rid of the video file of the current recording.

✔ **Send:** Share your current video recording. You have the option to send it as e-mail, as MMS, or through Bluetooth. If you have IM clients installed, such as Google Talk or Yahoo! Messenger, the IM client will be listed as one of the options for sending the video file.

Customizing the Video Camera

Your BlackBerry has a few settings you can tweak to change the behavior of the video camera. And as with every other BlackBerry application, to see what you can customize, don't look anywhere else but the application's Options screen — in this case, the Video Camera Options screen.

Follow these steps to get to the Video Camera Options screen:

1. **Open the Camera application.**

2. **Press the menu key and then select Video Camera (refer to Figure 13-6).**

3. **Press the menu key and then select Options.**

   The Video Camera Options screen appears, as shown in Figure 13-9.

Figure 13-9:
Customize
your video
camera
here.

Video Camera Options	
Video Light	Off
Color Effect	Normal
Video Format	Normal (240 x 180)
Store Videos	In Device Memory
Folder	
■	...Memory/home/user/videos/

The available options are easy to digest, but in case you need a little help, here's what you can tweak:

✔ **Video Light:** In case it's a little dim, you can turn on the video camera's lights. This is available only if you have the 8900. The Curve 8500 doesn't have a video light. While on the video camera screen, you can toggle this setting on or off simply by pressing the Space key.

Dropped something in a dark alley? This video light is a good alternative to a flashlight when you need one.

Video Light is the flash that you use when taking still pictures. It stays lit when you set the setting to On and open the Video Camera. The default is Off.

Using Video Light is a drain on your battery.

✔ **Color Effect:** The default color effect is Normal, which is standard color. If you're in the mood for effects, you can opt for Black & White or Sepia.

✔ **Video Format:** This option is the screen resolution size. The default here is Normal, at 240 x 180 for the 8900 and 320 x 240 for the 8500. If you're planning to send your video to friends through MMS, you can choose MMS mode, which has the smaller size of 176 x 144 and is optimal for MMS.

✔ **Folder:** You can use this option to change the default location where your BlackBerry saves the video file.

Chapter 14

Satisfy Your Senses with Media Player

*I*f one word describes today's phone market trends, it's *convergence*. Your BlackBerry Curve is among the participants in this convergence race. In addition to sending and receiving e-mail and being a phone, a camera, and a PDA, the Curve is an excellent portable media player.

In this small package, you can

✔ Listen to music

✔ Record and watch video clips

✔ Sample ring tones

✔ Snap and view pictures

These capabilities are bundled into an application with a name you'd recognize even after sipping a couple of pints of strong ale — Media.

Accessing Media

 To run Media, simply select the Media icon from the Home screen. The Media icon is easy to distinguish because it bears the image of a CD and a musical note.

Media is a collection of the following media applications:

- ✔ Music
- ✔ Video
- ✔ Ring Tones
- ✔ Pictures
- ✔ Voice Notes

When you open Media, you see that each application is represented with an icon, as shown in Figure 14-1. It's not that difficult to figure out what each one of these media applications is used for. Ready to have some fun?

Figure 14-1:
Explore
Media here.

Let the music play

You don't need a quarter to play music on your BlackBerry Curve. Just select the Music application from the Home screen (the left side of Figure 14-2) or Music from the Media screen (refer to Figure 14-1). Either method launches the same Music application.

Several potential views of your music collection appear, as shown on the right side of Figure 14-2. *Music* is the screen heading. The views are

- ✔ **All Songs:** Displays all your music files in alphabetical order.
- ✔ **Artists:** Lists your music files by artist so that you can play your John Mayer songs in one go.
- ✔ **Albums:** Views your music collection one album at a time.

✔ **Genres:** If you prefer not to mingle your country with your cutting-edge techno, navigate through this view.

✔ **Playlists:** Organizes and plays songs as you prefer — the perfect mix tape!

✔ **Sample Songs:** Go here when you're dying to check the player but haven't yet put your collection into the BlackBerry.

✔ **Shuffle Songs:** Life is all about variety, and when you're tired of the song order in your playlist, select this.

Figure 14-2:
Launch
Music from
the Media
screen (left),
and choose
how to view
your music
collection
(right).

 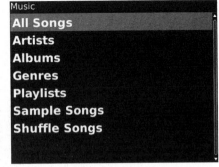

After you choose a view, select one of the songs to start playing it. After BlackBerry starts playing a song, it plays the rest of the music listed in the view you selected. The standard interface shown in Figure 14-3 doesn't require much explanation.

Figure 14-3:
The music
plays here.

The two small icons at the bottom left indicate repeat and shuffle:

- ✔ If you want the songs to be played again after the last song in the list is played, just press the menu key and select Repeat.
- ✔ Tired of hearing the same sequence of songs played? Press the menu key and select Shuffle. Your songs will be played randomly.

You can't fast-forward or rewind, but you can position where Curve is playing by dragging the progress slider. Use the trackball or trackpad to select the progress slider and then slide the trackball or trackpad to change the slider's position. Press the trackball or trackpad again, and the music starts playing from that position.

BlackBerry supports many music formats. The following list shows the supported formats, along with the file extensions:

- ✔ **ACC:** Audio compression formats AAC, AAC+, EAAC+, and AAC-LC (.aac and .m4a)
- ✔ **AMR:** Adaptive Multi-Rate–Narrow Band (AMR-NB) speech coder standard (.mmr and .3gp)
- ✔ **MIDI:** Polyphonic MIDI (.mid, .midi, and .smf)
- ✔ **MP3:** MPEG Part 1 and Part 2 audio layer 3 (.mp3 and .mp4)
- ✔ **WMA:** Windows Media Audio 9, Pro, and 10 (.wma and .asf)

The earpiece/mic combo that comes with your Curve is for one ear only. This is an issue when you're on a train. You may prefer using a stereo (two-ear) headset — or a Bluetooth headset is a good option.

The 8500 series has three media keys at the top. Starting from left, they are

- ✔ **Backward:** This is the standard two arrow keys pointing to the left, which you can use to go back to the previous song or movie in your playlist.
- ✔ **Play/Pause:** Pressing this middle media key launches the Media application. If the list of songs or videos is displayed, pressing this key plays the currently highlighted media file. If a media file is playing, pressing this key pauses the file.
- ✔ **Forward:** This is the standard two arrow keys pointing to the right. Press this key to go to the next media file.

Creating a playlist

Sure, you have favorites in your song library. Having a playlist would be nice, right? On your Curve, you can create two types of playlists:

✔ **Standard:** A bare-bones playlist in which you manually add the music you want.

✔ **Automatic:** You can specify a combination by Artists, by Album, by Genres, or any combination thereof.

To create a playlist, follow these steps:

1. **From the Music screen, select Playlists.**

   To get to the Music screen, select Music in Media or from the Home screen.

2. **Select [New Playlist].**

3. **Select Standard Playlist or Automatic Playlist.**

   The screen that follows allows you to enter the name of your playlist and either

   • Add songs you select (Standard Playlist).

   • Specify your playlist criteria (Automatic Playlist).

   Skip to Step 5 if you selected Automatic Playlist.

4. **If you select Standard Playlist, do the following:**

   a. **Press the menu key and then select Add Songs.**

      Your music library listing appears.

   b. **Scroll to your music list, and select the song you want to add to your playlist.**

      You return to the preceding screen, with the selected song added to your playlist. Repeat this step for each song you want to add.

   c. **After you've added all the songs you want in Standard Playlist, press the menu key and select Save.**

      You're finished!

5. **If you select Automatic Playlist, do the following:**

   a. **Select the + button to the right of the music type criteria, and select one of the listed combinations.**

      Again, you can choose by Artist, by Albums, by Genres, or a combination of any of the three options. If you choose by Artist, you'll be presented with the list of artists; the same is true for by Albums, where a list of albums will be shown for you to select.

   b. **Repeat Step 5a to add more values to your criteria.**

   c. **After you add all the criteria you want in Automatic Playlist, press the menu key and select Save.**

      You're finished!

From time to time, you may have played a song and happened to like it. Want to add it to your playlist? No problem. While you're playing the song, simply press the menu key and select Add to Playlist. Then select the playlist you want that song added to from the screen that follows.

Playing from your playlist

Playing your playlist is a no-brainer:

1. **From the Music screen, select Playlists.**

   To get to the Music screen, select Music in Media or from the Home screen.

2. **Scroll to highlight the playlist you want to start playing.**

3. **Press the menu key and then select Play.**

Now showing

Playing or recording a video is similar to playing music:

1. **From the Media screen, select Video.**

   You can launch Media by selecting the Media icon from the Home screen. The screen shows Video Camera, and a list of video files appears at the bottom. If you want to watch a video, skip to Step 5.

2. **To start video recording, select Video Camera.**

   A screen shows the image in front of the camera.

3. **Select the screen again to start recording.**

   Don't wait for "Cut!" You can pause the camera by pressing the trackball or trackpad. The familiar video and audio controls appear. From left to right, they are Continue Recording, Stop, and Play. The other buttons are Rename (for renaming the filename), Delete, and Send via e-Mail.

4. **Select the Stop button when you're ready to wrap up your home video.**

   You wind up at the previous screen ,with the video clip file listed. We know you're itching to watch it.

5. **Select the file to play it onscreen.**

Lord of the ring tones

Ah, the proliferation of ring tones. Nothing beats hearing a loud funky ring tone while you're sleeping on a bus or a train. You can wake other passengers, too, whether you want to use the Top 40, old-fashioned digital beats, or something you recorded.

To hear ring tones that come with your BlackBerry, do the following:

1. **From the Media screen, select Ring Tones.**

   You see three views: All Ring Tones, My Ring Tones, and Preloaded Ring Tones.

2. **Select Preloaded Ring Tones.**

   The preloaded ring tones are displayed.

3. **Select any one of them, and enjoy.**

   While playing a ring tone, select the right arrow to go to the next tone; select the left arrow to go the preceding one.

4. **Choose a ring tone you like.**

5. **Press the menu key, and select Set as Ring Tone.**

   That ring tone is what plays when your phone rings.

A ring tone is similar to a music file and includes many of the same music formats:

- **ACC:** Advanced Auto Coding format, used by iTunes

- **AMR:** Adaptive Multi-Rate, a popular audio format for mobile transmission and mobile applications

- **M4A:** A subset of ACC for audio only

- **MIDI:** Musical Instrument Digital Interface, a popular audio format for musical instruments

- **MP3:** MPEG Audio Layer 3, the most popular music format

- **WMA:** Windows Media Audio, a Microsoft audio file format

If you're familiar with any audio-editing software, you can make your own ring tones. Save the file in one of the formats in the preceding list and copy it to your Curve. You can also find many free ring tones on the Internet. The only possible harm from downloading one is being annoyed with how it sounds. The Browser default Home page (`http://mobile.blackberry.com`) has links to sources of ring tones as well. See the Fun and Pages link on the Home page.

Picture this

If you upgraded from an older BlackBerry, you may already know about Pictures, which you use to view, zoom into, and rotate pictures:

1. **From the Media screen, select Pictures.**

   Your options are similar to those for other Media applications.

2. **Navigate to the view you want.**

3. **Find the picture you're looking for.**

4. **Select the file.**

   Pretty easy, right? At this point, your photo file is displayed in the screen.

Check out Sample Pictures. Your BlackBerry comes with a collection of pictures that you can use as your Home screen background. Or assign one of the cartoons to a contact as a Caller ID until you get a chance to take the person's picture and use that instead. (We describe how to do that in Chapter 13.)

Your Curve supports the following standard picture formats:

- ✔ **BMP:** Bitmap file format (.bmp)

- ✔ **JPEG:** Developed by the Joint Photographic Experts Group committee (.jpg); typically compresses the image file to a tenth of its size with little perceptible loss of image quality

- ✔ **PNG:** Portable Network Graphics (.png), which is a bitmapped image format that employs a lossless data transmission

- ✔ **TIFF:** Tagged Image File Format (.tif), which is mostly used in scanners and is under the control of Adobe Systems

- ✔ **WBMP:** Wireless Bitmap (.wbmp) file format, which is optimized for mobile devices

View in Pictures

When you're in Pictures and navigating in a folder, the default view is always showing thumbnails. This allows you to quickly view many pictures at the same time before deciding which one to open.

Want to view all of them? Run a slide show. Press the menu key and select View Slide Show.

A convenient way to view pictures in OS 5.0 is to slide the trackball or trackpad sideways. Scrolling right transitions the view to the next picture, and you'll see a smooth sideways movement of the picture in the screen. Scrolling left transitions in the opposite direction until the preceding picture is displayed.

Zoom to details

To zoom in a photo, open it, press the trackball or trackpad, and then select Zoom. A tiny unobtrusive slider bar appears on the left side of the image. Now use your trackball or trackpad: Sliding up zooms in, and sliding down zooms out.

Rotating a photo

Want to view yourself upside down? Maybe not. But sometimes your pictures look better when viewed horizontally. If your Curve runs OS 4.6, you can rotate an image on the screen while you view it in Pictures: Just press the trackball or trackpad and select Rotate. The image rotates 90 degrees clockwise. By repeating the same steps, you can keep rotating it; each press is an additional 90-degree clockwise rotation. The Rotate feature isn't available in OS 5.0.

While you're scrolling, the slider bar indicates the degree of zoom. The exact center of this bar is the original image (no zooming applied). You can easily go back to the original zoom size by pressing the menu key and selecting Zoom All.

An image normally defaults to fit the screen, but you can toggle it by pressing the menu key and selecting one of these options:

✔ Fit to Screen

✔ View Actual Size

Pressing the trackball or trackpad while a picture is displayed is equivalent to zooming in 5.0. Once zoomed in, you can zoom out by pressing the escape key.

Record your voice

A feature-packed smartphone like your Curve *should* come with a voice recorder, and it does. Within Media, you can find Voice Notes, a neat recording application. Now you can record your billion-dollar ideas:

1. **Select Voice Notes (that little microphone icon) from the Media screen.**

   The Voice Notes application launches, sporting the simple and clean screen shown in Figure 14-4. At the top of the screen is a Record button, and the bottom part lists your previous recordings.

2. **Select Record.**

3. **Press the trackball or trackpad.**

   Your BlackBerry's microphone is designed to be close to your mouth, like any mobile phone's mic should be.

You can pause any time you want by pressing the Pause button. Familiar video/audio controls appear. From left to right, they are Continue Recording, Stop, and Play. Other buttons are Rename (for renaming the file), Delete, and Send via E-Mail.

4. **Press the trackball or trackpad and then select the Stop button to wrap it up.**

   You return to the preceding screen. Your recent voice recording appears in the list.

5. **Select the voice recording to play it.**

Voice Notes

Record

Find:

* No Voice Notes *

Figure 14-4:
Record your
voice here.

Viewing and Controlling Media Files

The previous sections show what types of files you can record or play on your BlackBerry. The following sections give you the lowdown on controlling those files when you're playing or viewing them.

Turning it up (or down)

Whether you're listening to music or watching a video, adjusting the volume is easy.

Your Curve comes with dedicated volume buttons on the upper-right side of the device. The top button (with the plus sign) turns up the volume, and the button below (with the minus sign) turns down the volume. The onscreen volume slider reflects anything you did with the volume buttons.

Media shortcuts

Taking the time to master the following short-cuts now will pay you back in time later. Here are the must-know Media shortcuts:

✔ **Mute:** Toggle between pausing and playing music and video. (The key is located at the upper right of the device and has a muted-speaker label.)

✔ **6:** Move to the next item.

✔ **4:** Move to the preceding item.

✔ **3:** Zoom in on a picture.

✔ **9:** Zoom out on a picture.

✔ **5:** Zoom back to the original picture size.

✔ **, (comma):** Rotate a picture counterclockwise.

✔ **Space:** Toggle between pausing and resuming a slide show.

Navigating the menu

Almost all Media applications have a common menu, with the exception of Pictures. The menu items are mostly self-explanatory, but the following sections quickly highlights what you'll see.

Navigating the Pictures menu

You can easily jump to the next item in the list. Press the menu key while you are viewing an image. In the menu that appears, you see the following items:

✔ **Next:** Jumps to the next item in the list. This item appears only if there's an item after this image file in the current folder.

✔ **Previous:** Jumps to the preceding item. This item appears only if there's a previous item in the current folder.

✔ **Delete:** Deletes the image file.

✔ **Move:** Moves the file to a different folder.

✔ **Rename:** Renames the image file.

✔ **Properties:** Displays a screen that shows the location of the image file, its size, and the time it was last modified.

Navigating the Music, Videos, Ring Tones, and Voice Notes menu

Whether you are watching a video, playing music, hearing a ring tone, or listening to a voice note, you see the following after pressing the menu key:

✔ **Replay:** Plays the media file again from the start.

✔ **Repeat:** Plays the same media after it reaches the end.

✔ **Show Playlist:** Displays the list of media files on the current folder or playlist.

✔ **Activate Handset:** Mutes the device's speaker. Use this if you want to use the earpiece. This menu item appears only if you have activated the speakerphone.

✔ **Activate Speakerphone:** Uses the device's speaker and mutes the earpiece. This menu item appears only if the handset is activated.

Using Explore

You can navigate to your media file in many ways, but Explore is probably the quickest way to find a file. It's easy to use because it has some similarities to Windows Explorer, and it also has a search facility similar to Find in other BlackBerry applications such as Contacts, MemoPad, and Tasks.

To launch Explore, simply select Media from the Home screen, press the menu key, and select Explore. The Explore screen starts with the device root folders: Media Card, Device Memory, and System.

Folders are in a tree hierarchy. You can get into the child folders (subfolders) by selecting from the parent folder, starting from one of the root folders.

If you've set a property of a picture to hidden, Explore is the only place in your Curve through which you'll be able to locate the file again:

1. **Navigate to the folder where your picture file is located.**

2. **Press the menu key and select Show Hidden.**

The default location for pictures taken by Camera is either `/Device Memory/home/user/pictures` or `/Media Card/BlackBerry/pictures`.

Changing the media flavor

Like the rest of your BlackBerry applications, you can customize Media:

1. **From the Media screen, press the menu key.**

2. **Select Options.**

    The screen looks like the one shown in Figure 14-5. Each media customization option is described in the following sections.

Media Options
Pictures
Sort By: Most Recent
Thumbnails Per Row: 4
Slide Show Interval: 2 sec

Exclude Folders

Figure 14-5:
The Media
Options
screen.

Media
Turn Off Auto Backlighting: Yes
Audio Boost: Off
Headset Equalizer: Off

Customizing pictures

You can change the Pictures application in the following ways:

- ✔ **Sort By:** Toggle file sorting based on recent updates or name.

- ✔ **Thumbnails per Row:** When your files appear as a grid of *thumbnails* (small versions of your photos), this number of thumbnails is displayed per row. The higher the number, the smaller the thumbnails.

- ✔ **Slide Show Interval:** When you're viewing your files in a slide show, a picture appears for this many seconds before moving to the next picture.

- ✔ **Exclude Folders:** Use this option when you don't want to display any pictures inside a particular folder. This makes it faster to load the list of pictures. (The fewer pictures you have, the faster the Pictures application can load the list.) This option isn't for your secret folders.

- ✔ **Set Convenience Keys:** A button available only in OS 5.0 allows you to change the settings for the right and left convenience keys, which are shortcut keys to an application. The defaults are for the right-side key to launch Camera and the left-side key to launch Voice Dialing.

Customizing media

You can finesse the rest of Media as follows:

- ✔ **Auto Stop Media Player When Idle:** You can set this to Off (the default), 5, 10, 20, 30, or 45 minutes. This can save you battery life if you get distracted and leave your Curve on a table playing video.

✔ **Turn Off Auto Backlighting:** The *backlighting* feature provides additional screen lighting when Curve detects that you need it. You'll notice it when you move your Curve from shade to direct sunlight. We find it bothersome when watching a movie. For that reason — and to extend battery life — toggle it Off here.

✔ **Audio Boost:** Allows you to increase the volume beyond the normal level. The default setting is Off. If you set it On, it gives you a fair warning about possible ear discomfort when you're using headphones.

✔ **Headset Equalizer:** The default is Off, but if you want to have a different audio setting, you have several options: Bass Boost, Bass Lower, Dance, Hip Hop, Jazz, Lounge, Loud, R&B, Rock, Treble Boost, Treble Lower, and Vocal Boost.

Chapter 15

Managing Media Files

*T*he ways that you can get your hands on media constantly evolve. Ten years ago, who would have thought that you could buy music from a tiny card or from an "all you can download" monthly subscription?

Someday, you'll wake up with a technology that doesn't require you to constantly copy media files to your handheld music player. But for now, enjoying music while on the move means managing these files.

Media, the BlackBerry application on your Curve, is a great music player, but without music files, it's as useless as a guitar without strings. And to satisfy your quest for mobile media satisfaction, this chapter gives you good information on ways to manage your media files.

This chapter is for PC users. BlackBerry Desktop Manager for Mac is not yet released at the time of writing, so it will not be covered in this chapter.

Working with Media Files

To acquire media files for your BlackBerry Curve, there are as many choices as there are ice cream flavors. The succeeding sections describe the most common ways.

Using your Curve as a flash drive

The most common way of manipulating media files into and out of your Curve is to attach it to a PC and use Windows Explorer:

1. **Connect your BlackBerry to your PC, using the USB cable that came with your Curve.**

   Only folders and files stored on the microSD will be visible to your PC. Make sure to have the microSD card in your BlackBerry Curve before you connect your Curve to the PC.

   When connected, the Curve screen displays a prompt for enabling mass storage mode.

2. **On the Curve screen, select Yes.**

   A screen appears on your Curve, asking for your password.

3. **On the Curve screen, type your BlackBerry password.**

   The device is now ready to behave like an ordinary flash drive. On your PC, the Removable Disk dialog box opens.

4. **On your PC, in the Removable Disk dialog box, click Open Folder to View Files and then click OK.**

   This opens the familiar Windows Explorer screen.

5. **Manipulate your media files as you want.**

   You can do anything you typically do with a normal Windows folder, such as drag and drop, copy, and delete files.

6. **Close Windows Explorer when you're finished.**

Meet and greet BlackBerry Desktop Media Manager

Roxio is known for its CD-ripping software. (*Ripping* converts music files in CD format to other popular compressed formats.) RIM licensed a portion of Roxio and packaged it with BlackBerry Desktop Software. Even though this version doesn't offer the entire Roxio software suite, you can still take advantage of fantastic features, such as

- ✔ Ripping CDs
- ✔ Converting files to get the best playback on your Curve
- ✔ Managing music files
- ✔ Syncing media files to your device

If you have an old version of Media Manager, just point your desktop Internet browser to `http://na.blackberry.com/eng/services/desktop` for directions on downloading the latest version for free and installing it on your PC.

In the following sections, we show you the Media Manager interface and how to copy a video file onto your Curve.

Accessing Media Manager

You can access Media Manager through BlackBerry Desktop Manager, which Chapter 16 describes in detail. Get to Desktop Manager this way:

1. **On your PC, click the Windows Start button.**

2. **Choose All Programs⇨BlackBerry⇨Desktop Manager.**

   BlackBerry Desktop Manager appears, as shown in Figure 15-1.

Figure 15-1:
Access
Media
Manager
here.

3. **Click the Media icon.**

   A screen appears, showing Media Manager and BlackBerry Media Sync sections. Each section has a Start button.

4. **In the Media Manager section, click the Start button.**

   The initial Media Manager screen is well organized and gives you the following options:

   - Manage Pictures
   - Manage Music
   - Manage Videos
   - View Connected Devices

5. **Click one of the options.**

Other features of Media Manager

Spend some time exploring Media Manager. It has interesting features you may find useful. Here's a quick rundown of what you can do with Media Manager:

✔ Import media files

✔ E-mail media files

✔ Enhance photos and apply special effects to photos by using PhotoSuite

✔ Set song info (such as title, artist, album, genre, year, or an image) to show as track art when playing a song

✔ Record audio

✔ Customize photo printing

The Media Manager screen (shown in Figure 15-2) is easy to use, plus it has the same interface as Windows Explorer:

✔ The left side is where you navigate to your folders and files.

✔ The right side displays the files in the folder you selected from the left side.

Figure 15-2: View your media files on this screen.

The top section looks the same as the bottom section. The top half — My Media — represents your desktop; the bottom — My Devices — represents your Curve. You can move or copy files easily. When you're copying, for example, one section can be the source, and the other section, the destination. By simply dragging the files between the two sections, you can copy on the same screen. Neat, right?

Importing media files to Media Manager

Here's a quick and easy way to import media files:

1. **In Windows Explorer, navigate to find the media files you want.**

2. **Drag and drop the files into Media Manager.**

You can drag and drop files to the folder in the left part of the screen (where the folder tree appears) or to the right part (where the files are listed). Just make sure that when you're doing the latter, the current folder in the tree view is the folder where you want the media files to be imported.

You can also use Media Manager to locate the files you want without going through Windows Explorer. The trick is to change the view to Folders. Check out the two tabs at the upper left. The first tab, My Media, is the default view. The Folders tab, just to the right of My Media, bears an icon of (go figure) a folder.

Click the Folders tab. You see a tree view, but this time, it looks exactly like you see it in Windows Explorer, as shown in Figure 15-3. The files can be on your local hard drive or in a network folder accessible by your desktop computer.

Figure 15-3:
Navigate to your desktop media files here.

Not all media file types are directly compatible with your Curve. This is especially true for video files. But Media Manager can convert most media files to a usable Curve format.

Adding a media file to your Curve

Time to copy files to your Curve. Here's the rundown:

1. **Connect your Curve to your PC, using the USB cable that came with your BlackBerry.**

2. **On the Media Manager screen, drag and drop your media files from the My Media view to any folder in My Devices.**

   You can drag and drop an entire album. After dropping a media file, you're prompted to convert the file to a format that's usable by your Curve, as shown in Figure 15-4.

Figure 15-4: Choose to convert your media files for optimum playback.

3. **Select a conversion option:**

   • Convert for Optimal Playback: This is the safest bet and is the default. This option is applicable to video files where the converter makes sure that the video fits perfectly with Curve's screen resolution.

   • Copy with No Conversion: Copies the file faster. The file is copied to your Curve as is, but it might not play on your Curve.

   • Advanced Conversion Options: From here, another screen lets you downgrade the quality to minimize the file size. It also allows you to crop video so that the entire screen is filled instead of seeing dark margins.

4. **Click OK to begin the transfer.**

Synchronizing with iTunes using BlackBerry Media Sync

If you have an iPod, you're probably using iTunes and maintaining a playlist and perhaps a subscription to podcasts or videocasts. Podcast files are downloaded to iTunes using RSS. (*RSS* — Really Simple Syndication — is a kind of digital file publish–subscribe mechanism. This is the mechanism iTunes uses to receive audio and video recordings, which most people refer to as *podcasts* and *videocasts,* respectively.)

To sync your Curve with iTunes, follow these quick and easy steps:

1. **Click the Windows Start button.**

2. **Choose All Programs⇨BlackBerry⇨Desktop Manager.**

3. **When BlackBerry Desktop Manager appears (refer to Figure 15-1), click the Media icon.**

   A screen appears, showing Media Manager and BlackBerry Media Sync sections. Each section has a Start button.

4. **In the BlackBerry Media Sync section, click the Start button.**

   In the dialog box that appears (such as the one shown in Figure 15-5), click the double-chevron icon in the lower left of the window to display options for the section of iTunes you want to synchronize.

Figure 15-5:
The
BlackBerry
Media Sync
screen.

5. **Click the Show iTunes Playlist icon (lower left).**

   A selection of what you have in iTunes appears, as shown in Figure 15-6. This is the part of the screen where you choose iTunes media file types.

6. **Select the iTunes media you want copied to your Curve.**

7. **Click the Sync button.**

   There you go. You see a progress bar showing the synchronization of the media files from iTunes.

Downloading sounds

RIM offer a Web site from which you can sample and download new ring tones, alarms, notifiers, and tunes. On your Curve, simply go to `http://mobile.blackberry.com`.

On this page, scroll down to the Personalize section, and click the Ringtones link. A list of available ring tones will be displayed. And did we mention that they're free?

Figure 15-6:
Choose
your iTunes
media here.

Clicking the ring tone link gives you an option to either play it or download to your Curve. Downloaded ring tones are filed in the My Ring Tones section when you open the Ring Tones inside the Media application.

RIM isn't the only site where you can find ring tones. The Web is a treasure trove, and ring tones and other media files are safe to download, so go hunting.

And the best place to find BlackBerry-related software — including ring tones — is to visit the ever-growing BlackBerry community on the Web. Check out `http://crackberry.com`, `http://blackberrycool.com`, and `http://blackberryreview.com`, to name a few.

Part V

Working with BlackBerry Desktop Manager

The 5th Wave — By Rich Tennant

"Russell! Do you remember last month when I told you to order 150 SMART phones for the sales department?"

In this part . . .

Here you discover essential information about some behind-the-scenes-yet-integral processes. Read all about BlackBerry Desktop Manager, which you direct to monitor and control database synchronization (Chapter 16). You'll also find out how to leverage Switch Device Wizard to migrate your existing data to your new BlackBerry Curve (Chapter 17). Find out how to back up your data (Chapter 18). And finally, discover the many ways of installing third-party applications (Chapter 19).

Chapter 16

Syncing the Synchronize Way

*W*hat better way to keep your BlackBerry Curve updated than to synchronize it with your desktop application's data?

Arguably, most of the data you need to synchronize is from your personal information manager (PIM) applications: notes, appointments, addresses, and tasks. The crucial piece for data synchronization to and from your device and desktop computer is Synchronize. This software within BlackBerry Desktop Manager allows you to synchronize your PIM data as well as upload and download media files between your PC and your Curve.

In this chapter, you explore Synchronize and see how to manually and automatically synchronize your Curve with your desktop computer. You find tips about which options you may want to use. Before all that, however, is a section on BlackBerry Desktop Manager.

If you're a Mac user, good news! The folks at Research In Motion have finally rolled out a Mac version of BlackBerry Desktop Manager. You no longer have to use PocketMac, which is way behind on features and capabilities compared to its Windows cousin BlackBerry Desktop Manager. In this book, we focus mainly on the PC version of BlackBerry Desktop Manager, but we also show screenshots of the Mac version of the application in different areas to let you Mac users out there know that you can do the same tasks in the Mac BlackBerry Desktop Manager.

If you're using a corporate BlackBerry Curve that's running under BlackBerry Enterprise Server, you can skip this chapter. BlackBerry smartphones running under BlackBerry Enterprise Server synchronize over the air (OTA), via serial bypass, or wirelessly.

Meeting BlackBerry Desktop Manager

The centerpiece of your desktop activities — such as data synchronization, switching smartphones, and data backup on the BlackBerry — is *BlackBerry Desktop Manager*, which is a suite of programs that includes the following:

- ✔ **Application Loader:** Installs BlackBerry applications and updates the BlackBerry OS.

- ✔ **Backup and Restore:** Backs up your Curve data and settings. Check out Chapter 18 for details.

- ✔ **Synchronize:** Synchronizes Curve data with your PC (um, the topic of this chapter).

- ✔ **Media Manager:** Uploads media files to your Curve from your PC and vice versa (another topic in this chapter).

- ✔ **Device Switch Wizard:** Helps you transfer data from your existing mobile device to your Curve. See Chapter 17 for details.

BlackBerry Desktop Manager is software loaded on the CD that comes with your Curve. Your Curve's packaging provides instructions on how to install BlackBerry Desktop Manager on your desktop computer. For corporate users, check with your BlackBerry system administrator for more details.

Installing BlackBerry Desktop Manager and Desktop Redirector

As we mention, use the CD that comes with your Curve to install BlackBerry Desktop Manager on your computer. At the same time, you can also install Desktop Redirector. (Read more about this in Chapter 8.) Desktop Redirector allows you to redirect e-mail that you receive in Outlook. This means that even if you get e-mails through Outlook (such as work e-mails), you can have those e-mails redirected to your Curve.

Only e-mails from mailboxes connected to your Outlook mailbox are redirected. Your PC and the redirector must run all the time to keep redirection active.

When you insert the CD, the installation wizard runs automatically. Follow the onscreen instructions. On one of the wizard screens, you choose whether this installation is for personal or work e-mail. Choosing the option for work e-mail enables you to use Desktop Redirector for both personal and work e-mail.

If you aren't using a corporate BlackBerry Enterprise Server, and you want to redirect your Outlook e-mail to your Curve, when you're installing BlackBerry Desktop Manager, make sure that you select the Redirect Messages Using the BlackBerry Desktop Redirector option on the installation screen, as shown in Figure 16-1.

Figure 16-1:
Configure the BlackBerry Desktop Manager installation to include Desktop Redirector.

If your Curve is running under a corporate BlackBerry Enterprise Server, your e-mail is already redirected to your smartphone wirelessly, and choosing the BlackBerry Desktop Redirector could really mess things up. So don't do it! Most companies are protective of corporate data, including your work e-mails. Make sure you aren't violating your company's policy before you decide to redirect your work e-mails to your personal BlackBerry.

Launching BlackBerry Desktop Manager

In most Windows installations, you find the shortcut to launch BlackBerry Desktop Manager through your computer's Start menu. Follow these steps to launch BlackBerry Desktop Manager:

1. **Choose Start⇨All Programs⇨BlackBerry⇨Desktop Manager.**

2. **Connect your Curve to your computer, using the USB cable that came with your device.**

   With the microSD card in your Curve, upon connecting to your PC, your Curve screen displays a prompt for enabling mass storage mode. It also asks for your Curve's password when you answer Yes to the prompt. Upon answering Yes and entering your password, your Curve will behave like a flash drive. A drive letter will be added to My Computer (or just plain Computer in Microsoft Vista) in Windows Explorer, allowing you to treat the microSD card as a normal flash drive.

3. **Launch BlackBerry Desktop Manager.**

The BlackBerry Desktop Manager opening screen appears (see Figures 16-2 and 16-3).

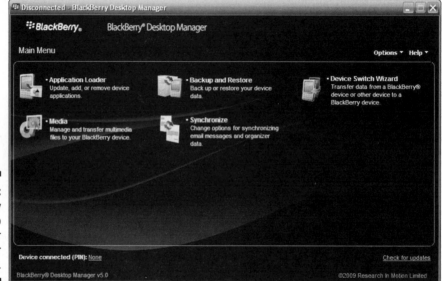

Figure 16-2:
BlackBerry
Desktop
Manager
under
Windows.

Figure 16-3:
BlackBerry
Desktop
Manager on
the Mac.

BlackBerry Desktop Manager installation can vary from phone provider to provider. You should see at least the following four icons, or applications:

✔ Application Loader (see Chapter 19)

✔ Backup and Restore (see Chapter 18)

✔ Media (see Chapter 15)

✔ Synchronize

Connecting BlackBerry Desktop Manager to your Curve

You establish a connection between your Curve and BlackBerry Desktop Manager through the USB cable. After BlackBerry Desktop Manager is running, it tries to find a BlackBerry (your Curve) on the type of connection specified. The default connection is USB, so you shouldn't need to configure anything.

Follow these steps to connect your Curve to BlackBerry Desktop Manager:

1. **Plug in your device to your desktop.**

   Keep your device on.

2. **Launch BlackBerry Desktop Manager.**

   BlackBerry Desktop Manager tries to find a BlackBerry (your Curve) on a USB connection.

3. **If your device has a password, BlackBerry Desktop Manager prompts you for the password.**

4. **Enter the password.**

   You see Connected as the screen heading. If, for some reason, you see Disconnected and no password prompt, one of the following is happening:

   • BlackBerry Desktop Manager can't find the device being connected via the USB cable. Make sure that the USB cable is properly attached at both ends.

   • The connection setting isn't set to use USB. To check this connectivity setting, go to Step 5.

5. **Choose Options⇨Connection Options on the right side of the BlackBerry Desktop Manager screen.**

   The screen shown in Figure 16-4 appears. Make sure that the connection setting uses USB.

6. In the Connection Type drop-down list, select the USB connection with your Curve's PIN.

Figure 16-4:
Possible
connec-
tion types
for your
BlackBerry
Curve.

Running BlackBerry Desktop Manager for the first time

If you're running BlackBerry Desktop Manager for the first time, the program does the following:

- Tries to make the initial configuration on your machine, which includes security encryption setup. It asks you to randomly move your mouse to generate security encryption keys.

- Checks which applications are on your device and which required applications need to be installed. If it can't find a required application on your device, it prompts you to install it. Of course, you have the option to cancel and install later.

- Looks at the settings you have for your Synchronize software. If auto-synchronization is turned on, BlackBerry Desktop Manager attempts to run synchronization for your PIM. This is discussed in the section "Synchronizing automatically," later in this chapter.

Setting Up Synchronize

Synchronize is the part of BlackBerry Desktop Manager that allows you to synchronize your data between your desktop computer and your Curve. (If your Curve is running on BlackBerry Enterprise Server, your data is already synced wirelessly, so you don't need your desktop for synchronization.) Synchronize is an icon on the BlackBerry Desktop Manager screen with two opposing arrows on top of two paper images. To launch Synchronize, simply double-click its icon. A screen like the one shown in Figure 16-5 appears.

Figure 16-5:
The
Synchronize
screen.

The Synchronize screen is divided into two sections. You can navigate through the links on the left:

- ✓ **Synchronize,** the default view, allows you to manually trigger synchronization (refer to Figure 16-5). See the "Using on-demand synchronization" and "Synchronizing Automatically" sections, later in this chapter, for more details and for when you use this screen.

- ✓ **Configuration** is where you can set up configuration and rules for reconciling data. Under the Configuration link are two subsections, Synchronization and Add-ins. These further help you organize the interface (see Figure 16-6). The first thing you need to work with is the Synchronization Configuration screen. The following section helps you do that.

Configuring PIM synchronization

The important item in the Synchronization Configuration subsection, as shown in Figure 16-6, is the Synchronization button. You use that button to configure PIM synchronization.

Click the Synchronization button to display the screen shown in Figure 16-7. You can see that the names correspond to the BlackBerry Curve applications, except for Contacts, which goes by the name Address Book. This screen is the entry point of the entire synchronization configuration for PIM applications. Selecting an application on this screen allows you to pair the PIM handheld application to a desktop application (most likely Outlook).

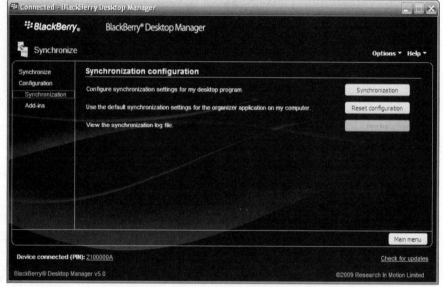

Figure 16-6:
The
Synchroni-
zation
Configura-
tion screen.

Figure 16-7:
The PIM
configura-
tion screen.

From the PIM configuration screen, select which application data you want to sync with your Curve. The following popular PIM applications can be synced to your Curve: ACT!, ASCII Text File Converter, Lotus Notes, Lotus Organizer, Microsoft Outlook, Microsoft Outlook Express, and Microsoft Schedule.

The types of application data that can be synchronized to your Curve are

✔ **Calendar:** Synchronize your appointments and events stored in your favorite PIM application.

✔ **MemoPad:** Synchronize any notes or text that you have been storing in your PIM application.

✔ **Address Book:** Synchronize any contact information with your Curve.

✔ **Tasks:** Synchronize your to-do list.

Follow these steps to set up your device's synchronization:

1. **Connect your Curve to BlackBerry Desktop Manager.**

2. **Click the Synchronize icon.**

3. **Click the Synchronization link.**

   (The link is below the Configuration link on the left side of the screen; refer to Figure 16-6.) In the Synchronization Configuration section is the Configure Synchronization Settings for My Desktop Program label.

4. **Click the Synchronization button.**

5. **Select the check box next to an application data type (Calendar, MemoPad, Address Book, or Tasks) that you want to synchronize.**

   For example, we selected the Calendar application data type.

6. **Click the Setup button.**

   This opens the Calendar Setup screen.

7. **Select a PIM application from which to retrieve application data by clicking your desired application.**

   BlackBerry Desktop Manager pulls your selected application data from the application selected from this screen. In Figure 16-8, we selected Microsoft Outlook. This means that when we synchronize the Curve, BlackBerry Desktop Manager retrieves Calendar data from Microsoft Outlook.

8. **Click Next.**

9. **On the Synchronization Options screen that opens, select which direction the synchronization will follow (see Figures 16-9 and 16-10).**

   Here are the three available synchronization options:

   • Two Way Sync allows you to synchronize changes in both your Curve and in your desktop application.

- One Way Sync from Device synchronizes only the changes made to your Curve. Changes to your desktop application aren't reflected in your Curve.

- One Way Sync to Device synchronizes changes made in your desktop application with your Curve. Any changes made in your Curve aren't reflected in your desktop application.

Figure 16-8: Choose the desktop application here.

Figure 16-9: Decide which direction synchronization follows (under Windows).

10. Click Next.

The Options screen opens for the PIM application you selected in Step 7. Figure 16-11 shows the Microsoft Outlook Options screen.

Figure 16-10: Decide which direction synchro- nization follows (on the Mac).

Figure 16-11: Select specific application settings here.

For synchronization to Microsoft Outlook, make sure that you select the correct user profile in the Outlook User Profile drop-down list. This is particularly pertinent in cases in which you have multiple user profiles in your computer. Choosing the wrong one may result in putting the wrong data into your Curve.

The amount of data that is reconciled or synchronized in a given application can also be controlled. For example, as shown in Figure 16-11, the center portion of the configuration allows you to specify whether to transfer all Calendar items, transfer just a set of appointments in the future, or transfer items within a range of dates you enter.

Select the Remove Alarm for Past Items check box if you don't want to keep the alarm setting for events that have already occurred.

11. Click Next and then click Finish.

Clicking the Next button brings you to the Calendar Setup Finish screen, and clicking the Finish button completes configuring the Calendar synchronization you selected.

Mapping fields for synchronization

For all four PIM applications, Synchronize is intelligent enough to know what information — such as names, phone numbers, and addresses in Contacts — corresponds to Outlook. A specific bit of information, or attribute, is a *field*. For instance, the value of a home phone number field in Contacts needs to be mapped to the corresponding field in Outlook so that information is transferred correctly.

But not all fields on the desktop side exist on the handheld (and vice versa). For example, a Nick Name field doesn't exist in Curve Contacts but is available in Exchange (Outlook) Address Book. In some instances, Synchronize provides an alternative field and lets you decide whether to map it.

If you ever need to change the default mapping, you can. The interface is the same for all PIM applications. To illustrate how to map and unmap fields, we use Contacts in the following steps :

1. From BlackBerry Desktop Manager, click the Synchronize link.

The Synchronize screen appears.

2. Click the Synchronization link.

3. Click the Synchronize button.

The PIM configuration screen appears (refer to Figure 16-7).

4. **Select the Address Book check box.**

   The Advanced button is enabled.

5. **Click the Advanced button.**

   The Advanced screen opens, as shown in Figure 16-12.

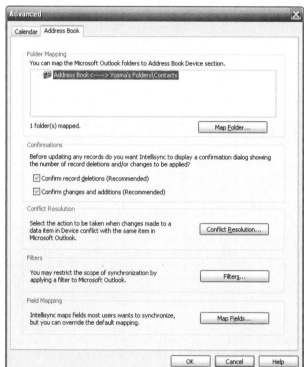

6. **Click the Map Fields button.**

   The Map Fields screen for the Address Book/Contacts application appears (see Figure 16-13). To map or unmap, click the arrow icons.

   If you aren't careful, you can inadvertently unclick a mapping (such as Job Title), and suddenly your titles aren't in sync. Double-check your mapping before you click OK. If you think you made a mistake, click Cancel to save yourself from having to restore settings.

7. **Click OK to save your changes.**

Figure 16-13:
The Map
Fields
screen for
Address
Book.

Confirming record changes

Face facts: Doing a desktop synchronization isn't a very interesting task, and few people perform it on a regular basis.

You can tell Synchronize to prompt you for any changes it's trying to make (or perhaps undo) on either side of the fence. The Advanced screen comes into picture here. To get to this view, follow these steps:

1. **From BlackBerry Desktop Manager, click the Synchronize link.**

   The Synchronize screen appears.

2. **Click the Synchronization link.**

3. **Click the Synchronize button.**

   The PIM configuration screen appears (refer to Figure 16-7).

4. **Select the Address Book check box.**

   If you want a PIM application other than Address Book, select that application from the list.

5. **Click the Advanced button.**

   The Advanced screen for Address Book appears (refer to Figure 16-12). This screen has a Confirmations section and gives you two options:

   • Confirm Record Deletions (Recommended)

   • Confirm Changes and Additions (Recommended)

Regardless of whether you select the first option, Synchronize displays a prompt if it detects that it's about to delete *all* records.

Resolving update conflicts

Synchronize needs to know how you want to handle any conflicts between your Curve and your desktop application. A conflict normally happens when the same record is updated on your Curve and also in Outlook. For instance, you change Jane Doe's mobile number on both your Curve and PC in Outlook. Where you resolve these conflicts is the same for all PIM applications. Again, for illustration, we use Address Book as an example:

1. **From BlackBerry Desktop Manager, click the Synchronize link.**

   The Synchronize screen appears.

2. **Click the Synchronization link.**

3. **Click the Synchronize button.**

   The PIM configuration screen appears (refer to Figure 16-7).

4. **Select the Address Book check box.**

   If you want a PIM application other than Address Book, select that application from the list.

5. **Click the Advanced button.**

   The Advanced screen for Address Book appears (refer to Figure 16-12). This screen has five sections, and the third section is Conflict Resolution.

6. **Click the Conflict Resolution button.**

   The Conflict Resolution screen is shown in Figure 16-14. From the Conflict Resolution screen, you can tell Synchronize to handle conflicts in a few ways. Here are the options:

   • Add All Conflicting Items: When a conflict happens, adds a new record to the Curve for the changes on the desktop, and adds a new record to the desktop for the changes on the Curve.

   • Ignore All Conflicting Items: Ignores the change and keeps the data the same on both sides.

   • Notify Me When Conflicts Occur: This option is the safest. Synchronize displays the details of the conflict and lets you resolve it.

   • Device Wins: Unless you're sure this is the case, you shouldn't choose this option. It tells Synchronize to disregard the changes in the desktop and use handheld changes every time it encounters a conflict.

   • Microsoft Outlook Wins: If you aren't using MS Outlook, this option is based on your application. This option tells Synchronize to always discard changes on the handheld and use the desktop application change when it encounters a conflict. We don't recommend this option, because there's no telling on which side you made the good update.

Figure 16-14:
Manage
conflicts
here.

7. **Select the option you want.**

8. **Click OK to save the settings.**

Ready, Set, Synchronize!

Are you ready to synchronize? Previously in this chapter, we show you ways to define synchronization filters and rules for your e-mail and PIM data. Now it's time to be brave and click the button. You can synchronize in one of two ways:

✔ **Manually:** Click the Synchronize Now icon.

✔ **Automatically:** Choose How Often on the calendar.

Using on-demand synchronization

On-demand synchronization is a feature in Synchronize that lets you run synchronization manually. Remember that even if you set up automatic synchronization, actual synchronization doesn't happen right away. So if you make updates to your appointments in Outlook while your Curve is connected to your PC, this feature allows you to be sure that your updates make it to your Curve before heading out the door.

Without delay, here are the steps:

1. **From BlackBerry Desktop Manager, click the Synchronize link.**

   The Synchronize screen appears (refer to Figure 16-5). The following four check boxes let you be selective:

   • Reconcile Messages: Synchronize your e-mails between Outlook and your Curve.

- Synchronize Organizer Data: Include notes, appointments, addresses, and tasks.

- Run Add-in Actions: You have third-party applications that require data synchronization between your PC and your Curve.

- Update Device Date and Time: You want both the PC and Curve to have the same time. This ensures that you're reminded of your appointments at the same time for both Outlook and your Curve.

2. **Select the check boxes for the data you want to synchronize.**

3. **Click the Synchronize button.**

   Synchronize starts running the synchronization, and you see a progress screen. If you set up prompts for conflicts, and Synchronize encounters one, a screen appears so that you can resolve that conflict. When finished, the progress screen disappears and the Synchronize screen reappears.

   If you turned on automatic synchronization (see the next section), the items you select in Step 2 automatically sync every time you connect your Curve to your PC.

4. **Click the Close button.**

Synchronizing automatically

How many times do you think you reconfigure your Synchronize setup? Rarely, right? After you have it configured, that's it. And if you're like us, the reason you open BlackBerry Desktop Manager is because you want to run Synchronize. So opening Synchronize and clicking the Synchronize button are somewhat annoying.

To make Synchronize run automatically every time you connect your Curve to your PC, simply make sure that you select the last check box on the Synchronize screen (refer to Figure 16-5) — Synchronize the Selected Items When Your Device Is Connected to the BlackBerry Desktop Manager.

You may be asking, "What items will autosynchronization sync?" Good question. Synchronize automatically syncs the items you selected in the top portion of the Synchronize screen. Note that if you make a change, selecting or deselecting an item on the Synchronize screen, only the selected items will be synced automatically the next time you connect your Curve to your PC.

Chapter 17

Switching Devices

*W*ouldn't it be nice if you could just make one device's data available to another? That's the future. But right now, RIM (Research In Motion) wants to make switching devices as painless as possible. That's why Device Switch Wizard is part of the suite of applications in BlackBerry Desktop Manager.

Device Switch exists in Windows, but we're sure that by the time you read this, a Mac version will be available. We included screenshots of the prerelease version of Device Switch on the Mac, but be aware that the actual release version may differ slightly.

Switching to a New BlackBerry

Switching from an older BlackBerry to your new Curve is no big deal. When you want to transfer application data (e-mails and contacts, for example) to your new Curve, BlackBerry Desktop Manager Device Switch Wizard backs up your old BlackBerry and loads that backup to your new device.

On your PC, the following steps help you transition from your old device to your new BlackBerry Curve:

1. **On your PC, choose Start➪All Programs➪BlackBerry➪Desktop Manager.**

   The Desktop Manager screen opens, where you can find Device Switch Wizard, as shown in Figure 17-1.

2. **Click the Device Switch Wizard icon.**

   The Device Switch Wizard screen lets you choose whether to switch from BlackBerry to BlackBerry Curve or from non-BlackBerry to BlackBerry Curve. The BlackBerry-to-BlackBerry section tells you to connect your current (old) BlackBerry to your PC.

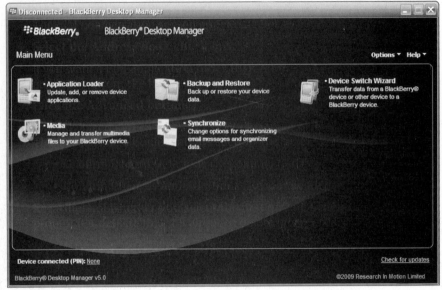

Figure 17-1:
Launch
Device
Switch
Wizard
here.

3. **Connect your old BlackBerry to your PC with the USB cable.**

   Keep your BlackBerry on when connecting.

4. **Click the Start button below Switch BlackBerry Devices.**

   The next screen lets you verify the PINs for both devices — the old BlackBerry on the left and your new Curve on the right, as shown in Figure 17-2. Because you connected only your old BlackBerry, it should be preselected.

    Your BlackBerry PIN isn't a password — it's your BlackBerry smartphone identifier. You can find the PIN by choosing Options⇨Status on your BlackBerry.

5. **Decide whether to include user data and third-party applications and then click Next.**

   If you want all the data, leave the screen untouched; this backs up everything. *Third-party applications* are all the programs you installed — the ones that didn't come with the device originally.

   A status screen appears, showing the progress of the backup operation. When the backup is finished, the next screen prompts you to connect your new BlackBerry Curve.

6. **Connect your BlackBerry Curve to your PC with the USB cable.**

   The next screen, as shown in Figure 17-3, lets you verify that your Curve is connected properly, with your Curve's PIN preselected in the drop-down list. It also asks for the password. Because data is already backed up from the old BlackBerry, the old device is no longer needed on succeeding steps, and it doesn't matter whether you keep the old one connected.

Figure 17-2:
Verify that your old BlackBerry is connected to the PC and decide what data to include here.

Figure 17-3:
Type your device password here.

7. **Enter the password of your Curve and then click OK.**

   A screen similar to Figure 17-4 tells you what will be restored to the new device. Nothing has been done to your new BlackBerry Curve yet, and this is your last chance to cancel the process.

8. **Click Finish.**

   A progress screen shows you the loading process.

9. **When the Success screen appears, click the Close button.**

Figure 17-4:
Confirming
loading
data onto
your new
BlackBerry
Curve.

Figures 17-5 and 17-6 show how to switch your device from an old BlackBerry to your new Curve on a Mac. Again, these screenshots are the prerelease version, so it's possible that the process is a little different on your version. After launching BlackBerry Desktop Manager, you can run Switch Device by going to the Device menu and selecting Switch Device. The screen shown in Figure 17-6 appears with a few options that allow you to move your old BlackBerry data to your new Curve.

Figure 17-5:
On the Mac,
choose
Switch
Device here.

Figure 17-6:
Switch
Device
on a Mac
version of
BlackBerry
Desktop
Manager.

Switch Device

This will allow you to switch the settings and information from this device (%NAME%) to a new device.

All of the data on this device will be copied to your computer. When it has completed, you will be prompted to connect your new device.

Options:

☐ Copy device data and options
☐ Copy third-party applications

☐ Update the software on the new device
☐ Allow me to select the applications to install or update

(Cancel)   (Start)

Switching from a Non-BlackBerry Device

This section is applicable only to Windows. The prerelease version of BlackBerry Desktop Manager on the Mac does not show support for any other devices.

Device Switch Wizard supports two types of non-BlackBerry devices:

- ✔ Palm
- ✔ Microsoft Windows Mobile

This doesn't mean that you can't import your old data if you have another device; Device Switch Wizard just makes it simpler for these two types of devices. Check Chapter 16 for synchronization options for your Desktop PIM application if your old device is neither a Palm nor a Microsoft Windows Mobile device.

Palm device requirements

Your PC and Palm have to meet three prerequisites for Device Switch Wizard to import data from Palm to your BlackBerry Curve:

- ✔ Your PC must be running Windows 2000 or later.
- ✔ One of the following Palm Desktop Software versions must be installed on your desktop: 4.0.1, 4.1, 4.1.4, or 6.0.1.
- ✔ The Palm Desktop software installed is synchronizing properly with the Palm device.

You can check your Palm user guide for more details about your Palm device and synchronizing it to your PC. You can also download the user guide from www.palm.com/us/support/index.hml. Navigate to this page by selecting the Palm model you have and the wireless network provider on which it runs.

Windows Mobile device requirements

You need the following for Device Switch Wizard to work properly with a Windows Mobile device:

✔ Your PC must be running Windows 2000 or later.

✔ Microsoft ActiveSync versions must be installed on your PC.

✔ The mobile device must run one of the following operating systems: Microsoft Windows Mobile 2000, 2002, 2003, 2003SE, or 2005/5.0 for Pocket PC or Microsoft Windows Mobile SmartPhone software 2002, 2003, or 2003 SE.

Running the wizard

Before you run the wizard, make sure that all the requirements for your device are in place.

We recommend hot-syncing or synchronizing your Palm or Windows Mobile device; this ensures that the data you're sending to your Curve is current. Palm Desktop Software, as well as Microsoft ActiveSync, should come with help information on how to hot-sync.

Although the following steps migrate Windows Mobile data to the Curve, the steps are similar for Palm. We indicate at what point the steps vary. Do the following to get your other device's data migrated to your new Curve:

1. **Connect both the Windows Mobile device and BlackBerry Curve to your desktop computer.**

2. **On your PC, choose Start⇨All Programs⇨BlackBerry⇨Desktop Manager.**

   The Desktop Manager screen appears (refer to Figure 17-1).

3. **Click the Device Switch Wizard icon.**

4. **When Device Switch Wizard appears, click the image next to Switch from Another Device to BlackBerry Device.**

   The Welcome screen, as shown in Figure 17-7, describes what the tool can do.

Figure 17-7:
Migrating
data from
a non-
BlackBerry
device.

5. **Click Next.**

A screen prompts you to decide whether you're migrating from Palm
or Windows Mobile, as shown in Figure 17-8. The wizard is intelligent
enough to enable the option associated to the connected device, which
in this figure is a Windows Mobile device.

Figure 17-8:
The wizard
has already
selected
which
device to
port.

6. **Click Next.**

Hot-syncing the Windows Mobile device kicks in at this point. You see
a series of screens for each of the application's data, such as Calendar,
Contacts, and MemoPad. A sample for the Calendar data is shown in
Figure 17-9. The screen indicates what to sync and will be empty if you
already performed a hot-sync before running the wizard. Otherwise,
it will take some time, depending on how much data there is to sync
between the device and the desktop software.

Figure 17-9:
A message
showing
hot-syncing
on your
device.

7. **Click OK.**

A progress screen appears. Before the data is applied to your Curve, the wizard prompts you about the change, as shown in Figure 17-10. Click the following buttons on this screen to either confirm or reject the change:

- Details: You want to know the records the wizard is trying to apply.

- Accept: You just want the data migrated.

- Reject: Ignore this data and continue.

- Cancel: Change your mind and cancel the whole operation.

Figure 17-10:
Confirm the
importing of
data here.

8. **Click the Accept or the Reject button on any confirmation screens that appear.**

The wizard migrates all the data you accepted. Obviously, the wizard skips everything you rejected. When the migration process is finished, a success screen appears.

9. **Click Finish.**

Chapter 18

Protecting Your Information

*I*magine that you left your beautiful Curve in the back of a cab. You lost your Curve for good! Okay, not so good. What happens to all your information? How will you replace all those contacts? What about security?

Take a deep breath, and relax a bit. One thing you don't need to worry about is information security — *if* you set up a security password on your Curve, that is. With security password protection enabled, anyone who finds your Curve has only ten chances to enter the correct password; after those ten chances are up, it's self-destruction time. Although the conclusion isn't as smoky as those self-destructing tapes from *Mission Impossible,* your Curve does erase all its information, thwarting your would-be data thief. Sad but safe.

If you haven't set up a password for your Curve, do it *now!* For information on how to do so, see Chapter 3.

Hmm. But how do you get back all the information that was on your Curve? That's what this chapter is all about. Vital information — clients' and friends' contact information; notes from phone calls with clients; and, of course, those precious e-mail messages — shouldn't be taken lightly. Backing up this information is a reliable way to protect it from being lost forever.

If your Curve isn't on a BlackBerry Enterprise Server, BlackBerry Desktop Manager is the only way to back up and restore information to and from your desktop PC. And SmrtGuard (pronounced *smart guard*) offers a wireless backup and restore service if you don't have the habit of plugging your Curve into your PC. If that sounds like you, go to the end of this chapter to find an introduction to SmrtGuard's backup and restore solution, which can give you peace of mind when it comes to protecting your data.

Accessing Backup and Restore

Backup and Restore — a BlackBerry Desktop Manager application — allows you to back up all the sensitive data on your Curve, including contacts, e-mails, memos, to-do's, and personal preferences and options.

For most users, your e-mails are already stored in accounts, such as Gmail or Yahoo! Mail. But you can still back up e-mails just in case.

To back up information on your Curve, follow these steps:

1. **Open BlackBerry Desktop Manager on your PC by choosing Start⇨ All Programs⇨BlackBerry⇨Desktop Manager.**

   If you haven't already installed BlackBerry Desktop Manager on your PC, see Chapter 16.

2. **Connect your Curve to your PC with the USB cable that came with your Curve.**

   If everything is set up right, a pop-up window on your PC asks you to type your BlackBerry security password. Make sure your Curve is turned on.

3. **Type your password.**

   The Curve connects to the PC.

4. **On the BlackBerry Desktop Manager screen, double-click the Backup and Restore icon.**

   The Backup and Restore screen opens (see Figure 18-1). You're ready to back up data from or restore information to your Curve.

Figure 18-1:
The Backup
and Restore
screen.

Backing Up, BlackBerry Style

Everyone knows that backing up data provides tremendous peace of mind. So
do the folks at RIM, which is why backing up your information is quite easy.
You can back up your Curve manually or by autopilot.

Backing up your Curve manually

To back up your Curve on demand, follow these steps:

1. **Connect your Curve to your PC with the USB cable. Then, from the
   PC's BlackBerry Desktop Manager screen, double-click the Backup
   and Restore icon.**

   The Backup and Restore screen appears (refer to Figure 18-1).

2. **Click the Back Up button.**

   The dialog box shown in Figure 18-2 appears, where you can name the
   backup file and figure out where on your PC you want to save it.

Figure 18-2:
Name and
find a home
for your
backup file.

3. **Name your backup file, and choose a place to save it.**

4. **Click Save.**

   BlackBerry Desktop Manager starts backing up your Curve information to your PC. Figure 18-3 shows the backup progress in the Transfer in Progress window. Depending on how much information you have on your Curve, the backup might take ten minutes to finish.

Figure 18-3:
A backup is
in progress.

Don't unplug your Curve from the PC until the backup is finished!

5. **When the Transfer in Progress window disappears, unplug the Curve from the PC.**

Setting up automatic backups

What's better than backing up your information once? Remembering to back up regularly! And what's better than backing up regularly? You guessed it — running backups automatically. After you schedule automated BlackBerry backups, you can really have peace of mind when it comes to preventing information loss.

Follow these steps to set up an automatic backup:

1. **From the PC's BlackBerry Desktop Manager screen, double-click the Backup and Restore icon.**

2. **In the Backup and Restore screen, click the Options button.**

   The Backup Options screen appears, where you can schedule automatic backups (see Figure 18-4).

Figure 18-4:
Set
automatic
backups
here.

3. **Select the Back Up My Device Automatically Every *xx* Days check box.**

   Choosing this option allows you to make more decisions (check boxes and options become active), such as how often you want BlackBerry Desktop Manager to back up your Curve.

4. **In the Days field, enter a number of days between 1 and 99.**

   This interval sets how often your Curve is backed up. For example, if you enter 14, your Curve is backed up every 14 days. Go figure.

5. **Select the Back Up All Device Application Data radio button.**

   This option backs up all the data on your Curve each time autobackup runs.

   Although you can exclude e-mail messages and information (such as from Contacts, to-do's, and memos), we recommend that you back up *everything* each time. That way, when it's time to restore to a new BlackBerry, you get everything where you left off, including e-mail.

6. **Click OK.**

   Now you can go on with your life without worrying when to back up.

To run a backup, you must have your Curve connected to your PC. Make sure that you plug your Curve into your PC once in a while so that autobackup has a chance to back up your information.

Restoring Your Data from Backup Information

We hope that you never have to read this section more than once. A *full restore* means bringing back all your BlackBerry information from a previous backup stored on your PC.

The steps to fully restoring your backup information are simple:

1. **Connect your Curve to your PC using the USB cable. Then, from the PC's BlackBerry Desktop Manager screen, double-click the Backup and Restore icon.**

2. **In the Backup and Restore screen, click the Restore button.**

   An Open File dialog box asks where the backup file is on your PC.

3. **Choose the desired backup file, and click Open.**

   A warning window appears when you're about to do a full restore (see Figure 18-5), alerting you that you're about to overwrite existing information.

4. **Click Yes to go ahead with the full restore.**

   A progress bar appears. It might take a while for the full restore to finish.

   Don't unplug your BlackBerry from your PC during this time!

5. **When the progress bar disappears, unplug the device from the PC.**

Figure 18-5: Be careful when overwriting existing info.

Protecting Your Data, Your Way

A certain burger joint and BlackBerry both say that you can have it *your way* with their products. Just like you can get your burger with or without all the toppings and condiments, you can choose to not back up and restore things that you know you won't need.

For example, say you accidentally deleted all your Internet bookmarks, and now you want them back. *Don't* restore all the information from your last backup, which could be more than 90 days ago (depending on how often your autobackup runs, if at all). You may unintentionally overwrite other information, such as e-mail or new contacts. You want to restore bookmarks only.

If you lose something in particular or want something specific restored on your Curve, use the *selective* backup and restore function in BlackBerry Desktop Manager to restore only what you need. The same goes with backing up. If you're a big e-mail user, back up just your e-mails, nothing else.

In the following sections, we use the term *databases*. Don't worry; this isn't as technical as you think. Just think of a database as an information category on your Curve. For example, saying "backing up your Browser bookmarks database" is just a fancy way of saying "backing up all your Browser bookmarks on your Curve."

Backing up, your way

To back up specific information — selectively — follow these steps:

1. **Connect your Curve to your PC using the USB cable. Then, from the PC's BlackBerry Desktop Manager screen, double-click the Backup and Restore icon.**

2. **In the Backup and Restore screen, click the Advanced button.**

   The advanced Backup/Restore screen appears, as shown in Figure 18-6. The right side of the screen shows different information categories, or databases.

3. **In the Device Databases list on the right side, Ctrl+click the databases you want to back up.**

4. **Click the left-pointing (backup) double arrow.**

   This step merely transfers the databases onto your PC; it doesn't save them. That's next.

   A progress bar moves while your Curve is backed up. When the backup transfer is finished, you can see the databases on the left side.

BlackBerry® Desktop Manager v5.0 ©2009 Research In Motion Limited

Figure 18-6: The advanced Backup/ Restore screen.

5. **Choose File⇨Save As.**

   A file chooser appears.

6. **Name your file, specify where you want to save it on your PC, and click Save.**

   Make sure to name the file something specific so that you know exactly what is in the backup.

You need to manually save the backup file on your PC even after you choose a location for the file in Step 6. Remember that a selective backup doesn't automatically save your backup on your PC.

Looking at backup BlackBerry files

Whether you use the one-button backup method or manually back up your files, backup files are saved on your PC as IPD files. Are you asking, "Can I read these backup files without a BlackBerry?" The answer is yes! With the third-party product ABC Amber BlackBerry Converter, you can view any nonencrypted IPD file. What's the point? Suppose you lost your BlackBerry but need to read an old e-mail or get contacts from your backup files. This tool allows you to convert anything in your backup file (e-mails, SMS messages, PIM messages, and contacts) to PDF or Word documents. For more information and to try ABC Amber BlackBerry Converter for free, go to www.processtext.com/abcblackberry.html.

Restoring, your way

When you're restoring selectively, you must already have a backup file to restore from. Although this may sound obvious, the point here is that you can selectively restore from any backup — auto or manual.

For example, say you have autobackup running every other day, and you want to restore only your e-mail messages from two days ago. You don't need to do a full restore; that would overwrite that new contact you put in Contacts yesterday. Rather, you can use the selective restore method and get back only your e-mail messages.

To restore your way, follow these steps:

1. **Connect your Curve to your PC with the USB cable. Then, from the PC's BlackBerry Desktop Manager screen, double-click the Backup and Restore icon.**

2. **In the Backup and Restore screen, click the Advanced button.**

   The advanced Backup/Restore screen appears (refer to Figure 18-6). The right side of the screen shows your different information categories, or databases.

3. **Choose File⇨Open.**

   A window opens so that you can choose which backup file you want to restore from.

   A BlackBerry backup file has the .ipd extension.

4. **Select a backup file.**

5. **Click Open.**

   The different information categories, or databases, appear on the left side of the screen. You are now ready for a selective restore.

6. **Select the database(s) you want to restore.**

   You can select multiple databases by Ctrl+clicking the databases you want.

7. **Click the right-pointing (restore) double arrow.**

   You see a warning window asking whether you want to replace all the information with the data you're restoring (refer to Figure 18-5).

   If your Curve has the same categories as the ones you're restoring (which is likely), you'll overwrite *any* information you have on your Curve.

   You can confidently move on to Step 8 (clicking the Yes button) if you know that the database you're restoring has the information you're looking for.

8. **Click Yes.**

   A progress bar appears while the selected databases are being restored. When the progress bar window disappears, the information categories that you selected are restored on your BlackBerry.

Clearing Curve information, your way

You can also selectively delete information on your Curve from BlackBerry Desktop Manager. Suppose you want to clear only your phone logs from your Curve. One way is to tediously select one phone log at a time and press Delete, repeating until all phone logs are gone. However, you could instead delete a database from the advanced Backup/Restore screen by using the Backup and Restore function.

To selectively delete databases on your Curve, follow these steps:

1. **Connect your Curve to your PC with the USB cable. Then, from the PC's BlackBerry Desktop Manager screen, double-click the Backup and Restore icon.**

   The Backup and Restore screen appears.

2. **In the Backup and Restore screen, click the Advanced button.**

   The advanced Backup/Restore screen appears (refer to Figure 18-6). The right side of the screen shows your Curve's databases.

3. **Ctrl+click the database(s) you want to delete.**

   The database is highlighted.

4. **Click the Clear button on the right side of the screen.**

   A warning window asks you to confirm your deletion.

5. **Click Yes.**

   A progress bar shows the deletion. When the progress bar disappears, the information categories you selected are cleared from your Curve.

Backup and Restore Wirelessly

You can even back up and restore wirelessly without being on the BES or going through the trouble of plugging your Curve to your PC via BlackBerry Desktop Manager. However, you do have to pay a little bit for this service.

SmrtGuard (`www.smrtguard.com/smrtguard.jsp`) offers software you can install on your BlackBerry that can wirelessly back up your data. Currently, SmrtGuard supports backing up contacts, memos, calendar items, call logs, to-do's, SMS, and e-mails.

In addition to its backup and restore capabilities, SmrtGuard has features to help you locate, recover, and destroy data on your device. SmrtGuard has a BlackBerry tracking feature (a similar concept to LoJack for cars), which helps you determine whether you simply misplaced your device or your device was stolen. If you determine that your device was stolen, you can send a signal to have your data destroyed via the SmrtGuard Dashboard on the SmrtGuard Web site.

SmrtGuard has three pricing plans:

✔ Monthly plan: $3.99 a month

✔ 6-month plan: $22.99

✔ 12-month plan: $44.99

Chapter 19

Installing and Managing Third-Party Applications

*T*hink of your Curve as a minilaptop where you can run preinstalled applications as well as install new applications. You can even upgrade the operating system. (Yup, that's right — your Curve has an OS.)

This chapter starts by introducing Application Loader, which you use to load applications (who'd have guessed?) onto your Curve. Next, you find ways to install and uninstall apps to and from your Curve. Then we explore the portion of Application Loader that allows you to upgrade the OS.

This chapter describes Application Loader, which is available only under Windows. As of this writing, BlackBerry Desktop Manager for the Mac is not yet available. The screenshots you see in this book and toward the end of this chapter are based on a prerelease version, which is subject to change. If you are a Mac user, some of the topics discussed in this chapter that relate to Application Loader will not be applicable to you. However, other topics should be able to assist you with regard to installing and uninstalling applications on your Curve.

In the Part of Tens, you'll find a few great applications that make your BlackBerry Curve that much more productive.

Accessing Application Loader

In this chapter, you work closely with your PC and your Curve. On your PC, you use the BlackBerry Desktop Manager application, which comes on a CD along with your Curve. You can find Application Loader in BlackBerry Desktop Manager.

For an introduction to BlackBerry Desktop Manager, see Chapter 16.

After installing BlackBerry Desktop Manager on your PC, do the following to access Application Loader:

1. **On your PC, choose Start⇨All Programs⇨BlackBerry⇨Desktop Manager.**

2. **In BlackBerry Desktop Manager, connect your Curve to your PC via your USB cable.**

   If the connection is successful, you see the password dialog box, as shown in Figure 19-1.

Figure 19-1:
The password dialog box on your PC.

If the connection isn't successful, see whether the USB cable is connected properly to both your PC and your Curve and then try again. If all else fails, contact the technical support department of your service provider.

3. **Enter your password.**

   Your Curve-to-PC connection is complete.

4. **On your PC, double-click the Application Loader icon in BlackBerry Desktop Manager.**

   The Application Loader screen opens, as shown in Figure 19-2. At this point, you're ready to use Application Loader.

Figure 19-2:
The
Application
Loader
screen.

Installing an Application

In this chapter, we show you how to install iSkoot for Skype for BlackBerry. iSkoot is a free application that connects to the Web directly and allows you to use Skype. You can download this application at

```
www.download.com/iSkoot-for-Skype-BlackBerry-/3000-7242_4-10797721.html
```

No matter what application you're installing from your PC to your Curve, the steps are the same. Use the following steps as a guide to installing the application of your choice:

1. **Install the application on your PC.**

   The installation varies, so refer to the manual.

2. **Locate the application's ALX file.**

   You can usually find a file with the .alx extension in the folder where you installed the application on your PC.

   The ALX file doesn't get installed on your Curve. It tells Application Loader where the actual application file is located on your PC.

3. **Double-click the Application Loader icon in BlackBerry Desktop Manager.**

   The Application Loader screen appears (refer to Figure 19-2).

4. **Connect your Curve to your PC, using the USB cable.**

   A screen appears, prompting you to enter your Curve password.

5. **Enter your password (refer to Figure 19-1).**

   After you enter your password, the Application Loader screen indicates that your device is connected.

6. **Click the Start button below Add/Remove Applications.**

   The screen listing of what applications to install appears.

7. **Click the Browse button, and locate and select the ALX file you want to install.**

   You return to the Application Loader screen, where iSkoot is one of the applications in the list, as shown in Figure 19-3.

Figure 19-3:
Your application is added to the list of installed applications and can be installed on your Curve.

8. **Select the application you want to install (for this example, select iSkoot Skype for BlackBerry) and then click Next.**

   A summary screen appears, listing only the applications that will be installed or upgraded.

9. **Click Finish.**

   The installation process starts, and a progress window appears. When the progress window disappears — and if all went well — the application is on your Curve. The application should be in the Applications folder of your Curve.

If you get an invalid signature error after clicking the Finish button, the solution depends on how you received your Curve:

- ✔ **You didn't get your Curve from your employer.** Something is probably wrong with the application. You need to contact the software vendor.

- ✔ **You got your Curve from your employer.** You don't have permission to install applications on your Curve. The IT department rules the school.

You don't have to use Application Loader to get the goods onto your Curve, though. You can install applications in other ways as well:

- ✔ **Wirelessly, through an *over-the-air (OTA)* download:** See Chapter 11 for more on wireless installations.

- ✔ **BlackBerry Enterprise Server wireless install (if your Curve was provided by your employer):** In this case, you have no control over the installation process. Your company's BlackBerry system administrator controls which applications are on your Curve.

- ✔ **Through the PC using Microsoft Installer:** Some application installations automate the preceding steps. All you need to do is connect your Curve to the PC and then double-click the installation file. The application installation's file using Microsoft Installer bears the `.msi` file extension.

Uninstalling an Application

You can uninstall an application in two ways:

- ✔ Using Application Loader
- ✔ Using your Curve

We use iSkoot as an example here and assume that you've already installed the iSkoot application. You can follow the same steps for uninstalling other applications.

Uninstalling with Application Loader

To uninstall a BlackBerry application, follow these steps:

1. **On your PC, double-click the Application Loader icon in BlackBerry Desktop Manager.**

2. **Connect your Curve to your PC, using the USB cable.**

   A screen prompting you to enter your Curve password appears.

3. Enter your password (refer to Figure 19-1).

If your handheld isn't connected properly, the PIN of your device won't appear in the Application Loader screen. Connect your Curve to the USB cable and then connect the USB cable to the PC.

After you enter your password, the Application Loader screen indicates that your device is connected.

4. Click the Start button below Add/Remove Applications.

The screen listing applications appears, similar to Figure 19-3, earlier in this chapter.

5. Scroll to the application you want to delete and then deselect its check box.

For example, when we deselect the iSkoot Skype for BlackBerry check box, the Action column for iSkoot indicates Remove.

6. Click Next.

You see a summary screen that lists the action of Application Loader. It indicates that iSkoot is to be removed from your Curve.

7. Click Finish.

The uninstall process starts, and a progress window appears. When the progress window disappears, you have uninstalled the application from your Curve.

Uninstalling with your Curve

When you don't have access to your PC, you can uninstall an application directly from your Curve. Follow these steps:

1. Locate the application icon on the BlackBerry Home screen.

By default, any applications you installed on your Curve are filed in the Downloads folder of the Home screen. However, you always have the option to move it.

2. Highlight the application icon and then press the menu key.

3. From the menu that appears, select Delete.

4. In the confirmation dialog box that appears, select Delete to confirm the deletion.

You're given a choice to restart now or at a later time. After restarting, the deleted application is uninstalled.

Upgrading Your BlackBerry Curve OS

The OS used by Curve has gone through a few revisions. The BlackBerry OS update comes from BlackBerry Handheld Software, which is available from three sources:

✔ Your network service provider

✔ The Research In Motion Web site

✔ Your BlackBerry system administrator

Because the handheld software might differ from provider to provider, we recommend getting it from the service provider's Web site. RIM has a download site for different service providers at

```
http://na.blackberry.com/eng/support/downloads/download_sites.jsp
```

In this section, we assume that the latest BlackBerry Handheld Software for Curve is already installed on your PC. For help with installing BlackBerry Handheld Software, refer to the instructions that come with it.

If you plan to upgrade your BlackBerry OS, and you've installed many third-party applications, check whether those applications support the new OS revision. Third-party applications work as is most of the time, but there is always a possibility of losing third-party application data.

Start the upgrade process by doing the following:

1. **Enter your Curve password (if you have set one) into BlackBerry Desktop Manager on your PC.**

2. **Double-click the Application Loader icon on the Desktop Manager screen.**

   The Application Loader screen appears (refer to Figure 19-2).

3. **Click the Start button below Add/Remove Applications.**

   A list of software appears, as shown in Figure 19-4.

4. **With your mouse, you can opt out of the upgrade by deselecting the OS portion.**

   This appears as BlackBerry 5.0 System Software in Figure 19-4.

The OS is listed only if you need an upgrade — meaning that your BlackBerry OS is out of date. If the OS doesn't appear in the list, the handheld software you installed on the desktop machine is the same as the one installed on your device or a previous version compared with the one installed on your device.

Figure 19-4:
Application
updates
that are
available.

You also need to back up your device in case something goes wrong with the upgrade. Backup options can be accessed through the Options button.

5. Click Options.

The Options screen appears, as shown in Figure 19-5. This is where you decide whether you want to back up your Curve content before upgrading your OS. We suggest that you do.

Figure 19-5:
Choose
whether
to back
up before
upgrading.

6. Select the Back Up Device Data Automatically During the Installation Process check box and then click OK.

You return to the screen shown in Figure 19-4.

7. Click Next.

A summary page confirms your actions — a final chance for you to proceed with the OS upgrade or not.

8. **Click Finish.**

   The BlackBerry OS upgrade starts, complete with a progress window that shows a series of steps and a progress bar. The entire process takes about ten minutes, depending on your PC model and the OS version you're upgrading to.

   At times during the BlackBerry OS upgrade, your Curve's display goes on and off. Don't worry; this is normal.

   When the progress window disappears, the OS upgrade is complete.

Finding and Installing Applications from App Stores

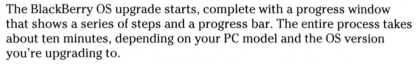

With the success of the iPhone App Store, several copycats sprouted up for other platforms, including the BlackBerry. Broadly, an "app store" is an online storefront that showcases applications that you can download directly to your device. Applications can be free or not:

- ✔ **Handango (www.handango.com):** Handango is one of the oldest storefronts that sells applications for mobile devices. It started selling apps through the Web but now has an app store that you can download from its Web site.

- ✔ **CrackBerry On-Device App Store (http://crackberryappstore. com):** Partnering with MobiHand, CrackBerry also provides an app store where you can find great applications to download.

- ✔ **BlackBerry Application Center:** This is software built by RIM, but the carrier has control over what shows up in Application Center.

- ✔ **BlackBerry App World:** RIM has full control over what applications are available. This is in contrast with BlackBerry Application Center, where the carrier has control.

   If you don't have App World on your Curve, you can download it from the RIM Web site at http://na.blackberry.com/eng/services/ appworld.

Just recently, RIM created a Web version of App World. Using your desktop Internet browser, you can visit the site at http://appworld.blackberry. com/. The site allows you to send an e-mail to your device with a download link for the app that you are interested in.

Managing Applications on Your Mac

Again, BlackBerry Desktop Manager for the Mac is not released as of this writing. The screen shown in Figure 19-6, which you see when you click the Applications button, is based on the prerelease version and is subject to change.

Figure 19-6: Install, remove, and update your applications here.

Note that although this screen shows an empty grid, your version will list all the applications installed on your device. When this software is completed and released, you will have options to add new applications, delete applications, and update applications.

Part VI
The Part of Tens

The 5th Wave — By Rich Tennant

PERSONAL TECH UPDATE:
THE CELL PHONE/PDA TOUPEE WITH
DISCREET VIBRATING PAGER FUNCTION

©RICHTENNANT

"Will you excuse me? I'd better take this."

In this part . . .

If the earlier parts of this book are the ice cream and hot fudge, this part is the whipped cream and cherry on top. Delve into these three short but sweet chapters to find out how to accessorize your BlackBerry Curve, boost your productivity, and max your BlackBerry experience with useful sites. And remember that you can always visit www.blackberryfordummies.com for updated lists.

Chapter 20

Ten Great BlackBerry Accessories

*T*he BlackBerry retail box contains a few essentials: a battery, a charger, a micro USB cable, a belt clip, and possibly a 1GB microSD card. If you're like most of us, though, you're not satisfied with what is included in the box. In this chapter, you find accessories that supplement your Curve — and find out where to get them.

Check out our companion Web site, www.blackberryfordummies.com, for an updated accessories list.

If you like to accessorize your Curve, check out site promotions. Every now and then, a site such as CrackBerry.com runs promotions and gives big discounts. Also look at RIM's Web site at www.shopblackberry.com. It usually offers accessory bundles.

Unify AV Solution

Unify AV Solution is an innovative product of Unify4Life that makes a smart-phone (including your BlackBerry) a universal remote control.

You can find a suite of features on the Unify4Life Web site, but a sample includes complete TV listings in your BlackBerry for informative channel switching. You can purchase it directly from `http://unify4life.com/products.html`.

microSD Card

Your new BlackBerry normally comes with external memory: a *microSD card*. But if you're not satisfied with its capacity, go hunt for a much bigger one. After all, you want to carry with you a boatload of music and video files, right? Many electronic gadgets use microSD cards, so they're easy to find.

A normal price range at the time of this writing is $20 for 8GB capacity and $40 for 16GB capacity. Special promotions come and go, but you can always find a good deal somewhere on the Internet. And for any Internet purchase, take into consideration the shipping and handling costs plus the vendor's return policy (or lack thereof).

Any brand will do, as long as you make sure that you're buying a microSD card.

Full Keyboards

As netbooks become more popular, people forget that the BlackBerry they already carry is a "mini netbook." Internet? Check! E-mail? Check! Microsoft Word docs and Microsoft Excel? Check! Sure, the screen is a bit smaller, and the keyboard is small, but with a little help from a Bluetooth keyboard, your BlackBerry will save you the cost of a netbook and still be productive.

We recommend the pFreedom Universal Bluetooth keyboard, which you can find under Bluetooth keyboards at `shop.crackberry.com` or `Amazon.com`.

You have the choice of Bluetooth and non-Bluetooth connection options. We recommend Bluetooth to minimize the clutter. A Bluetooth keyboard is the most convenient option for the obvious reasons: You don't have to carry cables, and you can position your BlackBerry any way you want.

For less than $100, you can own the cool iGo Stowaway Ultra-Slim Bluetooth keyboard, available at www.amazon.com. Or you can buy the ThinkOutside Stowaway Shasta Bluetooth keyboard for BlackBerry, available at http://yahooshopping.com for $45.

Stereo Headsets

Although your new BlackBerry is a stereo music player, it doesn't come with stereo headphones. You will definitely yearn for stereo sound the moment you listen to music or watch video clips. A quick search on the Internet for *BlackBerry + stereo headphones* yields many results. But you want to be able to talk, too.

You could spend $30 to $200. Several good headsets follow:

- BlackBerry stereo headset with noise-isolating ear gels
- V-MODA Vibe duo in-ear headphones with mic
- Motorola S9 stereo Bluetooth headset

The best place to get stereo headphones for your BlackBerry is good ol' Amazon: www.amazon.com.

Case and Belt Clip

You have plenty of cases to choose among, with looks ranging from sporty to professional. These cases can set you back anywhere from $20 to $40, which isn't too bad for looking hip.

Here's where you can buy a new case or belt clip:

- http://www.smrtcase.com
- http://shop.crackberry.com
- www.amazon.com
- www.bberry.com
- www.blackberryden.com
- www.blackberrysource.com

When you buy a new belt case or clip, buy one made specifically for your BlackBerry model. Also, it's important that the case or clip come with a small magnet. BlackBerry is holster-aware and conserves battery juice, and this magnet is the key for the BlackBerry to know that it is inside a holster.

Screen Protector and Skins

If the protector case described in the preceding section is a bit stressful for your wallet, try the Blackberry Pro high-definition screen protector with mirror effect. That's a mouthful, but for about $10, it protects your screen from scratches. Go to www.accessorygeeks.com.

Other popular bestsellers are skin cases. They come in many colors and keep your BlackBerry looking new. The price is usually between $9 and $12. Go to http://shop.crackberry.com or www.accessorygeeks.com.

Extra Battery, Charger, and Charging Pod

An extra battery for your BlackBerry will come in handy if you're a daily user.

Buy your battery only from Research In Motion, at www.shopblackberry.com, or an authorized RIM reseller, not from some unknown vendor. A faulty battery can damage your BlackBerry beyond repair.

Make sure that the battery you buy is for your BlackBerry model. You'll spend around $50 for the extra battery.

If you watch video on your BlackBerry, you know that the battery needs to be charged every couple of hours. And if you're always on the go, you'd better have a portable charger on hand. The charger included with your BlackBerry is great to carry around town (and the world) because it has multiple adapters for different countries' electric plugs.

If you're a road warrior, get the BlackBerry car charger. It will set you back around $30. To top it off, you can also get a power station or charging pod, which connects to a power supply for charging and at the same time holds your BlackBerry firmly in place on your desk or nightstand. On your nightstand, you can take advantage of sleep mode, which sets the device to not disturb you by doing things such as dimming the light and turning off the LED. The charging pod costs $12 to $30, depending on how fancy it is.

Make sure that the charger and the charging pod you buy are for your BlackBerry model.

You can get a BlackBerry car charger and charging pod from the following sites:

- ✔ http://shop.crackberry.com
- ✔ www.amazon.com
- ✔ www.blackberrysource.com
- ✔ www.shopblackberry.com (RIM's official store)

External Speaker

BlackBerry comes with a speaker, but if the sound quality just isn't good enough for your listening taste, an external Bluetooth speaker can bring your outdoor listening to the next level. We recommend the following:

- ✔ Blueant M1 Bluetooth stereo speakers
- ✔ Motorola EQ5 wireless travel stereo speaker

For about $110, you can get either of them from http://shop.crackberry.com.

Bluetooth Music Gateway

If you already have a great set of speakers or an audio entertainment system, using a RIM Bluetooth Music Gateway is the perfect way to stream music to your existing system. Simply pair your BlackBerry to the Bluetooth Music Gateway via Bluetooth (hence the name), and you are ready to go. What is even better is that this hockey puck–like Music Gateway can be paired with your PC or Mac, so you get more use out of it. Find it at http://shop.crackberry.com.

Car Mount

To complete your BlackBerry car experience, mount your BlackBerry in your car. The market offers many products, ranging from $15 to $30. You can search the major search sites. You can also get a car mount from these BlackBerry sites:

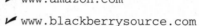

- ✔ http://shop.crackberry.com
- ✔ www.amazon.com
- ✔ www.blackberrysource.com

Make sure that the product you're choosing supports your BlackBerry model.

The latest wireless speakerphone from RIM is BlackBerry Visor Mount SpeakerPhone VM-605. It's a Bluetooth speakerphone that you attach to your car's visor, just like you attach your garage door opener. You can get one for $99 at www.shopblackberry.com.

Chapter 21

Ten Must-Have Applications

The availability of BlackBerry software is growing at a dizzying rate. In this chapter, we introduce ten must-have applications that make your BlackBerry Curve experience that much better.

We don't quotes specific reviews. These choices are the results of our quest to find programs that people use, discerned from discussions with BlackBerry users, postings on message boards, and commentaries in the public domain. The applications featured here are just the tip of the iceberg. By all means, feel free to surf the Internet, because by the time this book is published, more software will likely be available. And don't forget to visit our Web site at www.blackberryfordummies.com.

SmrtGuard, Your BlackBerry Guardian

If you lost your BlackBerry, have you wondered what would happen to your data, such as your sensitive e-mails, phone call histories, contacts, and appointments? It's scary to think of a stranger getting to know you through your e-mails and knowing what you're going to do next. These same thoughts haunt us as well. Fortunately, there's SmrtGuard (formerly known as BerryFinder.com), which provides the following tools:

- ✔ **Locate and "LoJack" your BlackBerry:** With no GPS signal required, you can track your Curve's approximate location to determine whether you simply misplaced it or someone stole it.

- ✔ **Wireless data backup:** This is another must-have feature that SmrtGuard provides. If you self-destroyed your data and don't have a backup, the scheduled wireless backup of your PIM data will come in handy. From the SmrtGuard Web site (www.smrtguard.com), you can even see and browse through your backed-up data and export it to a file (a Microsoft Excel file or a text file).

- ✔ **Sound the homing beacon:** If you simply misplaced your BlackBerry but can't find it by calling because you muted it, don't worry. Just send a homing beacon, and your BlackBerry will emit a loud sound regardless of your Profile setting. We wish our remote controls had this feature!

- ✔ **Self-destroy in five seconds:** Okay, perhaps not in five seconds, but you can decide when to destroy all your BlackBerry data. That includes e-mails, contacts, appointments, to-do's, memos, phone logs, text messages, and even all the files on your microSD card.

Always protect your BlackBerry Curve with a password. That way, if your Curve gets into the wrong hands, your data will be self-erased after ten unsuccessful password entries. However, the files on your microSD card aren't deleted. This is why SmrtGuard is so helpful.

With SmrtGuard by your side, you can concentrate on your business instead of worrying about your BlackBerry data being stolen. You can get SmrtGuard for $3.99 a month, or $49.99 for a whole year's subscription. There's also a 10-day free trial. Check it out at www.smrtguard.com.

TetherBerry

Subscribing to mobile broadband for your laptop is expensive. TetherBerry provides an inexpensive solution for connecting to the Internet from your laptop by using your BlackBerry Curve. You can check the details at www.tetherberry.com.

On the Web site, you can order the application for a one-time fee of $49.95. That's spare change considering that you get connectivity to your laptop using your Curve. There's also a 30-day money-back guarantee.

VibAndRing

Don't like the fact that you can't get your BlackBerry to alert you the way you want? Do you need custom vibration when a phone call comes in?

Time to get your hands on VibAndRing. With it, you can customize how many vibrate bursts you get before the Curve starts ringing and how long each vibration lasts.

To download a free trial, go to www.mobihand.com, and search for *vibandring.*

Viigo for BlackBerry

An application that you'll use on a daily basis is Viigo. Viigo is an RSS reader. The application is really a one-stop shop for almost all information you need, whether you want news, blogs, podcasts, weather info, entertainment, finance, flight info, or more.

Download Viigo for free from your BlackBerry at http://www.viigo.com.

PeeKaWho — E-mail and SMS Alerts

Ever find yourself in the middle of browsing or composing an e-mail, and all of a sudden a new e-mail finds its way to your inbox? Instead of stopping what you're doing and heading to the inbox, with PeeKaWho you can get a preview of the e-mail or SMS message that has just arrived, and you can dismiss, mark as read, go to your inbox, or delete the message — all from the alert pop-up.

To find out more, go to www.smrtguard.com/peek.jsp.

Zodiac

What's Zodiac? It's a simple yet addictive game where you match three or more cute animal figures; you hear a satisfying "bing" that will keep you going. The best part is that your spouse and kids will enjoy Zodiac as well. Try it for free by downloading it from http://www.mobihand.com/product.asp?id=29358&n=Zodiac.

Google Talk Mobile and Yahoo! Messenger Mobile

If you currently use Google Talk or Yahoo! Messenger on your PC, both mobile versions are must-downloads to keep up with your buddies no matter where you are. To download, point your BlackBerry browser to

- ✔ **Google Talk Mobile:** www.blackberry.com/GoogleTalk
- ✔ **Yahoo! Messenger Mobile:** www.blackberry.com/YahooDownload

WeatherEye

Numerous weather programs are available, but we like the one from WeatherEye for its simplicity. You set up the weather location you want, and WeatherEye displays an icon on your Home screen to indicate the current weather information, updated daily. This application is free; download it from http://blackberry.theweathernetwork.com.

Nobex Radio Companion

FM radio on your BlackBerry? That's right. With Nobex, you can get streaming radio on your BlackBerry for free (for now)!

More than a hundred stations are available for streaming. Nobex works best if you have a 3G or EvDo network (the faster the network, the better your experience with Nobex). To find out more, go to www.nobexrc.com.

Online Personal Music Players

Two applications, Pandora and Slacker, stream CD-quality music right to your BlackBerry. After you download and sign up for Pandora, you just search for the music that you like to hear, and Pandora will automatically feed you similar songs. If you indicate to Pandora whether you like or dislike a particular song that it feeds you, future Pandora selections should be more to your liking. Try Pandora for free at http://www.pandora.com/blackberry. To try Slacker for free, download it at http://www.slacker.com.

Chapter 22

Ten Important Types of Web Sites

*W*eb surfing with a BlackBerry has improved dramatically with the newer models. With higher screen resolution and bigger real estate, your BlackBerry Curve should give you one good mobile Web-browsing experience. And with a 3G connection, your Web browsing should be faster. Remember that by using Page view, where the Web page displays like it does in your PC Web browser, you can maintain on your BlackBerry the browsing habits you have on your PC, but in a smaller package. The Web site recommendations in this chapter are based on reviews in the public domain and sites that definitely help when you're on the go.

Weather

Weather changes often, but you can keep up with it at these sites:

- ✔ **AccuWeather.com** (www.accuweather.com): AccuWeather.com provides the local weather forecast.

- ✔ **Weather.com** (www.weather.com): Weather.com is smart enough to know that you're using a mobile device and displays a nice, trim version of its page with a few links to non-weather–related information.

If these two sites aren't enough, check out the "Search Engines, Directories, and Portals" section, later in this chapter. Major portals have weather information as well as traffic alerts and airport delays.

News

Most major news companies have mobile versions of their sites. This section gives you just a sampling of what's out there. We list the same Web address you'd expect when browsing from your desktop. These sites detect that you're using a smartphone and redirect you to the mobile-friendly version of their sites:

- **ABC News** (www.abcnews.com): Get ABC News on your BlackBerry.

- **BBC News** (www.bbc.com): You can read BBC News right from your BlackBerry, even if you're not in the United Kingdom.

- **CNN** (www.cnn.com): This is CNN's mobile-friendly Web site.

- **Reuters** (www.reuters.com): This is the mobile-friendly version of the Reuters site.

- **The New York Times** (www.nytimes.com): This automatically points you to *The New York Times'* mobile-friendly Web site, a site that's clean and easy to navigate, without a lot of advertisements.

- **USA Today** (http://usatoday.com): *USA Today,* one of the most popular newspapers, is now available for free from your BlackBerry.

- **Wired News** (http://mobile.wired.com): Wired News is the mobile version of this tech-news Web site.

Search Engines, Directories, and Portals

In this section we list *Web portals,* which are sites that contain various information or links to other sites:

- **Google** (www.google.com): The king of search engines works like a charm on your BlackBerry.

- **MSN** (www.msn.com): You can access MSN Hotmail, MSN Messenger, and an online calendar. MSN application for the BlackBerry has all the features that you can find in a Web portal, such as Web search, weather lookup, sports information, and news. Plus you get MSN's finance-related pages, which give you up-to-the-minute stock quotes.

- **RIM mobile home page** (http://mobile.blackberry.com): This is the default home page setting for most BlackBerry browsers. The service provider can customize it, though, so your BlackBerry browser may point to your service provider's home page. RIM's home page is definitely a place to start browsing the Web.

You should definitely bookmark this site.

✔ **Yahoo! Mobile** (www.yahoo.com): Yahoo! is a smart portal because it knows you're using a mobile device and formats the page accordingly — meaning a smaller page with no advertisements. The portal site allows BlackBerry users to employ regular Yahoo! functions, such as Yahoo! Mail, Messenger, Finance, and Games, as well as driving directions and weather.

This is another site you should bookmark.

Business

You can keep up with the latest news in the finance world from your BlackBerry. Visit the following sites for finance-related articles and news:

✔ **BusinessWeek Online** (www.businessweek.com): This is a place to get great finance information.

✔ **Fidelity** (www.fidelity.com): Fidelity is an online investment brokerage firm.

✔ **Yahoo! Finance** (http://finance.yahoo.com): This is a great site for checking the performance of your stocks.

Travel

Every site in the following list features flight status and gate numbers. Some allow you to log on (if you're part of the airline's frequent-flier program) to access frequent-flier benefits:

✔ Any airline: http://flightview.com

✔ Air Canada: www.aircanada.ca

✔ American Airlines: http://aa.flightlookup.com/omnisky

✔ British Airways: www.britishairways.com

✔ Cathay Pacific: www.cathaypacific.com

✔ Continental Airlines: www.continental.com

✔ Delta: www.delta.com

✔ JetBlue: http://jetblue.com

- Northwest Airlines: `http://nwa.com`
- United Air Lines: `http://ua2go.com`

In addition to these sites check out the following:

- **TripKick** (`www.tripkick.com`): Don't be so excited about getting a good deal on a hotel only to end up in a crummy room. TripKick tells you who has the best rooms and who doesn't.
- **WikiTravel** (`www.wikitravel.com`): This is one of the most up-to-date and complete travel guides on the Web.

Sports

Tired of missing updates on your favorite sport while on the go? You don't have to. Visit the sports-related sites that follow, and you'll get the scoop on what's happening to your favorite team:

- **CBS Sports Mobile** (`www.cbssports.com/mobile`): If you're active on CBS Fantasy Team, you'll be happy to know that you can log on and view your stats from this Web site. Popular U.S. sports are covered here.
- **ESPN** (`http://mobileapp.espn.go.com`): Everyone knows ESPN. This is the mobile version of its Web site.

Advice and Self-Help

Looking for ways to save time and get your questions answered? Check out these sites:

- **HowCast** (`www.howcast.com`): With a dose of humor, this site is a world of how-to videos.
- **Omiru** (`www.omiru.com`): This site offers practical fashion advice for the common person.
- **Yahoo! Answers** (`http://answers.yahoo.com`): Here, you can get all sorts of creative, amusing, and helpful responses to your questions — advice that's free.
- **Zeer** (`www.zeer.com`): There's no need to stand in the supermarket comparing nutritional labels; do it here.

Social and Virtual Networking

For those of you who are (or aren't yet) addicted to social networking sites, we list a few of the most popular ones here. If your favorite site isn't listed, don't fret; just search for it with a search engine:

- ✔ **Friendster** (www.friendster.com): This site is popular in Southeast Asian countries and is open to people 16 and older.

- ✔ **LinkedIn** (wwwlinkedin.com): LinkedIn caters to professional and business relationships. You'll find people publishing their bios on their profiles.

- ✔ **Multiply** (www.multiply.com): This site claims to focus on real-world relationships and is open to anyone 13 and older. It's a popular site for teenagers.

- ✔ **Orkut** (www.orkut.com): Orkut is a social networking site run by Google. It's open to anyone 18 and older, and it requires Google login credentials. This site is popular in Latin America and in India.

- ✔ **Windows Live Space** (home.spaces.live.com): This is a social networking site run by Microsoft. It's open to everyone and requires a Hotmail or Windows Live login.

MySpace and Facebook both have an application you can download from RIM's Web site. Point your browser to mobile.blackberry.com, and navigate to IM & Social Networking.

Shopping and Shipping Information

Shopaholics can keep it up online even when they're not in front of the PC. Check out these sites:

- ✔ **Amazon** (www.amazon.com): With Amazon Anywhere, you can shop and check your account information right from your BlackBerry.

- ✔ **eBay** (www.ebay.com): You can bid on goods from the convenience of your BlackBerry.

- ✔ **FedEx tracking** (www.fedex.com): This mobile version of the FedEx Web site allows you to track packages from your BlackBerry.

- ✔ **Gas Buddy** (www.gasbuddy.com): You can find the nearest gas station that sells the cheapest gas.

- ✔ **ILikeTotallyLoveIt.com** (www.iliketotallyloveit.com): This is shopping with a twist. Shoppers post things they like, from wasabi gumballs to DeLorean cars, and solicit opinions on posted sale items from members.

- ✔ **UPS tracking** (www.ups.com): Like FedEx, UPS has a mobile version of its Web site that allows you to track packages from your BlackBerry.

Other Browsing Categories

You can visit the following sites from your BlackBerry to get more information on various topics:

- ✔ **BlackBerry Cool** (www.blackberrycool.com): In the same category as CrackBerry (see the upcoming bullet) and in fact a direct competitor, BlackBerry Cool is one of the pioneers in providing great reviews of BlackBerry applications.

- ✔ **BlackBerryGoodies** (http://blackberrygoodies.com): Go here from your BlackBerry or your PC. You can get information on customizing your BlackBerry, read BlackBerry application reviews, and get answers to your BlackBerry-related questions — from the authors of BlackBerry-related *For Dummies* books!

- ✔ **CrackBerry** (http://mobile.crackberry.com): To experience the BlackBerry community, go to CrackBerry.com. From application reviews to the lively online forum, this site is one of the most active BlackBerry communities.

- ✔ **MiniSphere** (www.minisphere.com): You find useful links designed for mobile devices here.

- ✔ **MizPee** (www.mizpee.com): When you gotta go, you gotta go. This site locates the nearest clean public bathroom.

- ✔ **Starbucks Locator** (www.starbucks.com): This site helps you locate the nearest Starbucks so you can meet your buddies or get a dose of caffeine.

- ✔ **wcities** (http://pda.wcities.com): This site provides searches based on the city you select. You can search city information, dining, shopping, and sporting and local events.

Index

• **C** •

• D •